Astrology
Key to
Holistic Health

by

Marcia Starck

For Johnny, very special
One of the very special
people.... I'm glad
we're on the planet
at the same Time!
Love & Healing
to you,
Marcia

Astrology
Key to
Holistic Health

by

Marcia Starck

SEEK-IT PUBLICATIONS
BIRMINGHAM, MICHIGAN 1982

DEDICATED TO
the Great Mystery which surrounds us

Astrology: Key to Holistic Health
Copyright © 1982 by Seek-It Publications
P.O. Box 1074
Birmingham, Michigan 48012

Cover art work by Rohmana Harris
Edited by Arlene Robertson

ISBN: 0-930706-11-0

CONTENTS

FOREWORD

This book is a worthy beginning. We must, if we are to survive as a successful species, begin to heal the schism between body and mind. We have freed ourselves in this generation from utter slavery to the requirements of earning a living, and, with the advent of the microchip, we are close to a time when we will have more leisure than ever before. The dream that the machine will do most of the work is rapidly becoming a reality. It is time we began to work on ourselves, in order to integrate our souls with our bodies. This book will help us to find a way to do this.

Some of the medical part may be out of date almost before the printers' ink is dry, for the halflife of medical knowledge is approximately ten years. This is to say that in ten years, half of what we now think we know about the body will be found to be inaccurate, to some degree. The author has made a brave attempt to do that which is literally impossible: to explain the conditions of the human body as portrayed in the horoscopes. I suggest the reader let the charts speak for themselves. In their symbolic language, they will give us the truth forever. We can only be misled if we are too blind to perceive what we are being told.

A very useful part of this book is the information it contains which is otherwise not readily available in one place. The list of fixed stars which are associated with blindness, for example, can be found elsewhere, but not without going through a great many pages of a book on fixed stars to seek it out. The midpoints taken from Ebertins' "Combination of Stellar Influences" are arranged so that they can be readily referred to. There is also a great deal of original material in the book, and I found the remarks about Chiron to confirm what I have previously observed about this planet or planetoid. Chiron may very well be the key to the never-ending mystery of conception, epoch and birth, as anyone who has studied the conception and birth charts of the first "test-tube" baby, Louise Brown, realizes.

There is really nothing now in print like this book. For anyone interested in the subject, it is clearly written, easily readable, and is packed with useful information. The correlation of the eclipses with the beginning and progression of an illness is well shown. In my experience I have found no better tool than eclipses to see what is happening behind the scenes. In addition to the information imparted in this book, I have also found that an eclipse falling in aspect to the 8th or 12th Placidus cusp is very potent in its effects.

May all holistic health centers have a well-used copy of "Astrology: Key to Holistic Health."

Margaret Millard, M.D.
September 23, 1981

ACKNOWLEDGMENTS

The author wishes to thank the following people: Dr. Margaret Millard for her fine Foreword and detailed editing of the manuscript, Mitzi Perkins for proof-reading, editing, constant help and encouragement, Nalini Chilkov for assistance with the physiological material, Maureen Blumenthal for assistance with case histories, Stephen Arroyo for his professional advice over the years, Mary Vohryzek and Dr. Donald Wharton for their helpful comments on the manuscript, Astro-Computing Services for preparing the horoscopes used in research, Karen Harvey for the typing, Rohmana Harris for the beautiful cover, Ray Merriman for his wisdom and guidance, Frida Waterhouse for her spiritual sustenance, and my mother, Helen Cantor, for her continued belief in and support of this work.

"A physician without a knowledge of astrology
cannot rightly call himself
a physician"

Hippocrates

INTRODUCTION

I recently received a magazine from Hawaii in which there was an article on Kahuna healing. In the article, one sentence especially stood out: "For the low self, the Kahunas use herbs and physical therapy, for the middle self, psychology, and for the high self, prayer." That one sentence contains for me the essence of the healing process—the balance or integration of the subconscious, conscious, and higher self while working simultaneously with spiritual, psychological and physical therapies.

Helping individuals achieve this balance has been the aim of the Holistic Health movement in this country, the seeds of which were sown in the 60's with the Uranus-Pluto conjunction in Virgo. Among the diagnostic tools which came to the fore during this burgeoning movement was the astrological horoscope, a tool used for many centuries in the medical and healing arts.

Hippocrates stated, "A physician without a knowledge of Astrology cannot rightly call himself a physician." His instruction to his students included a thorough knowledge of the stars and planets. Following the Hermetic axiom, "As above, so below", Hippocrates contended that one could not accurately know the disposition and temperament of a man without an understanding of the greater environment in which he was born.

Though much of this astrological information has been lost to the Western world, we are slowly beginning to uncover and rediscover these ancient truths. Knowledge of the signs and planets which govern the organs of the body and our physiological processes is incorporated into many of the Oriental systems of healing. The Chinese equate each organ with a corresponding emotion (i.e., the liver is anger; the kidneys, fear, etc.) and no real therapy can take place in the physical body without understanding these emotional patterns.

Our Western world, on the other hand, has fostered the schism of mind/body (intellect/intuition) since the time of the Dark Ages. It is this schism which produced what is commonly termed "Medical Astrology" with its emphasis on assessment of *bodily* ailments, and dates and times for surgery, without reference to the psychological and spiritual state of the individual.

This book, then, is an attempt to begin to heal that schism in Western astrological thought with particular emphasis on physiological manifestations or what we in the Western world refer to as "dis-ease".

Much of the bridging of this gap in the astrological field in general has already been accomplished through the pioneering works of Dane Rudhyar. In 1934 Rudhyar wrote, "True astrology is the mathematics of wholeness. It is 'holistic logic' in opposition to the 'intellectual logic' of this present Western civilization. It deals with wholes. It studies the structural harmony, the growth, development, and the disintegration or transfiguration of wholes—whether these be the usual biological organisms or more transcendent mental and spiritual wholes."

Due to the vast amount of research still needed in this particular area of astrology, this book may at best be considered a "seed" book. It will undoubtedly undergo many revisions and additions throughout the years. It is being published at this time as a stimulus or guide for my students, friends and fellow astrologers who have requested the information in a more structured and permanent form.

The names of various dis-eases or unbalanced states as hypoglycemia, diabetes, cancer, have been used in an attempt to communicate a specific condition or set of symptoms. No doubt fifty years from now we will have different names for the same syndromes.

My hesitations in putting this material into print are twofold: the first is that any suggested patterns found in horoscopes manifesting a certain disease may seem simplistic and incomplete because of the need to consider the whole chart, and, secondly, a consideration for those sensitive individuals who may find in their own horoscopes a similar configuration to that being discussed. Finding these similarities in no way indicates that the same physical manifestation will occur. In fact, none of us ever need manifest any physiological symptoms of disease if we maintain that constant flow of energy between our spiritual, emotional, and physical selves. It is to this purpose, the manifestation of the harmony within each one of us, and to the rest of creation, that this book is dedicated.

CHAPTER ONE

THE USE OF ASTROLOGY IN HOLISTIC HEALTH

The astrological horoscope is one of the process tools which reflects the wholeness of the individual. Through the symbolic relationship of the entire solar system to the destiny of each individual, a cosmic blueprint is produced incorporating all aspects of one's life. We can live our horoscopes on a mundane level or on an extremely esoteric one.

Since the chart shows various psychological patterns and how they may or may not manifest in physiological symptoms, it can be an excellent aid in understanding health and in preventative health care. Studying the progressions (natal planetary positions progressed for the coming year) and transits (daily positions of planets) in the horoscope enables one to understand why certain tensions and conflicts arise at various time periods and how to channel this energy in the most constructive manner. In being aware of these cycles, an individual can also keep his body balanced through diet, herbs, exercise, and nutritional supplements.

For example, a person with several planets in the sign Libra may experience his kidneys to be a particular sensitive area. He is aware that when he becomes anxious or when he undergoes changes in relationships, it is that area of his body that bothers him. This realization is important and further steps can be taken to maintain his body balance. Through a study of the horoscope, suggestions may be made on how to resolve various problems in relationships and channel his emotional energy. There may be foods (which exacerbate the difficulty) that could be eliminated or herbs that would be helpful. Various types of exercise or physical therapies might also be recommended.

The value of progressions and transits in health assessment and preventative health is extremely important. A case in point is a client who has her Sun in 10° Taurus, her Moon in 9° Scorpio and her Ascendant in 10° Scorpio. Before the planet Uranus, by transit, approached these degrees, she was made aware of the possible effects on her nervous system this transit might bring, as well as the many changes in her life that would be catalyzed by Uranus aspecting these important points in her chart. Most of her time was spent at a desk job, so in order to get exercise and relieve tension she bought a bicycle and became more physically active. She also stopped drinking coffee due to its stimulating effect on the nervous system and substituted herb teas. And, perhaps most significant of all, she started practicing yoga and meditation. Consequently she was able to experience the unexpected and sometimes disruptive changes in her life in a calm and relaxed state of mind.

Many more examples could be given but the point has been made—the astrological horoscope serves as a road map through which each of us individually may attune to the cosmic energies and be guided through our transformations with as much insight as possible.

The horoscope is also an excellent tool in evaluating specific symptoms or disease-syndromes. Dr. William Davidson, in his *Lectures on Medical Astrology*, gives a beautiful example of this. Two doctors diagnosed a patient as having a tumor in the area of the stomach. When Dr. Davidson examined her and also saw her astrological chart he commented that it was not a tumor but a swelling of the stomach with fluids. Much to the surprise of the other doctors, the "tumor" disappeared in fourteen days!

In my counseling work I have had many clients who have been unable to conceive. Most of them have undergone fertility tests, or tried fertility drugs, dilatation and other procedures. A study of their astrological charts often revealed an under-active thyroid gland and hormonal imbalance which was later verified through tests administered by a doctor. Through the use of the horoscope it was found that several of the women had extremely difficult relationships with their mothers and it was necessary to work through these fears and anxieties before they were able to conceive.

Some of them also were unsure of their partner's support in bringing a child into the world. There are many complex factors at work here, all of which were pinpointed by using the horoscope.

Utilizing planetary cycles with progressions and transits is extremely important in the planning of children. It is much easier for a woman to have a healthy pregnancy if it is begun during harmonious aspects. Miscarriages and other difficulties may sometimes be avoided through this kind of planning.

One is thus made aware of the duration of planetary cycles to see what specific measures can be adopted. In a later chapter we will look at major transits and determine how they affect the body physically and what precautions can be taken at these particular times.

Timing is important in another way—in administering remedies, herbs and other preparations. Taking these remedies when certain aspects are exact or at particular times of the day by utilizing planetary hours can be helpful. One homeopathic physician uses a timetable, given him by a Hindu astrologer, which allocates the systems in the body to particular hours of certain days. He recommends that the remedies be taken at these times. In this manner the vibrational qualities of the remedies are enhanced.

CHAPTER TWO

ANALYZING THE HOROSCOPE

Before analyzing the horoscope for potential health problems and nutritional requirements, one needs to have an understanding of the *whole person* as shown by the chart. Each horoscope is different and all factors in the chart must be studied and the essence extracted before reaching any conclusions. It is important to consider all the subtleties. For example, an angular Mars may offset a water sign Ascendent, or several planets in the seventh house may provide the balance to a lack of air emphasis.

The first thing to consider is the Sun—its sign, house and aspects. The Sun represents the basic constitutional vitality; hard aspects from the Moon and Ascendant would alter the vitality in some way, as would hard aspects from Mars, Saturn, Uranus, Neptune and Pluto. Hard aspects include the conjunction (δ), opposition (8), square ($\square$), semi-square ($\angle$), and sesquiquadrate ($\square$ 135°); the quincunx, or inconjunct, (λ 150°), which is an important aspect in physical health, should also be noted.

Hard aspects from Mars increase the metabolism and indicate that the person burns up energy quickly; eating small amounts of food more frequently replenishes the energy. Hard aspects from Saturn slow down the metabolic rate—these individuals can exist on fewer meals eaten over a longer time interval; they need frequent exercise, however, to overcome the lethargy of Saturn and to strengthen their body structure. Sun-Uranus hard aspects affect the nervous system and indicate a tendency to have difficulty with the cardiovascular system since Uranus, as ruler of Aquarius, relates to circulation. Sun-Neptune hard aspects can deplete the vital forces through a leak of etheric energy which is like trying to fill up a balloon when the balloon has a hole in it.

Working with the breath through breathing exercises may be most helpful in sustaining energy; sunshine and sufficient amounts of vitamin D are also important. Sun-Pluto hard aspects refer to the regenerative or recuperative ability of an individual. With hard aspects one's body doesn't recuperate as quickly unless there is a fire sign rising or Mars is angular. The hard aspects between Sun and Pluto also tend to slow down the circulation.

The Moon in the horoscope shows how the vital forces flow through the body. Thus the Moon is our "amperage" whereas the Sun is our "voltage" (amperage is the flow of current; voltage is pressure behind the energy which makes it flow). With several hard aspects to the Moon, the individual may tend to be ill from time to time, though his vitality may be very strong. Conversely, those with easier aspects to the Moon and hard aspects to the Sun may rarely become ill, though they need to watch their energy level carefully by getting balanced meals and a sufficient amount of rest.

The Ascendant acts as the general conductor of energy throughout the body. It is primarily our outer covering or the physical image we present to the world at large. Fire signs on the Ascendant followed by the air signs are the best conductors of energy. Earth and water signs are weaker, though this may often be modified by Mars, Sun or Pluto within 10° of the Ascendant. Mars and the Sun provide energy and vitality and Pluto the regenerative or recuperative ability. Planetary aspects to the Ascendant are also important in determining how well the energy is conducted throughout the body.

ELEMENTS

In considering the balance of the elements, one should look at houses and planets as well as signs. The first, fifth and ninth houses are fire houses; second, sixth and tenth earth; third, seventh and eleventh air; and fourth, eighth and twelfth water. Sun, Mars and Jupiter are fire planets; Saturn earth; Mercury and Uranus air; Moon, Venus and Neptune water. Pluto may be considered a combination of fire and water. When these planets are angular or in close hard aspect to the Sun or Moon, they may balance out other factors in the horoscope.

With a lack of planets in the fire signs there is less physical vitality and a tendency to lethargy and depression. These individuals need much physical exercise and the practice of such disciplines as Tai Chi or yoga to keep the vital energy (chi or prana) flowing in the body. An example of a former landlord comes to mind: his Sun sign is Pisces with Moon and three planets in Taurus in the twelfth house and Gemini rising. He is a very sensitive individual with a love of philosophy but a tendency to be extremely serious and often depressed. One day, while putting summer screens on two houses he owned, he was in buoyant spirits and claimed he never felt better physically. After it was pointed out to him that this was due to exercising, he began to pay more attention to that area of his life and consequently became a much more lively and optimistic person.

Preponderance in fire indicates a person who often burns himself out and does not conserve his physical energy. These people are constantly on the go and rarely take time to reflect on life. One friend who has four planets in Aries and a Pisces Moon broke his foot (Pisces) shortly before the Christmas holidays. The doctor told him not to use it for a month but he wanted to work at a Christmas fair the next weekend. He worked at the fair and his foot got much worse—he was, in fact, de-*feated*, and forced to spend the next two months flat on his back. This turned out to be one of the most important periods of his life in terms of the inner work he did on himself and the issues with which he was forced to deal. Another client, with four planets in Aries, Leo Moon and Sagittarius Ascendant, was pregnant with her second child when she began to experience periods of extreme fatigue. She already had one child to take care of and expended a great deal of energy every day. Once she decided to slow down, she became involved in photography, writing poetry and listening to music. Consequently, the remainder of her pregnancy went well and she had an easy delivery.

A lack of the element earth frequently leads one to ignore the physical body. Often these individuals have pale sensitive skin unless they spend enough time outdoors. To them, buying groceries, cooking meals, exercising, can seem a chore and a waste of time. One such lady, a beautiful poet, remarked to me, "Wouldn't it be simpler if we could swallow a pill each time we needed to eat?" Another man, who lacks earth and has a deep awareness of his horoscope, has planted a large garden in which he works every day. His business is a company that sells clay for medicinal and cosmetic purposes.

An abundance of the earth element usually indicates those who enjoy taking care of their physical needs by exercising, cooking and other activities. Sometimes they tend to overdo this, especially with a strong Virgo or sixth house emphasis. A friend with several earth placements and Virgo rising experimented with different kinds of diets—one week he was eating raw foods, another week he followed a macrobiotic diet. He often alienated people by discussing in elaborate detail the various changes he experienced in his digestive system through these diets.

Lack of the air element may point to a weak nervous system and difficulty in communicating. A man who had no air planets developed a nervous stutter until he started working at a job where he had to communicate with people continually. As he became confident of his ability to express his ideas, his stutter disappeared.

Preponderance of planets in air signs tends to make one very mentally active. These people often develop symptoms such as tics and spasms which result from an overload on the nervous system and respiratory ailments. Working with yoga breathing techniques and exercising often relieves these symptoms.

An individual having few planets in water may find difficulty expressing his emotions; he also tends to lack fluids in his body. If this is not balanced out, toxins may accumulate. Drinking more liquids and going on frequent juice fasts are helpful in eliminating toxins. For many, living near the water provides the necessary balance as well.

With an excess of the water element, emotionally-caused conditions are prominent. These individuals are super sensitive and tend to absorb negative feelings from others as well. They need to learn detachment from personal feelings and to channel their emotions in a positive way. One lady who has eight planets in water signs was suffering from cancer. As she became aware of her tendency to take on other people's problems, she was able to become more objective and her condition improved.

CARDINAL, FIXED AND MUTABLE CROSSES

Cardinal signs initiate action. Aries begins projects; it rules the head and motor center of the brain, which conceives ideas. Libra, sign of relationships, is its polar opposite; it governs the kidneys and bladder. Cancer and Capricorn refer to home and profession, the structure of our lives. Cancer rules the abdominal area and body fluids while Capricorn rules the spine, bones, teeth, and cartilage. With strong cardinal sign emphasis, there may be problems related to body structure, the gastrointestinal system, the eyes, and kidneys.

Fixed Signs solidify energy. They can be intractable and stubborn thereby holding back feelings and retaining toxins in the body. Taurus rules the throat, thyroid gland, and process of cleansing through the oral cavities. Scorpio governs the reproductive system, excretory system, and cleansing through the anal opening. Leo refers to the heart and Aquarius the circulation; blocks in this area of the body affect the cardiovascular system and are often a result of holding back emotions. Fixed signs refer to chronic conditions.

Mutable signs are adaptable and flexible, though often times indecisive and wishy-washy as well. Gemini rules the lungs, tubes of the body, arms, hands, and nervous system, while Sagittarius rules the thighs, sciatic nerve, and expiration from the lungs (to balance the Gemini inhalation). Virgo governs the digestive system, the assimilation of foods and discriminatory processes that take place in the intestinal area, while Pisces governs the lymphatic system and the throwing off of waste materials. Gemini and Sagittarius refer to nervous and respiratory problems (if the breathing is not slowed and controlled) while Virgo and Pisces may indicate digestive disorders and upsets. Mutable signs tend to throw off toxins more readily and maintain a faster recovery process.

T-SQUARES

The T-squares in a horoscope are extremely important as they point to tension areas. The combination of planets in the T-square is significant in determining probable areas of health difficulties. These combinations are like midpoints (which will be studied in a later chapter) with one planet being roughly at the midpoint of the other two. The signs and houses in the T-square should be considered, but it is the planets that are most important.

SIGN AND HOUSE EMPHASIS

Often there are three or more planets in one sign or one house in the horoscope. The corresponding area of the body becomes more sensitive so these should be considered.

SIGNS OF THE ZODIAC

In addition to ruling the anatomical parts of the body, the signs also govern various physiological processes. If one is having difficulty with a certain physiological process, there are undoubtedly psychological problems to be looked at in those areas of life.

ARIES-LIBRA

Aries is the personal, the "I am", indicating individual energy and initiative. It rules the area of the head, the blood, and the muscular system. When one is too mental or too much "in his head" he often develops headaches. Polarizing Aries is the sign Libra, the "We are" of the Zodiac, referring to relationships and contracts. Libra rules the kidneys, which eliminate the liquid wastes of the body. Libra also governs the endocrine system whose secretions pour directly into the bloodstream thereby balancing the body. Aries and Libra together rule the adrenal glands, located above the kidneys. They are the body's tool which respond to stress. The adrenals have traditionally been associated with Mars. Arians may suffer from nephritis or kidney inflammation which causes headaches, eye problems, and mental stress. Stress stimulates the adrenal glands and this often leads to anger and irritability. The semicircular canal which maintains equilibrium (Libra) and is located in the inner ear, also comes under the jurisdiction of these two signs. Basically in Aries we take in (for ourselves) and in Libra we give out (to friends and relations). If our lives are not in balance through this taking in and giving out (the in-breath and the out-breath), we may develop problems in the area of the head (including the eyes), kidneys and adrenals.

TAURUS-SCORPIO

Taurus-Scorpio, fixed signs of desire and will, serve to feed the body as well as cleanse and purify by ridding it of waste material. Taurus rules the mouth and throat while Scorpio governs the rectum and excretory system. If we ingest any spoiled or poisonous food, our body immediately cleanses itself through one or both of these doorways. Likewise, if we become too emotional, or take in too many negative experiences, our body may seek to cleanse itself in a similar fashion. Taurus is associated with the thyroid gland in the throat while Scorpio is associated with the reproductive system. The thyroid is closely connected with genital development, and thus, during puberty, the voice changes. Mumps, an infectious disease characterized by a swelling of glands in the neck (♉), also attacks the reproductive organs (♏).

GEMINI-SAGITTARIUS

Gemini and Sagittarius, the body's communication network, control the nervous system for distributing messages. Gemini rules the arms, hands, shoulders, lungs and nerves, while Sagittarius governs hips, thighs, the sciatic nerve, pancreas and liver. The dualism of Gemini is shown by the fact that man has two arms, two lungs and two nervous systems. Breathing is also a dual process of inhalation and exhalation. Sagittarius rules the largest nerve, the sciatic nerve, and the liver, the largest internal organ of the body which was considered by the ancients to be the seat of the soul. Gemini transmits the messages and Sagittarius distributes them throughout the body. Our hands and arms may direct us but it is the torso and thighs that actually move us. If we are under pressure, nervous or tense, our breathing may become too shallow and we can develop problems in the area of the lungs; states of tension and anxiety may also lead to problems with the sciatic nerve.

CANCER-CAPRICORN

Cancer and Capricorn, the security-oriented signs, home and profession, provide us with the foundation and structure for our bodies. Capricorn rules the skeletal frame, the bones, teeth, cartilage and skin—Cancer, the viscera and softer parts such as the stomach, uterus, and breasts. When something goes awry in our professional work or our domestic or emotional life, it is often our body's structure that gives way with a broken bone or a slipped disc or one of our sensitive areas develops stomach ulcers or uterine infections. In general, the ventral (front) of the body is ruled by Cancer and the dorsal (back) side by Capricorn. One of the functions of a straight spine is to hold the abdominal organs in alignment.

LEO-AQUARIUS

Leo and Aquarius, creativity and the expression of it to humanity, govern circulation and oxygenation. Leo rules the heart, the center of the circulatory system, which in Aquarius sends out the energy to all the cells of the body. Aquarius also rules the ankles; swollen ankles often result from circulatory dysfunction. If we repress our feelings or block our emotions in any way, we tend to have poor circulation. If impaired circulation persists, it can lead to abnormal heart behavior. Aquarius and Uranus also govern electrical energy and brain waves, and many of the nervous diseases involving erratic brain functioning come under the jurisdiction of

Aquarius. Radiation and radioactive chemicals are also Aquarian-ruled.

VIRGO-PISCES

Virgo and Pisces are signs of health and healing, assimilation and digestion. Virgo rules the intestines and the entire digestive system, discriminating which foods are fit for assimilation. Pisces governs the duodenum, the first part of the small intestine, which is prone to ulcers. Pisces also rules the lymphatic system whose cells attack and neutralize invading bacteria. Thus Virgo purifies while Pisces immunizes. When we take on too many projects especially of a mental nature as Virgo is ruled by Mercury, we then have difficulty assimilating our experiences and often develop digestive problems.

HOUSES

Although the sixth and twelfth houses are particularly referred to as health and healing houses, all of the houses should be considered in making a medical evaluation of the horoscope. A stellium in the third house may take on a vibration similar to a strong configuration in Gemini, influenced, of course, by the particular planets and the signs they occupy. As examples, those with cardiovascular problems often have a predominance of planets in the succedent houses and those with respiratory illesses, the cadent houses, particularly the third and ninth.

The sixth and twelfth houses should be examined with reference to the signs on the cusps indicating particular areas of the body and physiological processes; the planets contained therein; and the rulers of the cusp signs and their placement. Planets in the sixth and twelfth houses and rulers of the cusp signs often indicate chronic and hereditary problems.

Heavy planetary emphasis in the sixth and twelfth houses suggests that this energy may be channelled through service work and healing others rather than turned inward upon the self as dis-ease. As the old maxim had it, serve or suffer!

PLANETS

The basic rulerships of the planets are:

⊙   Heart and circulatory system
☽   Fluids, mucous membranes, stomach storage organs and the bladder
☿   Nervous and respiratory systems
♀   Throat, thyroid gland
♂   Muscles, adrenal glands, blood
♃   Liver, pancreas
♄   Skeletal system, teeth, bones, joints, skin, gall bladder
♅   Nervous system, along with Mercury
♆   Cerebro-spinal fluid, pineal gland, lymphatic system
♇   Bowels, reproductive system

PHYSICAL SYMPTOMS ASSOCIATED WITH THE PLANETS ARE:

⊙   Cardiovascular diseases
☽   Inflammation of mucous membranes, imbalance of body fluids, (edema, dehydration), digestive problems
☿   Neuritis, respiratory ailments, impediments of speech
♀   Throat infections, thyroid imbalance, kidney problems
♂   Swelling and inflammation, fevers, infections, accidents, hemorrhage and blood diseases
♃   Liver diseases (hepatitis), pancreatic diseases (hypoglycemia, diabetes), obesity, abnormal growths, tumors
♄   Arthritis, rheumatism, fractures, spinal ailments, dental problems, skin diseases, gall stones
♅   Cramps, spasm, shocks, paralysis, epilepsy, radiation poisoning
♆   Obscure diseases, hallucinations, poisonings and overdoses, alcoholism and addictions, toxic conditions, schizophrenia

♀   Destruction of tissue, hidden cell changes, diseases of the reproductive organs

BODY REGION

♈	Head, face	Eyes, nose
♉	Neck, throat	Mouth, tonsils, vocal cords
♊	Arms, shoulders	Lungs
♋	Stomach, breasts	Diaphragm, uterus
♌	Cardiac region	Spleen, heart
♍	Lower abdominal area	Small intestine
♎	Small of back	Kidneys, bladder
♏	Pelvis	Reproductive organs, gonads, colon, rectum
♐	Thighs, hips, buttocks	Liver, pancreas
♑	Knees, bones	Gall bladder, teeth, cartilage
♒	Calves, ankles	Retina of eyes
♓	Feet	Lymphatic system

Since there are seven glands and twelve signs, there is no exact correspondence between the two, despite the efforts of many to impose some system of order on the glands. Research has shown that the glands are probably ruled by the following signs:

♈	Pituitary		♎	Adrenal
♉	Thyroid		♏	Gonads
♊	Thymus		♒	Para-thyroid
			♓	Pineal

CHAPTER THREE

OTHER ASTROLOGICAL DATA: ASPECTS, PARALLELS, SECONDARY AND SOLAR ARC DIRECTIONS, DECANATES, DWADS, ASTEROIDS, VERTEX, CHIRON, FIXED STARS, DEGREE AREAS

ASPECTS

The most important aspects to consider in Medical Astrology are the conjunction (two planets next to each other), the opposition (180°), the square (90°), the semi-square (45°), sesqui-quadrate (135°) and quincunx or inconjunct (150°). The quincunx is a first-sixth house aspect and thus its significance in health matters. Trines (120°), sextiles (60°), and semi-sextiles (30°) seem to be less important as they represent the division of the circle by three and are not particularly action-oriented.

The question of orbs is a subtle one inasmuch as larger orbs on the major aspects run into other harmonic divisions of the circle. The circle can be divided by any number to form another aspect: division by 2=180°, by 3=120°, by 4=90°, by 6=60°, by 8=45°, by 5=72° (quintile), by 7=51.26° (septile), by 9=40° (non-agen). Suggested orbs are 6° for conjunction, opposition, trine and square, 3° for sextile, and 2° for quincunx, semi-square, sesquiquadrate and semi-sextile.

PARALLELS AND CONTRA-PARALLELS

Parallels and contra-parallels are measured by declination rather than by longitude. Declination is the number of degrees a planet is North or South of the Equator. Two planets are parallel if their declination is the same (both 12° North); they are contra-parallel if their declination is opposite (12° North and 12° South). Parallels are interpreted like conjunctions and contra-parallels like oppositions. Since the range of possible declinations is only 26° North or South from the Equator, an orb of only 1° is used.

It seems very important in delineation to include parallels and contra-parallels. If two planets in the horoscope are in conjunction they are often in parallel aspect as well. However, sometimes a parallel or contra-parallel gives us additional information about the horoscope. For example, in the chart of the diabetic patient reproduced in this book, Neptune and the Moon are parallel and they are both contra-parallel to Saturn. Natally, the Moon is at 2° Aries, Neptune at 15° Virgo, and Saturn is at 21° Pisces. This person is a highly sensitive artist and has consumed a great deal of alcohol and various types of hallucinogenic drugs; he is also very insecure. The Moon parallel Neptune contra-parallel Saturn is perhaps the strongest indicator in the horoscope of these tendencies.

SECONDARY PROGRESSIONS

Secondary progressions (the day-for-a-year method) are important to calculate for additional information. The aspects by progression, especially to natal Sun, Moon and Ascendant, will provide insights into the health picture for the year ahead. For example, if Sun_P is conjunct $Mercury_R$ or $Mercury_P$ it is important to nourish the nervous system and to be aware of any allergic tendencies, if such tendencies are already present in the natal chart. Likewise, if Sun_P makes a hard aspect to natal Mars, there could be less vital energy and one could compensate for this by increasing the iron in the diet and doing exercises that build vitality. The sign and house of the progressed Moon are also important in showing the focus of the individual's life at the time. Monthly aspects of the progressed Moon combine with transits in determining energy level and tendencies to manifest physical symptoms.

Another factor to observe in progressions occurs when a progressed planet aspects one of the health midpoints. (These are listed in the chapter on Midpoints). In such a case, that combination of planetary energies would be important for the coming year. For example, in one horoscope Mars = Mars/Pluto midpoint the year a woman had a miscarriage. In another case, Venus = Saturn/Neptune midpoint at the time a client had difficulty with her thyroid gland.

SOLAR ARC DIRECTIONS

Solar arc directions often provide even more information than secondary progressions because so many more aspects are formed. Solar arc directions are determined by advancing each position in the natal chart by the arc of the progressed Sun. There are four methods of calculating solar arc directions:

1. *true solar arc*—difference in longitude between the natal Sun and the secondary progressed Sun, using the day for a year method.

2. *mean solar arc*—the average daily movement of the Sun, used uniformly for each year.

3. *birthday arc*—the 24 hour rate of movement on the day of birth used throughout the life.

4. *age arc*—one degree for each year.

Examples of solar arc are the following: For one client allergic attacks started when Mercury conjoined natal Neptune by solar arc. Another client manifested hypoglycemic symptoms when Neptune conjoined his natal Jupiter.

DECANATES AND DWADS

The zodiacal signs are divided into decanates of 10° each and dwads of 2½° each.

Decanates

The first third of each sign (0°–10°) represents the sign itself; the second third (10°–20°) carries the vibration of the next sign of the same element, and the last third of the sign has the overtones of the last sign of the same element. This quality is added as an additional factor in delineation. For example, 1° ♈ is the Aries decanate, 11° ♈ is the Leo decanate, and 21° ♈ is the Sagittarius decanate.

Dwads

Dwads or Dwadashamas are a Hindu division of the Zodiac; they divide the sign up into 12 sections of 2½ degrees each so that the whole zodiac is represented in each sign. The first 2½ degrees of Aries would be Aries, the next 2½ degrees Taurus, etc. When a new decanate starts, the dwad of the first 2½ degrees is associated with that sign. (The Leo decanate of Aries, 10–12½ degrees, would also be the Leo dwad; 12½–15 degrees would be the Virgo dwad, etc.) Dwads add another vibration or overtone to the meaning of the sign.

ASTEROIDS

In delineating a chart for health purposes, it is helpful to place the four major asteroids in the chart and to observe progressions and transits to them as well as to the planets. Several years of research work with these asteroids have convinced me of their importance.

In Medical Astrology, Ceres (?) and Vesta (⚶), both representing aspects of Virgo, seem particularly relevant. Ceres, the goddess of the grain and harvest, appears to be the indicator of child-bearing and fertility along with the Moon. The sign and house where Ceres is placed usually shows where and how one's nurturing capacities may manifest. One client has Ceres conjunct Neptune in Virgo in her eleventh house. She has no children of her own, but through her spiritual and healing work continuously mothers friends and acquaintances. Another client, with Ceres on her seventh house cusp, always wondered why she was forced into a mothering role with each of her mates. Another close friend has Ceres conjunct his Mars in Pisces near the Ascendant. He practices various forms of Oriental healing such as Acupressure and Jin Shinn, and thus nurtures people by working with their bodies and transmitting energy to them.

In the case of a client who was having difficulty conceiving a child, in the year she finally adopted one Ceres came by solar arc to her Sun. Another client had an abortion when

Ceres conjoined her Mars by solar arc. She had conceived the child when Pluto conjoined her natal Ceres.

Vesta represents the virginal goddess of the hearth, the serious or work side of Virgo. A strong Vesta in the natal chart indicates one who is constantly working and is very Virgoan in his habits—neat, orderly, and efficient, sometimes to the point of overemphasis. One lady, who has no Virgo planets in her chart nor any sixth house emphasis, has Vesta at her Nadir in a funnel formation (a single planet in a hemisphere acting as a focus through which all else in the chart flows). She does healing work and also maintains a bookkeeping job on the side, is extremely careful about her health habits and is very meticulous about her house, clothes and job.

Another friend has Vesta conjunct her Neptune in the third house. She is a spiritual therapist and channel, has written several books and is extremely particular about how each book is printed. Besides publishing her own books, she also distributes them and keeps precise records on all her accounts.

One client conceived a child when her Ascendant by solar arc squared Vesta; one month later she lost the child. Another client had glaucoma diagnosed when Saturn by solar arc conjoined natal Vesta. Overwork and tension were related to her contracting glaucoma.

Juno (⚵) and Pallas (⚴) represent aspects of Libra. Juno indicates more personal relationships and Pallas denotes counseling and sponsoring social and political causes. One student with Pallas conjunct Pluto in the ninth house maintains a practice in counseling using astrology and past life regressions. (Pluto represents the buried past or that which lies underneath the surface). Another client with Sun conjunct Juno always needs to be involved in a relationship.

In progressions, aspects to Juno and Pallas often occur when marriage or relationships come together or break apart.

Juno seems to be involved in childbirth as well. One friend had Juno conjunct her Ascendant when her son was born; another student had it conjunct her Sun, and a third client had it conjoined her Venus.

VERTEX

The Vertex-Anti-Vertex axis derives from the intersection of the ecliptic with the Prime Vertical. Most of the time the Vertex falls within the fifth through eighth houses; the Anti-Vertex is exactly opposite. (See Appendix for calculation of the Vertex.) The Vertex-Anti-Vertex axis, like the Ascendant-Descendant, is involved with relationships. The Anti-Vertex shows the individual's own actions whereas the Vertex symbolizes others in the life with whom the person is involved. The sign and house where the Vertex falls indicate the areas where we have lessons to learn in relationships with others. Any natal planets on this axis are strongly emphasized. When the Vertex is aspected by progressions or major transits, we may experience a different way of relating to others. We often attract people (friends, business associates, lovers) whose planets fall on this axis. Thus far, little work has been done with the Vertex in Medical Astrology, though it appears to be prominent by secondary and solar arc progressions at periods of crisis and turning points in the life.

CHIRON

Chiron, the new planet or planetoid, was discovered on Nov. 1, 1977. In size, Chiron is comparable to the asteroids though its orbit is between the planets Saturn and Uranus; thus it has been called the Maverick.

Chiron's discovery at this time is symbolic of the strong interest in holistic health with its emphasis on herbology and body therapies, and in terms of the recent studies being conducted on death and dying. From Chiron (Greek root, chir means hand) come our English words chirognomy, chiropractic, and chiropody, treatment of the diseases of the hands and feet from which podiatry arose.[1]

Those individuals who contract serious health problems as well as those who undergo a major healing crisis during their lives have Chiron prominent (angular or conjunct Sun or

---

[1]*Ephemeris of Chiron* 1890–2000 introduction by Tony Joseph, p. iii.

Moon). In the charts of doctors and healers, Chiron is strongly emphasized. (Several doctor's charts I have seen have Chiron on either the Ascendant or Midheaven.)

Chiron is usually found to be active by progression or transit whenever there is a strong manifestation of physical symptoms. It is often involved in conceptions, births, abortions and miscarriages. A client who was having difficulty becoming pregnant finally conceived when Chiron exactly trined natal Chiron. Her son was born with Chiron transiting her Moon. Another lady had an abortion with transiting Chiron exactly square her Sun. Five years later she adopted a child with transiting Chiron square Pluto. Still another client had a miscarriage of twins with solar arc Moon square Chiron and transiting Chiron semi-square natal Chiron. Later she had a premature child who died; Chiron was opposing her Neptune. When she finally gave birth, Chiron was exactly sextile Venus and trine Vesta. Another woman had a child born with transiting Chiron opposite her Moon; several years later she lost a child due to a serious uterine infection; Chiron was opposing Neptune.

FIXED STARS

The Fixed Stars of the Zodiac are an important factor to consider. However, much more research is necessary to determine the planetary qualities of each star. When a planet or angle of the horoscope conjuncts one of the Fixed Stars (the orb used is about one degree), that planet will be strongly influenced by the nature of the star; oppositions and, to a lesser extent, squares are also worth noting. Like the planets, the Fixed Stars have both a positive and negative vibration; the level of evolution of each individual determines the vibration of the star to which he is attuned.

The latitude of the particular star (latitude is the distance of the star from the ecliptic) should be noted as well as the declination (distance from the equator). Stars that are quite distant from the ecliptic or equator are weaker in their effects. The magnitude of the stars should also be taken into consideration. First, second and third magnitude stars have the strongest effects.

The Fixed Stars are particularly significant when they conjunct or oppose the Sun, Moon, or Ascendant. Falling on one of these three points, they should be considered in the overall health analysis, especially in cases of blindness and other eye disorders. (See chapter on Eye Disorders for more details.)

DEGREE AREAS

Certain degrees of the Zodiac relate to specific areas of the body and to particular physical manifestations or diseases. The degrees listed by Charles Carter (in the back of the *Encyclopedia of Psychological Astrology*) are often cited. In some cases these degrees have shown up many times; 4 and 18 of the mutables = asthma and allergies; 9 and 25 of the fixed = alcoholism.

Of great importance to the medical astrologer is the *Anatomical Correspondences to Zodiacal Degrees* by Elsbeth and Reinhold Ebertin (translated and adapted by Mary Vohryzek—see Bibliography). On this listing, each zodiacal degree is equated with an organ, muscle, nerve, vertebrae, or some area of the body. The Ebertins suggest that one check the areas occupied by the Ascendant, M.C., Sun and Moon, as well as Mars/Saturn midpoint and Mars/Neptune midpoint areas for body toxicity and weakness. The progressed Sun is another important factor to check.

CHAPTER FOUR

MIDPOINTS AND THEIR USE

The use of certain midpoints is particularly important in assessing health problems. Midpoints are those points located halfway between any pair of planets. The midpoint represents a focus of energy between the two planets and thus becomes an important point in the chart. Although there are seventy-eight midpoints, only six are utilized in a general health analysis while others are involved with specific disease syndromes. Eight midpoint coordinates are used for each pair of planets: the points opposite and square the midpoint are known as direct midpoints; those making 45° and 135° angles to the midpoint are the indirect midpoints. (See Appendix for calculation of midpoints.) For example, if 15°♎︎ is the calculated midpoint, 15°♈︎, ♋︎, and ♑︎ are also involved. The other four midpoints are those points 45° away from the direct ones or 0° of the mutable signs. (0♊︎, 0♍︎, 0♐︎, and 0♓︎). If a natal planet equals (equals means aspects) any of these eight coordinates, it is significant in a health analysis of the chart. The orb for midpoints is one-and-a-half degrees. By the configuration of midpoints to natal planets, one can begin to see psychological patterns and predispositions to physical manifestations. Certain midpoint patterns emerge in various disease syndromes. The midpoints are also activated by progression, both secondary and solar arc, and transit. Often a planet activating a midpoint by transiting any of these eight co-ordinates may signify the onset of an illness.

When I first started to experiment with these particular midpoints I looked over my own transits for the previous year. I noticed that the two times when I was ill (once with a cold, the other with swollen lymph nodes) the Sun had conjoined and opposed my ♄ / ♆ midpoint, the health axis. Pluto transiting the same midpoint in late 1975 and 1976 catalyzed my first fast and subsequent dietary change. When my ☉/ ☽ midpoint was transited by ♆, allergic reactions to several foods which I never had experienced previously occurred. I also caught a flu bug that persisted for a few months at the beginning of this transit. Neptune transits make one particularly sensitive. Transiting Neptune over the ♂/ ♅ point in a client's chart set off the worst bout of eczema she had ever suffered. (Neptune rules allergies and ♂/ ♅ the nervous system.)

IMPORTANT HEALTH MIDPOINTS

☉/ ☽ — This is the most important midpoint in the horoscope. The soli-lunar angle reflects the phase of the moon under which a person was born. A planet or angle falling on the ☉/ ☽ midpoint is involved in the soli-lunar angle and thus receives much emphasis. ☉/ ☽ equals the basic vitality and balance of body fluids.

For example, if ♅ = ☉/ ☽ midpoint, the person may have an extremely nervous temperament. With ♄ = ☉/ ☽, there would be difficulty in expressing the emotions, lack of vital energy, and the body would be prone to the type of crystallizing effect found in arthritis or rheumatism.

♄/ ♆ — This is the health axis or cardinal point of disease. When a planet equals the ♄/ ♆ midpoint, it *may* signify difficulty with the organ or organs ruled by that planet. For example, if ♃ = ♄/ ♆ there is often trouble with the liver or pancreas. This may manifest in several ways— the individual may be diabetic or hypoglycemic at some point in life, or could contract hepatitis or some other liver disease, or may simply have a sluggish liver or pancreas, and need to be careful about what he eats and drinks. How this manifests depends upon the rest of the horoscope and whether the individual takes care of himself in regard to diet, exercise, sleep patterns, and any emotional stress.

A friend had hepatitis during Neptune's transit of her Moon. When calculating her midpoints, I found her ♄/ ♆

midpoint equaled ♃, indicating the tendency for problems in the area of the liver and pancreas. The transit itself could have manifested physiologically in many ways such as allergies or the flu. A client, injured in an accident at age fourteen and crippled as a result, has his ♄ / ♆ midpoint = ♀, indicating conditions of a more serious or chronic nature.

♂ / ♄ — Mars and Saturn in combination refer to the body structure as well as the inhibition or restriction of some bodily function. When ♂ / ♄ = ♀, there may be thyroid problems or restricted glandular functioning. In the horoscopes of some of the women who have had difficulty conceiving, the ♂ / ♄ midpoint = ♀.

♂ / ♅ — This midpoint corresponds to the nervous system, injuries, accidents, or operations. People with sensitive nervous systems or diseases of nervous origin often have their Sun, Moon or Ascendant equal this midpoint. This is true of those who are accident-prone and suffer many injuries.

♂ / ♆ — This is the point of toxicity, susceptibility to infections, epidemics, toxic conditions from poisons, and drugs. An important point in the chart equaling ♂ / ♆ indicates a person who contracts infections easily. In a medical astrology class, a student told us about her son, who was sent home from school in his early years whenever anyone else in the class got ill because he would invariably get the same illness. On calculating his midpoints, she found that his ☉ = ♂ / ♆, and realized his supersensitivity to infections and toxins.

Another client whose ♂ / ♆ midpoint = ☽, had a serious staph infection in her uterus, which was caused by an intra-uterine device (the Moon rules female organs).

♂ / ♀ — This midpoint refers to heavy accidents, destruction of cells, destruction of life in some form.

I have noted this midpoint active in horoscopes of women who have had miscarriages or abortions. In most cases the ♂ / ♀ midpoint = ☉, ☽, asc.—in one or two cases, ♀ or ♆.

MIDPOINT EQUIVALENCIES

Listed here are a few suggestions for the meaning of midpoints when they equal natal planets or when they are activated by progression or transit. It is important to remember that these are *only* potential meanings; by keeping one's body in balance the negative implications do not have to manifest. Also, as always, it is essential to examine the rest of the horoscope.

☉ = ♄ / ♆ — Health problems throughout the life; the person may be involved with healing.

☉ = ♂ / ♄ — Weak vitality; need for work on body structure; strong power of endurance.

☉ = ♂ / ♅ — Sensitive nervous system; a strong body capable of making sudden efforts; possible accidents or surgeries when aspected by progression or transit.

☉ = ♂ / ♆ — Susceptibility to infections and toxins; allergic tendencies; capable of working with higher vibrations of energy.

☉ = ♂ / ♀ — Serious or chronic conditions; strong will and regenerative power.

☽ = ♄ / ♆ — Disorder of female organs; emotional depression; ability to channel emotions into higher states

☽ = ♂ / ♄ — Inhibition of feelings or emotions; for women possible difficulty in conceiving; good control and focus of emotions

☽ = ♂ / ♅ — Highly sensitive nervous system; possible surgeries involving female organs; intuitive and inspirational abilities

☽ = ♂ / ♆ — Tendency to infections especially of female organs; sensitivity to allergies and toxins; possible hypoglycemic tendency; strong psychic and intuitive powers

☽ = ♂ / ♀ — Problems with female reproductive cycle; emotional upheavals; powerful and deep emotional encounters

☿ = ♄ / ♆ — Diseases of nervous system, respiratory ailments, allergies; intuitive and structured thought processes

☿ = ♂ / ♄ — Problems with hearing; possible blockage in respiratory system; organized and powerful mind

☿ = ♂ / ♅ — Possible injuries and accidents to neurological system; highly sensitive nervous system; respiratory allergies; quick and inspirational mind; independence in ideas

☿ = ♂ / ♆ — Nervous conditions resulting from use of drugs or alcohol; highly intuitive thinking and psychic faculties

☿ = ♂ / ♀ — Tendency to overstimulation of nervous system; hyper-activity; deep and probing mind

♀ = ♄ / ♆ — Glandular disorders; kidney problems; a more compassionate love nature

♀ = ♂ / ♄ — Inhibited function of endocrine glands particularly the thyroid; possible problems in conception for women; ability to structure creative energy

♀ = ♂ / ♅ — Hormonal imbalance; erratic functioning of thyroid gland; possible surgery involving reproductive organs; creative inspiration

♀ = ♂ / ♆ — Infections in reproductive system; venereal diseases; kidney and bladder infections; compassionate and sympathetic nature

♀ = ♂ / ♀ — Problems involving reproductive system; hemorrhoids and problems with excretory system; ability to transform sexual energy

♂ = ♄ / ♆ — Lack of energy; low vitality; depletion of adrenal energy; problems with spine and body structure; arthritis; rheumatism; hard worker with strong motivations

♃ = ♄ / ♆ — Possible dysfunctions of liver or pancreas; weight loss; focus on inner and spiritual growth

♃ = ♂ / ♄ — Metabolic problems; restricted functioning of liver and pancreas; protection in cases of broken bones and other problems with body structure

♃ = ♂ / ♅ — Erratic functioning of liver and pancreas; protection in accidents or surgeries

♃ = ♂ / ♆ — Difficulty metabolizing carbohydrates; tendency to hypoglycemia; personal expansion through study of metaphysical and spiritual disciplines

♃ = ♂ / ♀ — Strong regenerative and recuperative ability; chronic problems with liver and pancreas

♄ = ♂ / ♅ — Blockage of energy in neurological system; serious accidents; long term surgeries; ability to use new and unusual ideas

♄ = ♂ / ♆ — Low vitality; body structure out of alignment; arthritis; rheumatism; ability to utilize higher metaphysical concepts

♄ = ♂ / ♀ — Severe and chronic conditions; chronic problems with reproductive system; hard worker with strong motivations

♅ = ♄ / ♆ — Sudden or unexpected illnesses; problems with nervous system; independence and inventiveness

♅ = ♂ / ♄ — Possible blockage in neurological system; body structure out of alignment; manifests new ideas

♅ = ♂ / ♆ — Diseases of neurological origin; paralysis; changes in energy level; involvement with metaphysical and psychic studies

♅ = ♂ / ♀ — Long-term surgeries and disabling conditions; ability to transform nervous energy

♆ = ♂ / ♄ — Lowering of vitality through toxic conditions, use of drugs and alcohol; ability to ground physical energy while working in states of higher consciousness

♆ = ♂ / ♅ — Possible infections resulting from surgery or injuries; channeling of energy into metaphysical and psychic studies

♆ = ♂ / ♀ — Poor ability to recuperate or regenerate body; transforming patterns related to alcoholism or drugs

♀ = ♄ / ♆ — Serious illness; chronic disability; changing health patterns through diet and other healing techniques

♀ = ♂ / ♄ — Serious defects in body structure, such as missing organs or limbs; transformation of body structure through exercise and other physical therapies

♀ = ♂ / ♅ — Possible long-term surgery and disabling conditions; transformation of nervous energy to manifest in a creative way

♀ = ♂ / ♆ — Infections and toxic conditions leading to long-term illnesses and disabilities; transforming allergic tendencies

MIDPOINT COMBINATIONS

The following meanings apply when the three planets are found in a T-square or involved in a midpoint equivalency. These eight combinations are commonly found.

♂ / ♃ / ♆ — Difficulty metabolizing carbohydrates (one of the hypoglycemic signatures), adrenal depletion, toxic conditions resulting from the liver and pancreas, (often found in horoscopes of alcoholics). These people generally need frequent small meals of whole grains and vegetables, easily digested proteins like fish, bean curd, yogurt and other soured milk products, a small amount of fruit and fruit juice (no citrus fruits, tomatoes, cranberries, or green apples), no sugar or honey (barley malt or rice syrup may be substituted), no salt, no alcohol and small amounts of heavy carbohydrates.

♀ / ♃ / ♆ — Difficulty metabolizing carbohydrates, craving for sweets, prone to excesses in diet, often found in horoscopes of alcoholics. Diet same as above.

♂ / ♄ / ♆ — Prone to certain conditions arising from body structure as arthritis and rheumatism, and dental problems. These individuals need high amounts of calcium, magnesium, and B complex vitamins and a diet of whole grains such as brown rice, buckwheat and millet, soured milk products, sesame seeds, sesame butter and tahini (high in calcium), cashews and cashew butter (high in magnesium), herbs such as comfrey (high in calcium), borage and red raspberry leaf (high in magnesium), and wintergreen and sarsaparilla root. No red meats.

♂ / ♀ / ♆ — Faulty glandular functioning; need for extra iodine. Fish, dulse, kelp, and other sea vegetables are particularly good. The herb, nettles, is rich in iron and iodine.

♄ / ♆ / ♀ — May indicate a tendency to diabetes, or a restriction of the thyroid gland. Diet should include a small amount of fruit, whole grains and vegetables, fish, dulse, kelp, and other sea vegetables. No sugar or honey.

♂ / ☿ / ♅ — Nervous and respiratory conditions. Need for good B-complex supplement and magnesium as found in chlorophyll, almonds, cashews, green leafy vegetables; few dairy products if allergies or respiratory conditions are present; herbs as borage and red raspberry leaf for magnesium content.

♂ / ♀ / ☽ — Lack of iron with possible anemic tendencies; occasional irregularities of the menstrual function and miscarriages. Need iron-rich foods such as organic calves' liver, wheatgrass, beets, raisins, prunes, cherries; grains and B-complex vitamins; vitamin E and selenium.

☉ / ☽ / ♆ — Lack of tone and vitality which may manifest as a pranic leak or "leaky aura"; hard to maintain the vitality at an even level. An adequate amount of sleep and rest is needed; also exercises like yoga and Tai Chi involving deep breathing are beneficial. A balanced diet with sufficient protein and whole grains is important.

CHAPTER FIVE

TRANSITS, INCLUDING LUNATIONS AND ECLIPSES—HOW THEY MANIFEST PHYSIOLOGICALLY

Through progressions and transits to planets, angles, and midpoints, we undergo many changes—physically, emotionally, and spiritually. If we are aware of the transits beforehand, we can do much to handle them in the most positive way.

An example of how the energy of a transiting planet can be transformed for positive growth is the following: A client with Neptune crossing her Ascendant was experiencing low blood sugar, fatigue, and general listlessness. She had been having bad dreams in which memories of a bout with Hodgkin's disease ten years before were bothering her. After several consultations, she was able to see that she could channel this energy out into the world by working as a healer rather than manifesting it through her physical body. She began to focus more on her spiritual disciplines and soon after had a business card printed. Within a few months, she was serving out in the world rather than sitting home with her own physical problems.

The physiological effects of the various transits follows (only the hard aspects are included):

TRANSITS OF SATURN

Saturn transits teach us lessons. If we have been ignoring our physical bodies the transits of Saturn may seem restrictive and limiting in terms of health. Since Saturn rules calcium, calcium deficiencies are often prominent at this time bringing on problems with teeth, bones or various parts of the skeletal frame. For calcium depletion, chelated calcium tablets, calcium cell salts, and the herbs comfrey root and comfrey leaf have proved helpful. Magnesium and vitamin D are important in assisting the calcium to assimilate. Foods high in calcium include sesame seeds, kelp, dulse, green leafy vegetables, almonds and soybeans.

Aspects from **Saturn** to the **Sun** usually indicate low vitality; there is a need to build up the system with nourishing food and physical exercise to overcome the inertia of Saturn. The cardiovascular system can be affected, with poor circulation and heart problems as a result.

Saturn transiting the **Moon** affects the emotions and may manifest physiologically as a period of lowered resistance to colds and flus and crystallizations in the body resulting in arthritic and rheumatoid conditions. When Saturn conjoined my own Moon in Gemini I had colds frequently. One client had acute bursitis in her shoulder when Saturn hit her Cancer Moon. Many of these conditions have been helped by calcium and magnesium supplements which also alleviate the depression brought on by this transit.

Transits from **Saturn** to **Mercury** relate to the nervous system, speech and hearing. One of my clients developed a nervous stutter under a square from Saturn to Mercury. Foods rich in B-vitamins, such as whole grains and wheat germ, plus a B-complex supplement were effective in controlling his symptoms once he understood the emotional reasons for the stutter. Others have had allergies and hives under this transit especially when Saturn is in a mutable sign and transits Mercury.

Venus and **Saturn** combinations often manifest as skin conditions, kidney problems and thyroid deficiencies. A student of mine had Saturn conjunct her Venus over a long period. During this time her face broke out in a rash which continued to bother her throughout the transit. She also experienced a good deal of depression and limitations in her social life. Another client developed hyperthyroidism when Saturn squared Venus.

Saturn—Mars combinations can bring frustrations of various kinds. They are somewhat like driving a car with the brakes on. The lesson from these transits is one of *patience* but it may take an accident, some broken bones or high blood pressure to get the point across. Arthritis, rheumatism and hardening of the arteries may manifest during this time. The iron in the body may be lowered during this transit and it is neccessary to supplement with foods rich in iron (beets, cherries, prunes and dark red foods), herbs like nettle leaves, wheatgrass juice, and liquid dulse.

With **Saturn** making aspects to itself, hard testing and inner struggle are often experienced. Weak knees and knee problems may develop during this transit. When Saturn squared my natal Saturn in the sixth house, I experienced discomfort in my knees, especially while driving. Although I was taking a calcium supplement at the time, I still had a deficiency and needed a stronger supplement. A friend snapped her kneecap while bowling under a square from Saturn to natal Saturn.

Saturn transits to **Uranus** exacerbate mental tensions and frustrations It is extremely important at this time to examine any aspects of the personality which have become crystallized and rigid. Breaking through these old habit patterns may release much of the tension. Foods rich in B- vitamins and some of the nervine herbs (herbs that help relax the nervous system) like spearmint, camomile, catnip, scullcap and wood betony have helped cool down Uranian vibrations.

Saturn in combination with **Neptune** brings symptoms which are difficult to diagnose. One is more susceptible to toxins and has a lowered resistance under this transit; adequate rest, regular meals, and exercise are especially important. If an individual is ill and a drug is administered, it should be done with caution because of increased sensitivity at this time. Many people have developed allergies to drugs as a result. Respiratory and food allergies and hypoglycemic reactions have also started with Saturn transiting Neptune. One of my clients reported a very strong reaction to drinking wine during this period with Saturn conjunct her natal Neptune in Virgo.

Under **Saturn-Pluto** aspects one may take on more than one can handle; overwork and extra burdens drain the physical vitality. Transformations in diet and lifestyle are frequent at this time, often as a result of some illness or operation. When Saturn conjoined my natal Pluto in Leo I had a problem with the colon (ruled by Pluto) and with assimilating food. I was able to heal myself through fasting and subsequent change to a lighter diet.

TRANSITS OF URANUS

The most common physical manifestations of Uranus are nervous conditions and accidents. The energy of Uranus needs to be grounded through exercise and meditative practices so that it can be used in a positive way—in new ideas, projects, and inventions. For all transits of Uranus it is advisable to nourish the nervous system by eliminating coffee and regular tea (orange pekoe and black teas contain caffeine) and substitute the nervine herb teas: spearmint, camomile, catnip, scullcap, wood betony, vervain and hops. The mineral magnesium is usually depleted during Uranus transits and therefore more conditions involving pain and spasm result. Foods high in magnesium include kelp, wheat germ, almonds, cashews, and soybeans. Supplemental means of obtaining magnesium include liquid chlorophyll, chelated magnesium tablets, the magnesium cell salt, and the herbs borage and red raspberry leaf. A liquid B-vitamin supplement may also be recommended during this transit. Most tablets and capsules are difficult to assimilate and also have a yeast base, to which many people are allergic.

Aspects from **Uranus** to the **Sun** often lead to heart disease and hypertension (the Sun ruling the heart and Uranus the electrical system). This is true especially when Uranian energies are suppressed and tension builds up within. One client with Sun conjunct Mars in Libra had a heart attack when Uranus transited this conjunction. He was in his early 40's at the time and experiencing tension and frustrations with his job. His heart problems lasted several years until he made the big breakthrough and completely changed his vocation. A student with her natal Sun in the eighth house had an automoblie accident in which her car was totally demolished when Uranus exactly opposed her

Sun. Fortunately, she experienced no serious bodily injuries except for a whiplash and some nerve damage in one hand.

Uranus-Moon combinations have produced many unwanted pregnancies as well as a few desired ones. One client who conceived with Uranus opposite her Moon later miscarried. Another client, who had been trying to conceive for several years, finally was successful through the use of artificial insemination when Uranus was opposite her Moon. Emotional upsets from this transit have thrown many into states of nervousness and confusion.

Uranus-Mercury combinations may produce extreme nervous problems and spasms. Epileptic seizures have often started under this influence. A former student of mine ran a home for disturbed children, several of whom were epileptic. She noticed that many of them had seizures under Uranus-Mercury transits.

Transits from **Uranus** to **Venus** often manifest in skin conditions, kidney and bladder problems, and malfunctioning of the thyroid gland. Dulse, kelp, and other seaweeds high in iodine, iron, and other minerals have been helpful to many who experience erratic functioning of the thyroid.

Uranus-Mars combinations arouse restless physical energy which sometimes leads to mishandling of machinery or carelessness in driving. One can also experience a good deal of sexual restlessness. One friend, who had Uranus conjuncting her Mars in Scorpio, went swimming every day to release her physical and sexual energy. She also became pregnant twice during this transit. Another client with Uranus conjunct Mars developed a skin rash with itching and blisters as a result of repressing sexual energy. Surgery can also occur during this transit. Several female clients had hysterectomies when Uranus conjoined their natal Mars in Scorpio.

Uranus-Jupiter transits often relate to erratic functioning of the liver and pancreas. One client with Uranus transiting her Jupiter had severe pains in her stomach. Doctors diagnosed it as indigestion resulting from nervous tension and prescribed tranquilizers. Finally a Chinese doctor discovered that not enough bile was being produced (bile is produced by the liver); he gave her some herbal teas and put her on a diet of grains, vegetables and fish. The condition soon cleared up.

With **Uranus** transiting **Saturn,** the opportunity for breaking up old patterns is present. In the course of these changes, bones often get broken, back problems may often occur (re-structuring of the body) and occasionally conditions like arthritis and rheumatism develop when there is great resistance to these changes.

Uranus making aspects to its own place can bring out nervous conditions that may manifest in all parts of the body as one goes through the cycle of change. With Uranus' transit of Libra (1968–75), bladder and kidney problems were frequent. In Scorpio (1975–81), Uranus has stirred up problems in the reproductive system and colon. (Scorpio rules the colon and excretory system.) There has also been an increase in venereal disease. Many women receiving the opposition of Uranus in Scorpio to their natal Uranus in Taurus have experienced pre-menopausal symptoms and irregular menstrual cycles. Herbs for toning the female system, blessed thistle and raspberry leaf, and herbs that contain estrogens are helpful for this cycle, also supplements of magnesium, Vitamin B-6 and Vitamin E.

Uranus-Neptune combinations catalyze change in the higher consciousness. Often under these transits consciousness-expanding drugs have been used and occasionally side effects have resulted. In older people there may be a tendency to withdraw from the world with the mind lapsing into a kind of dormant state, often termed senility. Proper nourishment of the nervous system is important in aiding one to stay grounded and not be carried away with too many unrealistic plans.

Uranus aspecting natal **Pluto** brings about transformation on many levels. Change of diet and lifestyle may occur, along with alterations in one's physical appearance. Often there is a weight loss as one gets involved in more exercise and a lighter diet. Sometimes skin tone, hair texture, and other physical features are changed. One client practiced yoga during this transit and reported that a body area which had been rigid all her life became supple as a result.

TRANSITS OF NEPTUNE

With transits of Neptune there is a greater tendency to disease and infection. Since Neptune rules the auto-immune system susceptibility to toxins becomes stronger. One is also more predisposed to develop symptoms that are difficult to diagnose. It is important to meditate during this transit in order to discover what is happening and to gain clarity.

Malfunctions in the metabolism often develop during Neptune's transits. One client had her first severe symptoms of hypoglycemia when Neptune transited her Sagittarian Ascendant. The symptoms continued while Neptune conjoined her other Sagittarian planets.

Sensitivity to the outside world makes one feel more reclusive during Neptune transits and often one builds up anxieties and fears. The wearing of crystals and other gems may prove helpful in neutralizing any negative energy. One should be careful to take additional protective measures in doing any kind of healing work or spiritual readings.

Caution should also be exercised regarding the use of drugs, chemical or otherwise, or alcohol. Habit patterns that are started during Neptune transits may be difficult to break. Treating ailments (as much as possible) with natural substances is best.

Transits of **Neptune** to the **Sun** may bring about allergic reactions and increased sensitivity. One of my students developed an allergy to fish when Neptune conjoined her Sagittarian Sun. Still another developed nasal allergies.

With **Neptune-Moon** combinations eye problems have often become prevalent since the Moon deals with fluids in the body and Neptune vision. A friend had an eye operation with Neptune conjunct her natal Moon. If you are having any difficulties have your eyes examined during this transit. Also the kidneys, which are a reflex of the eyes and balance the fluid intake, should be checked. With the Moon ruling Cancer (the stomach) Neptune transiting the Moon has also brought about some digestive disturbances and food allergies.

Neptune-Mercury combinations can produce extremely nervous states, often associated with confusion. It is helpful to be able to relax as much as possible under this transit—to go away for a few weeks, if possible, and tune in to the Earth Mother. Films, music and poetry can be a source of inspiration at this time. Foods and supplements rich in B Vitamins as well as the nervine herbs are important. In extreme conditions, this combination can produce considerable strain, resulting in a nervous breakdown. Two clients were hospitalized when Neptune conjoined natal Mercury in Sagittarius.

Neptune transiting **Venus** can cause problems with the thyroid; the metabolism can also be thrown off with subsequent sugar imbalance. Curb any tendency to overindulgence in sweets and alcohol at this time . Fish and sea vegetables—dulse, nori and kelp— should be part of the diet during this transit.

Neptune-Mars combinations can, on occasion, cause anemic conditions. Foods rich in iron—organic calvers liver, wheatgrass, dulse, raisins, beets, seaweeds, cherry and prune juices—should be increased and nettle leaf tea and the cell salt Ferrum Phos should be taken if necessary. Infections that have been difficult to diagnose and cure have started under this transit.

Neptune aspects to **Jupiter** often catalyze metabolic disturbances like hypoglycemia. Additional toxins may also be present in the liver at this time and bile production may be low. Excesses in diet and drink are common since the individual often does not understand what is happening in the life. One student developed hepatitis when Neptune squared his natal Jupiter; he had to calm down and make changes in his diet and exercise pattern in order to maintain his health.

The influence of **Neptune** on natal **Saturn** may manifest in several ways. Often conditions of crystallization such as arthritis have developed because people were unwilling to release old habit patterns. Many children with natal Saturn in Gemini have their teeth coming in crooked with the opposition of Neptune in Sagittarius. Feelings of lethargy and the tendency to lay back have been experienced with the transit of Neptune over natal Saturn. One student with Neptune square his natal Saturn in Virgo started jogging because of this lethargic feeling; he ended up injuring his *foot*

(Neptune) and then decided to surrender himself to the lethargy.

Neptune-Uranus combinations stimulate the nervous system. Often individuals experiencing these transits are bewildered by the events occurring in their lives.

Confusion and disorientation in thinking have resulted, and on occasion some people have resorted to drugs or alcohol as an escape mechanism. Allergies have often manifested during this transit, especially in those with natal Uranus in mutable signs.

The first square of **Neptune** to its own place occurs in the early 40's when one has already completed the Uranus opposition and now needs catalyzation on the inner planes. This can be an upsetting emotional period or a very productive, creative and spiritual time. Several clients experienced a recurrence of childhood allergies. One person was working out an emotional relationship and kept repeating old patterns. He came down with the worst case of hay fever in twenty years. Another friend developed an allegy to a dog that he bought for his children and had to resolve some of his own childhood fears regarding dogs.

Transits of **Neptune** to **Pluto** relate to a period of intense inner and spiritual growth. Often old habit patterns are left behind and new ways of eating and taking care of the body are adopted. Many with natal Pluto in Gemini experienced surgery (removal of one of their organs) with the opposition of Neptune in Sagittarius.

TRANSITS OF PLUTO

Transits of Pluto can often lead to a transformation of health patterns and diet. Through some illness or physical breakdown, one is forced to go through a period of purification and purging, a rebirth on a physiological level. Surgery, involving the removal of one part of the body with another organ taking over that particular process, often occurs. Many women have undergone hysterectomies, especially with Pluto squaring its natal position.

Hidden transformations in the body that have not manifested physiologically prior to this time often come to the surface. One young client had cancer diagnosed when Pluto hit his Ascendant, though the process inevitably started prior to the actual conjunction.

The reproductive system is often involved under Pluto transits with infection and diseases flaring up. Problems with the excretory system may also manifest at this time.

Transits of **Pluto** to the **Sun** affect changes in the entire body, especially the circulatory system since the Sun rules the heart. Squares and oppositions of Pluto to the Sun often bring on poor circulation. Additional exercise and the herbs red clover blossoms and cayenne can be helpful.

Pluto-Moon combinations may indicate digestive disturbances (Moon governs the stomach) and require a change of diet. Transits of Pluto to the Moon can also aggravate allergies since the Moon rules fluids and mucous. One client with Moon conjunct Neptune in Libra in her natal chart developed an extreme case of eczema when Pluto transited this conjunction. The exacerbation of her condition forced her to seek out the help of a homeopathic physician, which resulted in an alleviation of the symptom.

Under **Pluto-Moon** combinations miscarriages and still-births have occurred. As Pluto rules birth and death, many situations are possible which force the individual to undergo some kind of transformative process. Someone asked a doctor, who assisted in home deliveries, how he felt about his responsibility in delivering children that were stillborn. He replied that he had seen both the mother and father undergo as much of a personal transformation through the delivery of a dead child as through a live one.

Pluto transiting natal **Mercury** can lead to nervous exhaustion and, in extreme cases, breakdowns. Under a Pluto transit one tends to go so deeply into the study of a subject that one experiences acute strain. Relaxation, meditation and physical exercise will help to balance out the intense mental energy.

Pluto contacting the **Venusian** energy may stir up sexual repression which often results in channelling the energy in a new manner. Skin eruptions and venereal diseases, such as gonorrhea and syphilis, may occur under this transit.

Mars-Pluto contacts can bring out the expression of violent explosive energies. Accidents are common under this transit. The individual can become physically exhausted from overdoing. Repressed sexual energy often manifests in the excretory system with symptoms of hemorrhoids.

Transits of **Pluto** to **Jupiter** mark a time of strong transformation and growth. This signifies the time to clean up any excesses in the life style. Problems with the pancreas and liver may surface during this transit, particularly if there is a need to cleanse the body and purify the diet.

Pluto-Saturn combinations often mark dramatic periods of change in the life when old structures are released and transformed. This may necessitate new dietary habits, exercise routines and other daily regimes. Cancer has often been diagnosed during Pluto-Saturn transits. When Pluto uncovers fixations that have been dormant it is an opportunity to release old patterns, emotional and otherwise, and evolve new ones.

Pluto transiting natal **Uranus** is certain to bring some new events into one's life. With Pluto in Libra, kidney problems and eye problems have become prevalent. One client, with Pluto opposing her natal Uranus in Aries, developed swelling under her eyes, and also discovered she had kidney problems. Another student had her fallopian tubes tied when Pluto squared her natal Uranus in Cancer.

The energy of **Pluto** transiting **Neptune** is responsible for many inner or spiritual transformations. Certain inherent sensitivities which, on the physical level, often lead to allergies or hypoglycemic tendencies may be brought out by this transit. The increased responsiveness toward the environment may bring about conditions that are common to many individuals.

Pluto aspecting natal **Pluto** often leads to a change of appearance; releasing old habit patterns and replacing them with new ones. If surgery is performed it may involve a new medical technique or replacing a diseased organ with an organ from another person. Many women clients underwent hysterectomies when Pluto squared their natal Pluto in Cancer and brought about changes in their hormone levels and menstrual cycles. Unfortunately, in many cases, surgery only compounded the difficulties and they still had to deal with their emotional and physical changes through diet, exercise and other therapies.

LUNATIONS AND ECLIPSES

In a study of the transits to the natal horoscope, lunations and eclipses play a strong part. Lunations occur monthly at new moon when the Sun and Moon are conjunct; solar eclipses occur twice yearly at lunations; lunar eclipses often occur two weeks after a solar eclipse. Some years, however, there are no lunar eclipses. It is important to note the planets, angles and midpoints that are aspected by the lunation or eclipse and the house in which it falls. An orb of about three degrees is recommended for lunations and eclipses.

When the lunation makes a hard aspect to a planet, particularly the conjunction or opposition, it may indicate the beginning of a cycle in regard to the functioning of a specific organ or the physiological process represented by that planet. With the full moon, some physical symptom may manifest for the first time since full moons bring the energy out into the open. As with all other transiting influences no negative effects may be experienced by the physical body. The cycle could as well indicate increased physical energy or the start of a new exercise program or dietary change.

Eclipses amplify the effect of lunations. Some eclipses are partial, some are total, some are annular, and each eclipse traverses a different path through the world.*

The pre-natal eclipse point refers to the *solar* eclipse prior to birth. The degree of the pre-natal eclipse should be included in the horoscope as significant time periods in one's life occur when a major progression, transit or eclipse make a hard aspect to this point. Note whether the eclipse point conjoins the North or South node. Individuals born with the South node conjunction seem to experience more serious

___

*The pamphlet on Mundane Data published by the American Federation of Astrologers or any good almanac will give the specifics on each eclipse. In order for an eclipse to occur, the Sun and Moon must conjunct one of the Moon's nodes.

health problems. As the South node functions more as a release point, the working through and releasing of old psychological and psychospiritual patterns give rise to a stronger physical manifestation.

In my studies of children's horoscopes those who have manifested cancer at an early age had the South node conjunct the eclipse point.

In my experience there are no hard and fast rules for the duration of an eclipse. The effect of the eclipse depends upon other transits and progressions operating at the time and, as always, how the *individual* responds to the influence. A health crisis can transform itself into a time of healing and energy renewal; are we then discussing the duration of the health crisis or the entire period of healing?

In terms of affecting particular organs of the body, it is possible that an eclipse making a hard aspect to the Sun *may* involve the heart or circulatory system but, more likely, will involve those bodily parts and systems where the individual is particularly vulnerable.

EXAMPLES OF ECLIPSE ACTION

Case history of the heroin addict: (see Chapter XII) When he was caught stealing and was put in the county jail the Solar Eclipse made a sesquiquadrate to the eclipse point and the Lunar Eclipse conjoined it. When he went to Synanon, a rehabilitation home for alcoholics and addicts, the Solar Eclipse conjoined his Moon and Ascendant at 20° Taurus and the Lunar Eclipse conjoined Mars at 4° Sagittarius.

Another example is the lady with eczema (see Chapter VI). Her symptoms started around her eleventh birthday with the Solar Eclipse opposed sixth house Pluto. At the age of fifteen, when her hand became very swollen and infected, the Solar Eclipse conjoined Mars (swelling). At the time she began working with a homeopathic doctor, which led to a healing crisis, the Solar Eclipse conjoined her Moon-Neptune conjunction in the eighth house.

A third example is the woman who was blind for four and a half years (see Chapter IX). When she began losing her sight, the Solar Eclipse made a sesquiquadrate to Neptune and the

Lunar Eclipse squared it. Neptune refers to sight as well as inner vision. The year she underwent her operation for glaucoma, the Solar Eclipse in January made a sesquiquadrate to her Jupiter (growth, success) and the Lunar Eclipse conjoined it; in July, the Solar Eclipse opposed her M.C. When she got her prescription for glasses after the operations the Solar Eclipse opposed Neptune.

CHAPTER SIX

HOLISTIC HEALTH INCLUDING HOMEOPATHY AND CELL SALTS

What is Holistic Health? The first factor to recognize is that the human body is capable of healing itself and each of us helps in that process as we care for ourselves each day. Holistic Health, then, is that which includes the body, mind, and spirit in its true sense. It is a system that functions in accordance with the universal laws and maintains the flow of healing energies. Holistic Health is not just treatment, but *prevention* and *maintenance.* In this sense, we are constantly practicing Holistic Health.

The most important concept in Holistic Health is individual responsibility—we must assume responsibility for our own being. Part of this is in learning to maintain a balanced diet, in exercising our bodies each day, in dealing with our emotional problems, and in balancing our spiritual side through prayer and meditation. In this way we attune ourselves to the cosmic flow.

Practices in Holistic Health that require treatments like body work, or various stress reduction techniques are conducted by a person trained in that area. He may be an M.D. who is using these tools as an adjunct to Western medicine, he may be an N.D. (Naturopathic Doctor), or D.C. (Doctor of Chiropractory), or he may simply be a Holistic Health practitioner. His title is not important—what *is* important is that this individual function as more than just a doctor for the body—he must be a true shaman or medicine man who is capable of conducting healing on all levels of the being. Only such an individual can truly call himself a Holistic Health practitioner, and even then, he is only a *catalyst* to our own healing process. First and foremost, it is *we* who heal ourselves.

NUTRITION

Assuming responsibility for the food we put into our bodies is a primary concern—where it is grown, whether it has been sprayed with pesticides, as well as its preparation and combination with other foods. Diet is truly an individual matter. Roger Williams has shown in his book, *Biochemical Individuality*, how different and varying are the needs of our bodies. Each of us requires particular nutrients in different proportions as is easily seen through the Astrological chart; many of us have food allergies or difficulty assimilating certain foods. To follow any one diet such as a Raw Food Diet or a Macrobiotic Diet is to shift that responsibility to another human being—the responsibility for tuning in to our own physical vehicles and determining our individual needs, regardless of what is in vogue at the time. There is a great difference between *desires* and *needs* when it comes to food. What we desire may not always be what is best for our bodies. If we can distinguish between the two, we can balance ourselves accordingly.

Lack of proper nutrition has been found to be an important cause of our major disease-syndromes—arteriosclerosis and heart disease, diabetes and hypoglycemia, as well as cancer. Diet also plays a significant role in alcoholism and drug addiction as well as asthma and allergic conditions.

There are several ways of determining an individual's nutritional needs. Laboratory blood tests and urinalysis may be helpful in checking for vitamin and mineral deficiencies and overloads. According to Chinese medical diagnosis and the five element theory, through the taking of the pulses it is possible to read not only the health of the organism as a whole but that of each organ separately. The colors and lines that are revealed through Oriental facial diagnosis show the dis-ease in the body and indicate dietary imbalances. Studying the iris of the eye through the science of Iridology is also a fine diagnostic tool in understanding what parts of the body are out of balance.

In terms of specific methods for checking foods and nutritional supplements, applied kinesiology (known as muscle testing or Touch for Health) is one way. Applied kinesiology uses a system of simple muscle testing procedures to assess the energy levels of the life forces which control the body. Through the relationships of each specific muscle group and organs, it is possible to discern where structural imbalances lie, to assess dietary deficiencies and allergies, and to detect organ dysfunction. Another way is through the science of Radiesthesia—the use of the pendulum to test various foods and supplements in order to determine which foods are best for each individual. With this method, one can also determine doses on vitamins and minerals, cell salts, and herbs.

EXERCISE

Man has always recognized the need for physical exercise as a necessary adjunct to his health. In an age of increasing mental activity and machines which perform most of our heavy tasks, we must turn to gymnasiums and exercise classes to fulfill important bodily needs. Regardless of how sound our diet is, if we are not spending enough time in physical activity, we are not absorbing and assimilating the nutrients from our foods. Many of us need to start building up our bodies slowly to the point where we are able to run further each day or swim more laps. Those who have been in ill health can gradually regain their strength through yoga therapy—simple physical postures that emphasize breathing and relaxation. Unity of mind, body, and spirit is an important concept in yoga and the postures aim at integrating these. Tai Chi is another ancient practice from the Orient which works with the integration of breath and movement to balance the body and increase the "chi" or vital energy.

Other exercises which are of great benefit are the Feldenkrais exercises. Developed by Moshe Feldenkrais, these exercises work on re-aligning body structure. Again, they do not require heavy physical exertion but work in a more subtle manner.

In addition, running, jogging, swimming, tennis, golf, and dance are all important ingredients in keeping one's body tuned up.

MEGAVITAMIN THERAPY

Megavitamin or Orthomolecular Therapy is a term which is often misunderstood. It does not necessarily mean the taking of large amounts of vitamins. It merely means providing the body with the proper elements to create the correct molecular environment for optimal health. This may be large doses of certain vitamins in the case of a schizophrenic personality or an alcoholic, but it may also be a small amount to correct a particular deficiency. Megavitamin therapy has been used most often in psychiatric cases— schizophrenia, depression, and alcoholism. These conditions are often based on biochemical disturbances or defects. Orthomolecular Psychiatry, as it has been called when used in conjunction with other psychiatric methods, believes that mental illness can result from a low concentration in the brain of the following vitamins: Thiamine (B-2), Niacin (B3), Pyridoxine (B6), B-12, Biotin, Folic Acid, and Vitamin C (Ascorbic Acid). Orthomolecular Therapy developed during the 1960's when the importance of treating hypoglycemia in schizophrenia and alcoholism was studied. At the same time allergies and allergies to environmental chemicals which are often the cause of psychiatric symptoms were researched. Megavitamin Therapy has now been expanded to other types of illness and symptoms resulting from body imbalances.

HERBS

Herbs have been used as healing agents since the beginning of time. Many roots, barks, and seeds of plants have medicinal value. Early pharmaceutical medicines were derived from botanicals. In our time, chemists from many major drug companies are studying herbs in hopes of finding effective healing agents to replace some of the harmful chemical medicines in modern drugstores.

Herbs can be used in many ways. The most common way is in the form of teas whereby an infusion or decoction is prepared. Infusions are teas prepared from leaves by steeping the leaves in boiling water. Decoctions are teas made from the root, bark, or branch of the herb. These are simmered or boiled in water for a certain period of time. Poultices and ointments for external use are made from herbs along with tinctures, a concentrated alcohol extract of the herb that is taken a few drops at a time. Each individual herb has many properties so it is important to have a thorough knowledge of what that herb does before combining it in mixtures with other herbs. It is also important, when possible, to pick herbs fresh and dry them oneself. By the time they get to the store, they may have lost some of their potency. If they are kept in tightly sealed jars they may be stored for quite some time. Using herbs in tea bag form has little medicinal value because most of the potency has been lost and a beverage tea, rather than a medicinal dose, results.

As external ointments, herbs have been effective in treating poison ivy and oak, eczema, psoriasis, and a variety of other skin infections. Internally, their use has proven effective in complaints including constipation and diarrhea, congestion and respiratory ailments, hemorrhoids, digestive problems, diabetes, and many more ailments and disease-syndromes.

BODY WORK

One of the most important areas to develop out of the Holistic Health movement is that of body work. Essentially, body work can be classified in three ways:
1. sensual and relaxing types of massage
2. massage techniques for relieving stress based on deep tissue work which breaks down body armor and releases pent up emotions
3. techniques which work with the electro-magnetic currents in the body and balance the "chi" force or vital energy

The first area is the most widespread and refers mainly to Swedish massage techniques which work on the muscles of the body in an effort to relax them and release tension. Another function of this type of massage is to work with the body in a way that is caring and nurturing. Traditional Swedish massage uses fast, quick movements to stimulate the heart and get the circulation going.

Included in the second category of stress-releasing techniques are Rolfing, or Structural Integration, and Bio-energetic Therapy. Rolfing or Structural Integration involves the application of heavy and concentrated pressure to parts of the body by using a knuckle or an elbow. Their purpose is to change the body posture by realigning the muscular and connective tissue. In order to do this, a Rolfing session brings out many deep-seated or repressed emotions that have been stored in the body. Bioenergetic Therapy (often known as Reichian massage) also works to release muscular constriction that has occurred as a defense against feelings and emotions the individual has not been able to handle. Body manipulations are accompanied by a verbal analysis of the emotions involved. There are other techniques like Postural Integration and Lomi Body Work that operate in a similar fashion. Of prime importance in this type of work is the strong desire of the individual to break up old patterns and transform his being.

Perhaps the most exciting kinds of body work are those techniques that deal with electromagnetic energy, which seek to polarize the various electrical currents in the body. The system of meridians, or lines of force running through the body, comes from the Orient. Each meridian is connected to one of the vital organs, and the organs, in turn, are related to one of the five elements. (There are *five* elements in the Oriental system). Each organ is also connected to another organ in the opposite part of the body by reflex action. Thus a polarity is established.

These body therapies deal with what the Chinese call the "chi" or vital energy (called ki in Japan, prana in India, orgone energy by Wilhelm Reich, universal life force, etc.). One of the laws that has to do with health and well-being states that all illness and injury are created through stagnation of the flow of the "chi". When the "chi" is made to flow again, the body heals itself. The body receives "chi" energy through the air we breathe, the food we eat, and every thing visible and invisible in our environment, including our thoughts.

Acupressure, Shiatsu, and *Jin Shinn* are all techniques which work with balancing the "chi" energy. Various pressure points along the meridians of the body are used to release bottled-up energy and muscular tension. Acupressure works more with finger pressure; Shiatsu is a massage technique utilizing the meridians and pressure points, and Jin Shinn works with the synchronization of pulses along the meridian.

Polarity Therapy is the name given by Dr. Randolph Stone to his own integration of a number of massage and manipulation techniques which seek to balance body energy. Polarity therapy derives from India and works with polarizing the electrical currents within the body.

Reflexology deals primarily with the feet (although there is also hand reflexology). It is based on the principle that pressure points on the bottom of the feet have reflexes in other points of the body. In the case of a headache, the underpart of the big toe might be massaged; for a stomach ache it would be another area. The points on the foot that are tender indicate difficulty with corresponding regions of the body.

Not included in any of these three categories is *chiropractic work*, which is concerned more with the body structure. Chiropractic is based on the theory that when the vertebrae of the spine are not in alignment, an unlimited amount of symptoms can occur. Chiropractors work mostly with adjusting the spine, and manipulating the vertebrae and the nerves. Some chiropractors also work with the muscles as well as the skeletal frame.

ACUPUNCTURE

The theory behind acupuncture is based on the balance of energies. By inserting needles at various points along the meridians which run through the body, it is possible to balance the energy flow and restore health. Various techniques of acupuncture are used. Some acupuncturists use ariculotherapy, in which needles are inserted into various points of the ear. (The ear, like the foot in Reflexology, is a microcosm of the entire body.) Another technique is the use of a very small amount of electric current which is fed into the needle to achieve a greater stimulating effect. Many conditions have been treated successfully with acupuncture— particularly arthritis, asthma, and migraine headache.

MEDITATIVE TECHNIQUES

Visualization

Most important in the Holistic Health movement is the utilization of such meditative techniques as Visualization, Biofeedback, and Color and Music Therapy. These techniques help to change mental attitudes of the patient toward his illness. The ability of the mind to bring forth positive images and to visualize the body as healed is very powerful. Visualization therapy was developed by Dr. O. Carl Simonton through his treatment with cancer patients. Dr. Simonton, working together with his wife, had patients mentally picture their disease and see how their bodies were interacting with the treatment so that they could hasten the recovery process. For example, he would have them visualize an army of white blood cells overcoming the cancer cells. The results of this type of treatment have been profound, and visualization is now being used to deal with a variety of disease syndromes.

Autogenics

Autogenics, which was developed by the German psychiatrist Johannes Schultz in 1932, is a relaxation technique with comparable goals to those of Eastern meditation. Specific exercises are used which induce states of deep physiological and mental relaxation. Having worked with hypnosis, Schultz noticed that people in a hypnotic trance experienced two physical sensations—one was a feeling of warmth throughout the body, and the other a feeling of heaviness in the limbs and torso. He therefore designed certain exercises to induce these two conditions where the individual would be in a passive state and not exercising conscious will. Through these exercises, people learn to abandon themselves to their own bodily processes, thereby improving physical functioning and eliminating many neurotic and psychosomatic symptoms.

After achieving physical relaxation, and once the individual can enter the relaxed state easily, he can advance to the more subtle psychological aspects of autogenic training, through which higher states of consciousness may be developed as well as a marked degree of autonomic control. Feats similar to that of Eastern yogis have been reported such as self-anesthetization against a third degree burn produced by a lighted cigarette on the back of the hand. The appeal of autogenic training to many Westerners is that it begins on an easily understandable level and then slowly progresses to a more esoteric state.

Biofeedback

Using a biofeedback machine is a significant aid in teaching people to relax and enter a meditative state. A GSR device (galvanic skin response) is attached to a person's fingertips; this measures the amounts of perspiration on the skin. The more tense one is, the more perspiration. This is then attached to a machine which uses a light or a buzzing sound. As the device picks up more perspiration, the buzzing sound becomes louder. When the person relaxes more and sinks into a deeper state of consciousness, the sound becomes softer. By the intensity of the sound, a person can feel what it's like to be in a relaxed state. In similar fashion, he can work on lowering his blood pressure or any other physiological process, through using the machine as a monitor.

Music Therapy

Music and dance have been known throughout the centuries to heal many who are in a tense or emotional state. Ancient tribal rituals emphasized music and dance as a way of emotional release, muscle relaxation, and the tightening of the social unit. In cases of mentally distraught individuals, certain types of music have been found to be very soothing. There is, in fact, a correspondence between the planets, colors and specific notes or tones.

Color Therapy

Wearing clothes of various hues or spending time in a room of a certain shade has a marked effect on one's attitude. In utilizing the spectrum of color through slides, theatrical gels, and colored waters, one can reduce pain and swelling, cure headaches, break up congestion, and balance out many body conditions. Colors are related to the meridians and organs within the body. Muscle testing and Radiesthesia are both helpful in choosing colors for various conditions.

Radiesthesia

Radiesthesia describes the detection of vibrations or waves of force which emanate from all objects in the physical universe and from levels of consciousness that lie beyond the range of physical sense perception. In order to detect and measure these forces, various implements have been employed as the dowsing rod and pendulum. These vibrations can be detected by any person who takes time to develop this skill or ability.

The higher intelligence communicates through the nervous system. A pendulum acts to amplify the neuro-muscular response in providing a clear set of signals. The signals supply important data for the radiesthesist—concerning water, minerals or in the healing field, the correct remedy.

Medical Radiesthesia can detect some of the hidden causative factors of disease that are not always identified by means of standard clinical tests.

Witnesses, or substances symbolizing the person are often used—a lock of hair, a blood spot, or saliva, or even the name of a person written on a card. (My own innovation has been to use the Astrological chart). The physical remedy itself can be used or its name can be written down.

The pendulum can respond by answering yes, no, or neutral to the remedy (or food or herb) or the remedy can be measured on a circular scale of 360 as to its potency.

Radionics

Radionics is a form of Radiesthesia that uses an instrument or machine for detecting the vibrations. Like Radiesthesia, it seeks to determine the cause of the disease before it is clinically identifiable. Once the cause is established, the instrument can then send or broadcast to the patient a particular vibration which may be in the form of a homeopathic remedy, a color, herb, or flower remedy.

HOMEOPATHY AND CELL SALTS

Homeopathy or the homeopathic system of medicine treats the individual person, not the symptoms or dis-ease. Allopathic medicine, most commonly practiced in this country, treats the symptoms of the illness, usually with chemical drugs. In the homeopathic system, it is not just the physical body that is being treated but the mind, emotions, and spirit. To this end, the homeopathic physician attempts to find a remedy that has a similar vibration to the person being treated and will stimulate his vital energy.

Homeopathic remedies are based on the principle that "like cures like" (thus the remedy, rhus tox, which is the extract from the poison oak plant, would be given for poison oak). Both allopathic and naturopathic medicine are based on the law of opposites. For example, in naturopathy, cold foot baths would be given to break a fever. This system of medicine also finds the law of the minimum dose most effective—therefore a homeopathic remedy is administered only a few times over a given period.

Medicines are prepared for homeopathic use by diluting one part of the original substance (if a solid) or tincture (if a liquid) in nine parts of milk sugar or in a solution of alcohol and distilled water. The mixture is triturated (ground into a fine powder) in a mortar or shaken in a bottle for some time until the medicinal substance is uniformly distributed throughout the dilutent. The process can be repeated as many times as desired. The high dilutions are usually felt to be more powerful than the low dilutions.

Homeopathy has proved particularly effective in chronic conditions such as allergies, asthma, arthritis, bursitis, and rheumatism. There are also homeopathic remedies for acute conditions such as cuts, burns, and shock.

Homeopathy can be correlated well with astrology by studying the personality type as represented through the chart. One homeopathic doctor I know gives his remedies in

timing with astrological hours of the day—hours that relate
to certain types of disease through the Hindu system of
Astrology.

BIOCHEMISTRY

The Biochemic system of medicine was developed by Dr. W.
M. Scheussler of Germany in the late 1800's. Dr. Scheussler
explained disease and body imbalance as a result of the
molecular disturbance in certain cell salts of the body. The
possibility of curing such functional disturbances was
through prescribing the individual salts which were found to
be deficient in the individual. Scheussler demonstrated by
experiments that the mineral salts vitally concerned in
carrying on functional activity in the cells of the human body
are twelve in number and he called these tissue salts. He was
able to describe the type of disorder due to the disturbance of
the physiological balance of each salt. He made it understood
that tissue salts were to be selected on the basis of individual
symptoms of each patient and not as remedies for a
particular disease.

The importance of the cell salts was first scientifically
determined by Dr. Samuel Hahnemann and his colleagues
through their investigation into homeopathic remedies.
These salts are listed in the standard homeopathic repertory,
the Materia Medica.

Since each person's chemistry and metabolism are
different, so the proportion of tissue salts varies in each of
our bodies. We may have an inherent tendency to lack one or
more of the salts, and at various periods in our life, we may
develop deficiencies of one or more of the salts. We should
view these salts as nutritional supplements rather than as
medicines.

In preparing the cell salts, Dr. Scheussler used the homeopathic principle of trituration, reducing the mineral salts to
fine particles, and putting them in a lactose (milk sugar) base
so they would be easily assimilated. These small tablets are
taken without water and simply placed under the tongue
where they immediately dissolve.

The twelve salts correspond to the twelve Astrological

signs. Many books have been written on this zodiacal correspondence, notably Inez Perry's *The Zodiac and the Salts of Salvation.* There are many existing theories about which salts are most easily depleted in our body—Sun sign, sign opposite Sun, Moon sign, etc. Again, I have found it to be an individual matter, although the signs containing Saturn and the South node are usually important. A thorough examination of the chart must be made before any salts can be recommended. A description of the twelve cell salts follows:

Kali Phos (Potassium Phosphate) Kali Phos is found in all the tissues and fluids of the body, particularly the brain and nerve cells. It is a great nutrient for the nerves. A deficiency of Kali Phos may produce irritability, timidity, fearfulness, and sleeplessness. It is a good remedy for headaches, depression, insomnia, and diseases of nervous origin.

Nat Sulph (Sodium Sulphate) The principal function of this salt is to regulate intracellular fluids in the body by eliminating excess water. It is important in the digestive process where it controls bile production and also in the proper functioning of the kidneys.

Kali Mur (Potassium Chloride) This salt unites with albumin, forming fibrin, which is found in every tissue of the body with the exception of the bones. Fibrin helps cells retain their shape. Kali Mur is helpful in treating any respiratory problems such as colds, hay fever, allergies, as well as sore throats and tonsilitis.

Calc Fl (Calcium Fluoride) Calc Fl appears in the surface of the bones, the enamel of the teeth, and in the elastic fibers of the muscle tissue. Its deficiency causes these tissues to lose their elasticity. It is useful in treating diseases of teeth, bones, hardening of arteries, and, an important aid for digestion.

Mag Phos (Magnesium Phosphate) Mag Phos is anti-spasmodic as its work relates to the nerves. A deficiency of this salt in the fiber of the body allows it to contract so it produces spasms and cramps. The contraction puts pressure on the sensory nerves which give rise to sharp, shooting pains. This salt is especially good for painful cramps associated with menstruation and has been used for spasm and epilepsy.

Kali Sulph (Potassium Sulphate) Kali Sulph carries oxygen to the cells of the skin and distributes oil in the body which aids in perspiration and the elimination of body poisons. Kali Sulph is excellent in the treatment of acne and other skin conditions, including dandruff.

Nat Phos (Sodium Phosphate) Nat Phos has as its function maintaining the acid-alkaline balance in the blood. Lack of this salt may produce a yellow coating on the tongue. Nat Phos is helpful in relieving acid stomach and in treating ulcers.

Calc Sulph (Calcium Sulphate) Calc Sulph is a blood purifier which builds the epithelial tissue in the body. It is effective in all healing processes and is used in elimination problems such as constipation.

Silica (Silicon Dioxide) Silica is present in the blood, bile, skin, hair, and nails. It is also found in connective tissue, bones, nerve sheaths and mucous membranes. In proper amount it gives bones, fingernails, and hair a glossy appearance, especially the teeth. It is helpful in cases of pus formation to promote suppuration. It helps to minimize scar tissue formation after surgery or injury.

Calc Phos (Calcium Phosphate) Calc Phos is a constituent of the bone tissue. The body requires large amounts when it is growing or recovering from fractures. It is also an essential ingredient in the digestive juices for food to be digested properly. This salt plays an important role in the clotting mechanism of the blood. Insufficiency causes skeletal problems such as rickets, curvature of the spine, teeth problems, rheumatism, arthritis, and swollen or painful joints.

Nat Mur (Sodium Chloride) Nat Mur is found in every cell and fluid where one of its most important roles is to maintain the proper degree of moisture within the body. Symptoms of the lack of Nat Mur are dryness of the mouth, constipation, shingles and slowed healing from insect bites. It is helpful in treating blisters, swelling, itching, eczema, and redness and burning of the skin, as in sunburn. With the exception of Calc Phos, the body requires more Nat Mur than any salt.

Ferrum Phos (Iron Phosphate) Found in the blood, Ferrum Phos is an essential component of the hemoglobin which carries oxygen to all parts of the body. It is the most frequently needed of all the tissue salts because most diseases start with inflammation of one kind or another. It is required for red blood cells and its lack can cause anemia. Insufficient oxygen can cause other body processes to slow down so the lack of Ferrum Phos may make the individual tire more easily.

BACH FLOWER REMEDIES

A Chapter on holistic health would not be complete without mentioning the Bach Flower Remedies. Homeopathically prepared, the Bach remedies use the healing power of wildflowers to create within us a condition in which we are more emotionally balanced and less prone to disease. Dr. Edward Bach, a pioneer in this field, roamed the English countryside to find flowers that would be suitable as healing essences.

Each of the Bach preparations responds to a particular emotional-spiritual imbalance and works in a very subtle way. By studying the thirty-eight remedies, each individual can decide for himself, or with the help of someone familiar with the remedies, his need at the moment. There is a handbook on the flower remedies, as well as another pamphlet which lists various emotions and moods and classifies the remedies in that way.

A few remedies at a time can be put into one preparation, which is then mixed with spring water. The remedy is taken four drops at a time, several times a day.

In addition to using a flower remedy, it is important to be doing inner work on oneself to balance out the emotional and spiritual energy. One American healer who works with the remedies has created a set of affirmations or positive statements for each remedy.

Besides the Bach flower remedies, there is also a set of American flower remedies created by Richard Katz and the Flower Essence Society (Box 459, Nevada City, California 95959). The purpose of the Flower Essence Society is to utilize the healing power of plants all over the world, to do research on the properties of the flower essence, and to network those practitioners throughout the world who are working with flower remedies. To this end, they publish a members' newsletter several times a year and a yearly journal.

There are also other individuals who have created essence remedies from flowers, roots, vegetables, fruits, and gems.

CHAPTER SEVEN

ALLERGIC DISORDERS
AND ASTHMA

Allergic disorders range from those which affect the respiratory passages (asthma, hay fever, allergic rhinitis) to skin allergies (eczema, hives), gastro-intestinal allergies (often causing diarrhea), and allergies affecting the neurological system (resulting in migraines, fatigue, and other symptoms). Certain physical types have sensitivities in particular areas of the body which manifest when their energy is low and during stressful periods in the life.

Stress affects the body in so many ways that it would be helpful to have an understanding of the many physiological changes that take place as a result. The most complete exploration of the phenomena of stress is given by Dr. Hans Selye in his book, *The Stress of Life*. Here are some of the basic concepts.

During stress reactions, the *kidneys* are affected because they regulate the chemical composition of the blood and tissues by selectively eliminating certain chemicals from the body. The kidneys can also adjust blood pressure. The *thyroid* is also affected; it releases hormones which stimulate the metabolism of every other tissue. The *liver* participates as well in most of the biochemical adjustments to stress. It regulates the concentration of sugar, protein and other important tissue foods in the blood; it destroys the excess of corticoids when the adrenals make too much, and it plays an important role in detoxifying environmental pollutants or poisonous substances that arise in the body. The *white blood cells* regulate immune reactions and allergic hypersensitivity resulting from exposure to various foreign substances.

Allergies create a hypersensitive state where the body overreacts to foreign substances; this reaction may stimulate the immune system and histamine production. The substances, known as allergens, can be detected in several ways.

The traditional way of determining allergic sensitivity was through the use of sub-dermal patch tests. Allergens were scratched on the surface of the skin to determine which ones were offensive. These tests did not always prove to be accurate, especially in the case of food allergens.[1] Other methods of testing include sub-lingual tests where the extract is placed under the tongue. This is an effective test since the food gets a chance to go through the digestive tract. Another method is cytotoxic testing, which measures the destruction of white blood cells caused by exposure to foods and chemicals.

Attempts have been made in allopathic medicine to desensitize the individual through injecting the allergens responsible. This has not always proved successful as often other chemical reactions take place in the bloodstream. A more thorough approach has resulted in the complete treatment of the glands and organs in a natural manner. This approach includes the following:

1. **Nourishing the adrenal glands so that they produce the required hormones.** The adrenal cortex releases a natural cortisone to destroy white blood cells and thus inhibit inflammation, as well as the hormone aldosterone which fights stress and prevents fatigue. In order to produce these, a sufficient amount of B-Complex is recommended; if in vitamin form, one which does not have a yeast base. Nutritional yeast has an extremely acidic effect on the body; yeast also contains little pantothenic acid. In addition to the B-Complex, B-6 tablets may be needed.

   Magnesium is another important nutrient for the nervous system. Liquid chlorophyll is high in magnesium (a dose of one teaspoon in half a glass of water twice daily) and provides vitamins A and C. If liquid chlorophyll is not obtainable, a magnesium tablet may be taken. Iodine is an ingredient necessary for the production of thyroid hormones. Sea vegetables, especially dulse, nori

---

[1]*Dr. Mandell's 5-Day Allergy Relief System,* Dr. Marshall Mandell & L. W. Scanlon, Simon & Schuster, N.Y. 1979, p. 35.

and kelp are high in iodine. However, a supplementation of liquid dulse may be necessary for a few weeks to stimulate the thyroid. An undersupply of thyroid hormones usually results in exhaustion, susceptibility to colds and flu, and other more serious conditions.

The sodium-potassium balance is also extremely important. Aldosterone, a hormone produced by the adrenals, causes the body to retain more sodium than usual, thus increasing the blood pressure and forcing nutrients into the tissues to meet the demands of stress. When the adrenals are undernourished, aldosterone is not produced, and fatigue and exhaustion result. Table salt should be avoided since there are many natural sources of sodium. Too much miso, (soybean paste) and tamari, (soy sauce) also cause a sodium-potassium imbalance.

2. **Detoxifying the liver.** The liver produces an enzyme called histiminase which serves as a natural antihistamine. If the liver is congested with fats or accumulated toxins, it cannot produce histiminase. Avoiding food additives in canned or packaged foods, artificial coloring, chemically grown or sprayed food, refined foods, alcohol, sugar, coffee and tea will help to keep the liver free of toxins. In addition, frequent juice fasts with a colonic irrigation or high enema will cleanse the liver of toxins and help purify the blood as well.

3. **Aiding the digestive system to assimilate proteins and starches.** Many people with allergies have difficulty assimilating proteins and starches and lack digestive enzymes, especially pancreatic enzymes. With frequent juice fasts the body is better able to produce its own enzymes. However, in certain cases it may be necessary to take additional enzymes and also increase vitamin B-6 which helps to break down proteins for easy assimilation. Specific digestive problems may be helped by a tablespoon or two of aloe vera juice from the aloe vera cactus.

4. **Maintaining the health of the mucous membranes.** Since allergic reactions often result in inflammations of the mucous membranes, it is important to maintain these in a healthy state. Mucous protects all the organ linings from invasion by bacteria. When this is not being

produced, membranes are vulnerable to irritation by germs and this irritation may result in an uncontrolled increase in the production of mucous. Vitamins A, C, D, and E may be necessary for certain people. Large amounts of vitamin A are found naturally in chlorophyll, wheat grass, alfalfa sprouts, alfalfa tea, and carrot juice, and in other yellow-orange and deep green vegetables and fruits. These sources usually supply the correct amount. If more vitamin A is needed, it should be taken in the dry form, not the fish liver oil capsule, but the tablet made from lemon grass. This is true of vitamins D and E as well. The oil-based form is not assimilated by the liver in some individuals. All fruits and especially green leafy vegetables contain vitamin C. If additional vitamin C is called for, it should be used in the form of calcium or potassium ascorbate. Potassium absorption helps maintain the acid/alkaline balance. Many people are deficient in vitamin D which aids assimilation of calcium and vitamin D absorption may be hampered because of smog and other pollutants in the atmosphere. Vitamin D should also be utilized in its dry form which is derived from mixed vegetable sources. Vitamin E helps deliver oxygen to the cells; it is found in the unrefined oils, grains and lecithin. If it is necessary as a supplement, it should not be used as an oil-based capsule, but in tablet form.

Various herbs are also healing to the mucous membranes; mullein and comfrey are particularly good for the nasal and bronchial mucosa while slippery elm is soothing to the stomach and intestinal linings. Other natural therapies that should be considered in controlling allergies include the following:

A) Homeopathic remedies have been extremely effective. They work on the biochemical level and are chosen according to the individual's sensitivities. (See Chapter Six).

B) Acupuncture, acupressure, Jin Shinn, shiatsu, and other oriental therapies. These systems have proved helpful in controlling allergic reactions and asthma. By working on the meridians of the body through needles or finger pressure the energy going to each organ is increased and the glands may be stimulated to produce the necessary hormones. (See Chapter Six).

C) Biofeedback, autogenics and other meditative techniques have been helpful in handling allergic reactions due to stress by enabling the individual to enter into a state of progressive relaxation to slow down heartbeat, pulse, etc. (See Chapter Six).

PSYCHOLOGICAL

Traditional medicine recognizes a strong psychosomatic element in allergies. Allergic individuals are hypersensitive people (Neptune, Moon, and Water sign emphasis) who react to external substances. These individuals often lack self-confidence and tend to suppress their feelings so that the allergic reaction provides a release for pent-up emotions. Many of them also have restrained their hostility, emotional expression and aggressions. Note that swelling, itching, and redness which accompany certain allergic reactions are ruled by Mars, the god of war!

Let's examine the personality traits of the asthmatic, perhaps the most complex of the allergic syndromes. Breath is the first requisite of life and respiration is an important step towards biological independence. Difficulty in breathing may be a subtle protest at being separated from the mother and needing to be independent. In fact, dependency on the mother seems to be a prime characteristic of asthmatics. There is often a conflict here between the *need* to be independent and the security of the dependency relationship.

Asthmatic children often have difficulty adapting to new surroundings and events. This kind of change may catalyze an asthma attack or a period of breathing difficulty. Asthmatics tend to be extremely rigid and need to plan for changes many years ahead of time. They may also tend to be compulsive in their habit patterns.

As teenagers, they often experience conflicts of a sexual nature which reappear later in life. In fact, it has been suggested by several authors that the asthma attack itself may be a source of sexual excitement. The attack definitely provides an outlet for emotional release and often is substituted for crying.[2]

Many types of events serve to trigger allergic episodes— moving away from a known environment, change of job, entering into a new relationship (marriage, for example) or separating from an old one, death or separation from the mother or other family members, accidents, health problems, and continuous anxiety and worry.

ASTROLOGICAL

With respiratory allergies and asthma, there is a predominance of mutable signs; with allergies involving the gastro-intestinal and neurological systems cardinal signs are usually emphasized.

The planet Neptune has much to do with one's sensitivities and often is angular, conjunct the Sun or Moon. Pluto is the other planet that is relevant to allergic reactions; Pluto may be angular or strong by progression or transit. The Moon rules fluids and has much to do with mucous and swelling; the Moon may be angular in the horoscope and the sign Cancer strong.

In cases of respiratory allergies, Mercury often appears as a dominant planet and the signs Gemini and Sagittarius are strongly involved. Four degrees of Virgo and Pisces and eighteen degrees of Gemini and Sagittarius are common in cases of respiratory allergies.

Venus and often Saturn are usually implicated in cases of skin allergy. Hard aspects from Venus to Saturn are found in the case of eczema; to Pluto where there are skin growths, warts or tumors; to Mars where there is swelling or blistering.

Midpoints that are important to check are Mars/Neptune which shows proneness to toxins and infections and Moon/Neptune, which shows overaccumulation of water in body tissues and hypersensitivity.

---

[2]"The Psychosomatic Approach to Bronchial Asthma" in *The Psychosomatic Approach To Primary Chronic Rheumatoid Arthritis*, Dr. J. J. G. Prick & Dr. K. J. M. Van DeLoo, F. M. Davis & Co., Philadelphia, p. 137-155.

CASE HISTORIES

CASE HISTORY #1

A woman in her early forties had asthma most of her life. Her symptoms began shortly before her fifth birthday and she remembers being taken to a doctor at this time and given some medication. During her college years the symptoms lessened and she took no drugs for seven years, from 1960-1967. In 1967, after a broken engagement and her brother's subsequent marriage, she again developed asthma attacks and resumed her medication. During this time she was undergoing psychotherapy. In June 1972 her symptoms became more severe, jeopardizing her teaching job. She continued to see her allopathic doctor and was given various antihistamines to help control her malady. In March 1977 I saw her as a client. She was already involved in the study of astrology and had gained further insights into her own make-up through her natal chart. Several things came out of this initial interview: first she needed to make some diet changes, eliminating coffee and replacing it with several herbal tea blends and cutting down on her consumption of dairy products (dairy products form excess mucous in the lungs); the second was to get more exercise by using yoga techniques; and the third was a referral to a homeopathic clinic for an interview; certain remedies and vitamin and mineral supplements were also recommended.

She disliked cutting down on dairy products but found it easy to replace her coffee with herb teas. She reported to the clinic for two months and has been feeling much better since that time. She no longer needs the antihistamine drugs, has changed her diet somewhat though is still erratic about it, and is getting more exercise. She still sees a psychotherapist and has been experiencing some stress in her job recently. Several years ago she stopped teaching, is presently taking care of a few older handicapped persons and is amazed to find that this stress is not producing any asthmatic symptoms.

Case History #1

Grand □ in mutables	Gets involved in too many projects; over-stimulated; needs to finish projects; problems with nervous and respiratory systems
☉ ♀ ♂ in ♊ in 11th house	Group work in communications; writing ability strong
☉ in ♊ ☍ ♃ in ♐	Tendency to overdo mental projects; spreads energy in too many directions
♃ ☌ ♂	Unusual types of writing and unique way of expressing personal philosophy
♄ □ ☉ ♀ ♂ in ♊	Difficulties in manifesting creative abilities especially in writing; frustrations in relationships, limitations in expressing love and sexual energy
♄ in 8th house in ♓ ∠ ♅ in 9th house	Strong spiritual drive and desire to relate to opposite sex in more cosmic way; vague fears in sexual area
♄ ☍ ♆ in ♍	Feelings of inadequacy and need to clarify things through a strong sense of order; potential problems with digestive system
♆ in 1st house	Not sure of her own identity or the way people perceive her
☽ in ♋	Emotional sensitivity; nurturing quality especially toward friends
☽ ☌ ☊	Difficulties with mother; needs love and support of mother; possible problems with mucous in the body and balance of body fluids
☊ dwad, ☽ ∠ ☊ asc.	Difficulty in expressing nurturing qualities because of personal ego needs
☿ in ♊ in 10th house	Need to teach, write, and work with people
☿ □ ♆	Link with intuitive side of her nature, less certain of her writing and teaching abilities
☿ Q ♄	Good ability for organizing material and presenting it to others

♀ in ♋ in 12th house	Possible emotional repression; working through old emotional patterns and subconscious programs
♀ △ ♄ in ♓ in 8th house	Ability to communicate subconscious material and transform old feelings
♅ in ♉ in 9th ♂ mc	Interest in unusual philosophies, metaphysical and occult studies; rebellious, holds to her own unique ideas; highly sensitive nervous system
♅ ∠ ♀ ♂	Manifesting ideas through writing and creative resources
♅ ∠ ♄	Somewhat restrictive in expressing her individuality
? on nadir	Strong desire to nurture and care for others
? ⬓☉, ⬓ ☽, □ asc, ∠ nodes	Difficulty in expressing the nurturing tendency
♃ in 18° ♐	Degree involved with respiratory problems
Nodes in 3° cardinal	Adrenal degree

MIDPOINTS

♄/♆ - ♃	Restrictions with liver and pancreas; with ♃ in ♐ lungs involved
♂/♆ = ♃ inverse	Tendency to hypoglycemia, difficulty metabolizing carbohydrates
☽/♆ = ♀ ♂ inverse	Emotional sensitivity, difficulty with love relationships, craving for sweets, artistic nature

Secondary Progressions	Solar Arc Directions	Transits	Eclipses
1. November 1941—five years old—first asthma attack			
☿ ∠ ♀	♆ □ ♃		March L. E. ☍ ♄
♂ ∠ MC	♃ □ ♄		Sept. L. E. ☍ ♆
☽ ♂ ♆ November			Sept. S. E. □ ☉
2. 1967—aggravation of symptoms			
MC ∠ ♀		♅ ☍ ♄ □ ♀ ♂ ☉	May S. E. □ asc.

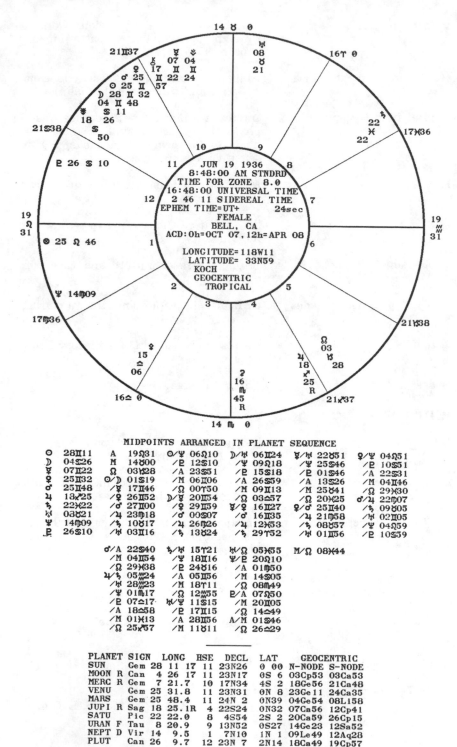

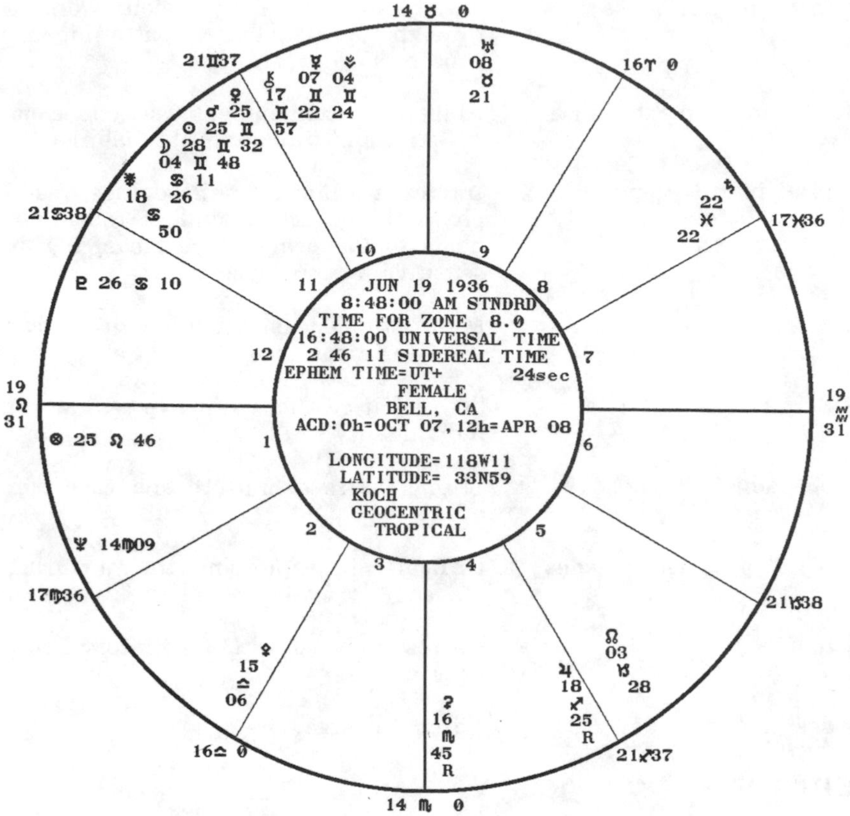
JUN 19 1936
8:48:00 AM STNDRD
TIME FOR ZONE 8.0
16:48:00 UNIVERSAL TIME
2 46 11 SIDEREAL TIME
EPHEM TIME=UT+ 24sec
FEMALE
BELL, CA
ACD:0h=OCT 07,12h=APR 08
LONGITUDE= 118W11
LATITUDE= 33N59
KOCH
GEOCENTRIC
TROPICAL

MIDPOINTS ARRANGED IN PLANET SEQUENCE

☉ 28♊11	A 19♌31	☉/♆ 06♌10	☽/♅ 06♊24	☿/♅ 22♉51	♀/♆ 04♌51
☽ 04♋26	M 14♉00	/♇ 12♋10	/♆ 09♌18	/♆ 25♋46	/♇ 10♋51
☿ 07♊22	☊ 03♑28	/A 23♋51	/♇ 15♋18	/♇ 01♋46	/A 22♋31
♀ 25♊32	☉/☽ 01♋19	/M 06♊06	/A 26♋59	/A 13♋26	/M 04♊46
♂ 25♊48	/☿ 17♊46	/☊ 00♈50	/M 09♊13	/M 25♉41	/☊ 29♓30
♃ 13♐25	/♀ 26♊52	☽/☿ 20♊54	/☊ 03♎57	/☊ 20♓25	♂/♃ 22♍07
♄ 22♓22	/♂ 27♊00	/♀ 29♊59	☿/♀ 16♊27	♀/♂ 25♊40	/♄ 09♉05
♅ 03♉21	/♃ 23♍18	/♂ 00♋07	/♂ 16♊35	/♃ 21♍58	/♅ 02♊05
♆ 14♍09	/♄ 10♉17	/♃ 26♍26	/♃ 12♓53	/♄ 08♉57	/♆ 04♌59
♇ 26♋10	/♅ 03♊16	/♄ 13♉24	/♄ 29♈52	/♅ 01♊56	/♇ 10♋59
	♂/A 22♋40	♄/♅ 15♈21	♅/☊ 05♓55	M/☊ 08♓44	
	/M 04♊54	/♆ 18♊16	♆/♇ 20♌10		
	/☊ 29♓38	/♇ 24♉16	/A 01♍50		
	♃/♄ 05♒24	/A 05♊56	/M 14♋05		
	/♅ 28♒23	/M 18♈11	/☊ 08♏49		
	/♆ 01♏17	/☊ 12♒55	♇/A 07♌50		
	/♇ 07♎17	♅/♆ 11♋15	/M 20♊05		
	/A 18♎58	/♇ 17♊15	/☊ 14♎49		
	/M 01♓13	/A 28♊56	A/M 01♋46		
	/☊ 25♐57	/M 11♉11	/☊ 26♎29		

PLANET		SIGN	LONG	HSE	DECL	LAT	GEOCENTRIC N-NODE	S-NODE
SUN		Gem	28 11 17	11	23N26	0 00		
MOON	R	Can	4 26 17	11	23N17	0S 6	03Cp53	03Ca53
MERC	R	Gem	7 21.7	10	17N34	4S 2	18Ge56	21Ca48
VENU		Gem	25 31.8	11	23N31	0N 8	23Ge11	24Ca35
MARS		Gem	25 48.4	11	24N 2	0N39	04Ge54	08Li58
JUPI	R	Sag	18 25.1R	4	22S24	0N32	07Ca56	12Cp41
SATU		Pic	22 22.0	8	4S54	2S 2	20Ca59	26Cp15
URAN	F	Tau	8 20.9	9	13N52	0S27	14Ge23	12Sa52
NEPT	D	Vir	14 9.5	1	7N10	1N 1	09Le49	12Aq28
PLUT		Can	26 9.7	12	23N 7	2N14	18Ca49	19Cp57

Asc. ☌ ♆   ♀ □♃   Oct. L. E. □♀
☉ ☌ ♀ P

3. 1972—teaching job jeopardized

♀ ∠ ♂   ♄ ☌ ☉♀♂   Jan. S. E. ☍ ♀
♀ □ ♅   Jan. L. E. □ ♄
☉ ⊓ ♃
Asc. □♃

4. March 1977—began consultations on health at homeopathic clinic

Asc. ☍ ♄   ☽ □ ♄ April   ♀ □ ☿
☉ ⊓ ♄   ☽ □ ♆ May   ♅ ☍ ♃
MC ∠ ♅
☿ □ MC

CASE HISTORY #2

This woman had eczema since her eleventh year and also suffered from hay fever when a child. The eczema appeared only on the inside of her arms. Her doctor at the time prescribed a steroid cream, which did not help much. In high school at the age of fifteen, the rash broke out on her calves and her right hand. The swelling on her hand was so severe that she was unable to use it for several years. When she moved to Washington D.C. a doctor cleared up the eczema on her hand by soaking it in ice water and in various kinds of baths. During her college years she had few problems with eczema but, as she says, channelled her stress to other areas by gaining weight and suffering from a bad complexion.

She came to the San Francisco area at twenty-two and experienced the eczema breaking out on her arms. During the summer months and warm weather her condition has always improved. In December 1977, however, the eczema became severe. Her entire body was covered and her right hand was badly affected. Presently she is working with her diet, attends a homeopathic clinic, and is involved in both psychotherapy and stress reduction techniques.

In her family both her mother and brother have had eczema and allergic reactions. Emotionally she is now working through her own tensions and fears. Her life is fairly stable; she teaches classes in art and does work in calligraphy.

Case History #2

The chart roughly occupies one half of the houses with the majority of planets below the horizon, indicating an extremely receptive and intuitive nature. There are no squares or oppositions to the Moon-Neptune conjunction (Venus-Uranus is wide) to release the energy of that combination.

☉ ☌ ♂ in ♉ (♑ decanate)	Practicality, strong drive and motivation
♓ dwad	Reinforces the ♓ asc. in emphasizing sensitive nature and idealism
☉ △ ♄ in ♍ in 7th house	Good sense of discipline; handles details well; partner is more conservative than romantic
☽ ♆ in ♎ in 8th house	Romantic ideals in relationships, feeling for poetry and music as transformational tools; with ♆ ruler of asc., allergic tendencies
☽ △ ⚷	Strong healing ability
☽ △ ⚴ in 12th house	Able to work things out in relationship through psychotherapeutic and spiritual approach
☽ contra ‖ ☿	Emphasis on nervous system; changes mind often
Angular ⚷	Hard working; tendency to be compulsive; strict attention to details
♓ Asc. (♈ dwad)	Sensitive physical vehicle; has difficulty confronting people but needs to initiate action
⚵ ☌ Asc.	Strong nurturing tendency
♀ ♅ in 5th house	Artistic inclinations; romantic affairs provide an outlet to ♄ in 7th house and break up routine; erratic functioning of thyroid gland
♀ □ ♃ in 1st house	May get carried away by too many creative projects; desire for sugars and car-

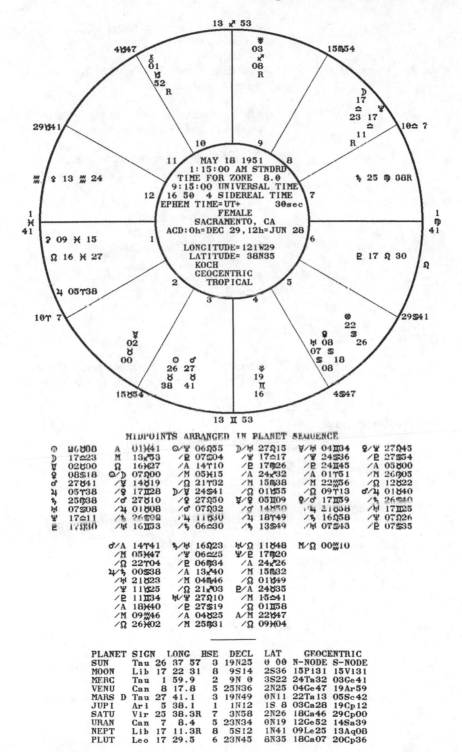

MAY 18 1951
1:15:00 AM STNDRD
TIME FOR ZONE 8.0
9:15:00 UNIVERSAL TIME
16 50 4 SIDEREAL TIME
EPHEM TIME=UT+   30sec
FEMALE
SACRAMENTO, CA
ACD:0h=DEC 29,12h=JUN 28

LONGITUDE=121W29
LATITUDE= 38N35
KOCH
GEOCENTRIC
TROPICAL

MIDPOINTS ARRANGED IN PLANET SEQUENCE

PLANET	SIGN	LONG	HSE	DECL	LAT	GEOCENTRIC	
SUN	Tau	26 37 57	3	19N25	0 00	N-NODE	S-NODE
MOON	Lib	17 22 31	8	9S14	2S36	15P131	15V131
MERC	Tau	1 59.9	2	9N 0	3S22	24Ta32	03Ge41
VENU	Can	8 17.8	5	25N36	2N25	04Ge47	19Ar59
MARS D	Tau	27 41.1	3	19N49	0N11	22Ta13	05Sc42
JUPI	Ari	5 38.1	1	1N12	1S 8	03Ca28	19Cp12
SATU	Vir	25 38.3R	7	3N58	2N26	18Ca46	29Cp00
URAN	Can	7 8.4	5	23N34	0N19	12Ge52	14Sa39
NEPT	Lib	17 11.3R	8	5S12	1N41	09Le25	13Aq08
PLUT	Leo	17 29.5	6	23N45	8N35	18Ca07	20Cp36

	bohydrates; involvement of liver and pancreas with the thyroid
☿ in 2nd house in ♉	Practical type of mind which could be utilized in business
☿ ⁎ ♀ ♅	Able to utilize her artistic skills through teaching and communication
♇ in 6th house	Transforming energy and working on her own health; possible healing work
♇ □ ☉♂ (broad)	Tendency to be somewhat compulsive; overdoing; poor circulation
♂ in 10th house in ♑	Profession will be unusual
♂ △ ☿ in 2nd house	Ability to make money and provide for herself through her profession

MIDPOINTS

♄/♆ = ♅, ♀	Tendency to hold back emotions; thyroid and other hormones may be off balance at times
♂/♅ = nodes ☿ (inverse)	Nervous system reacts when overstimulated emotionally

Secondary Progressions	Solar Arc Directions	Transits	Eclipses
1. May 1962—eleventh birthday, developed eczema			
MC □ ♄ ☿ ⊼ MC	♅ □ ☽ ♆	♅ □ ☉♂	Feb. S. E. ☍ ♇
☽ ⚹ ☍ ♄ April	♅ □ ☿		(6th house)
	♇ □ ♂		
	☊ ☌ ♄		
2. July 15, 1966—right hand swollen			
♃ □ ♀	Asc. ☌ ♌	♅ ☌ ☊	Dec. '65 L. E. □♌
☽ ⊼ ♆ July		♀ ☌ ☊	May S. E. ☌ ♂
☽ □ ♇ July			(swelling and
☽ ⊼ ☽ July			irritation)

3. **December 1977—severe eczema over body**

MC ☌ ♀   ♀ □ MC   ♀ ☌ ☽ ♆   Oct. S. E. ☌ ☽ ♆

♂ □ ☊   ♆ □ ☊ ☌ ♂/♅

☽ₚ ☌ ♃ Nov.

CASE HISTORY #3

The next horoscope is a very interesting example of gastrointestinal and respiratory allergies. From an early age this female was allergic to many foods. Her mother remembers that she vomited after eating malted milk, pineapple, eggs, and green pepper. At age ten the first bad allergic episode occurred with a sinus infection when she tried to keep a pet cat. She recovered from the infection after the cat disappeared but still continued to miss about one day of school a week through junior high and high school. No one seemed to know what was wrong with her or how to help her.

In 1963 she attended graduate school and developed a bad sinus infection. The doctor put her on anti-histamine drugs which she continued to use for the next ten years. She also had a bad throat infection for which she was treated with antibiotics.

In early 1969 she married and moved to California. She states in her case history, "That was when the eight-year long nightmare started." She relied on anti-histamine ther apy for awhile, then used penicillin for a virulent sinus infection. She also had recurrent bladder infections. Several cortisone shots were given in 1971 and 1972. In the summer of 1973 she went to an allergist who did some skin testing and treated her with a mixture of allergens that were administered by drops under the tongue. She wrote: "I tried a number of different formulas with always the same results—a period of improvement followed by a period in which I was much worse. This roller-coaster effect was wreaking havoc with my emotions and it was a time in which I was very close to suicide because I was so miserable. Eventually they concluded that I was having an allergic reaction to the phenol they were using in the solutions as a preservative, so I never did try a program of injections because I was afraid to let anyone inject phenol into my system."

In the spring of 1974 she moved to another county, which alleviated the situation somewhat. She had some more cortisone shots which were administered locally in her nose. In the summer of 1975 she experienced symptoms of acute hypoglycemia. She says she realized from her reading that hypoglycemia was at the root of many of her problems. This was confirmed by a glucose tolerance test and her diet was changed to eliminate both sugar and alcohol. In January 1976 she consulted me regarding her medical history. On February 26, 1976 she saw a homeopathic physician, who took her off anti-histamine drugs and treated her with homeopathic remedies; there was no noticeable improvement. On April 2, 1977 the use of arsenicum, a homeopathic remedy, caused obvious and immediate aggravation, and the situation has been improving since that time. Homeopathic medications often aggravate the situation first. She says that the fall pollen season of 1977 proved to be less of a discomfort than any of the past eight years had been.

Concerning the gastro-intestinal allergies, it is still necessary to be cautious with foods. She has also had migraine headaches since 1965. By being careful of her diet and eating at regular intervals these headaches have been minimized.

Delving into her family background, I found that her grandmother was a strong healthy woman but she suffered from occasional migraines, suggesting perhaps some allergic involvement. Her mother, however, has been the sickly type and has undergone two significant nervous breakdowns. My client underwent psychotherapy for about a year at age nineteen, and again in 1967 for six months before separating from her husband. She has many fears, anxieties and emotional problems. Her own description of her work with her health problems follows:

"About the summer of 1975 I started studying astrology and began to get some perspective on the karmic nature of my health problems. I also began to realize that illness can serve a positive purpose in your life by putting you in a position of having to get in touch with things that you might tend to avoid in a more healthy incarnation. Indeed, the more I studied, the more clear it became that the purpose of my being ill was to focus my attention away from worldly accomplishments towards a more spiritual orientation." In fall of 1976 and winter of 1977 she did some past life regressions to gain further insight into her problems. "All of the things I have been specifically allergic to in this lifetime are things that have been associated with my deaths in the past. In one lifetime, I was running around with a bunch of renegades in a forest and I died at the camp where horses and people were milling around stirring up a fine, powdery dust. When I was tested for allergies I had a very severe reaction to dust allergens. On another occasion I died in a feather bed covered with a down quilt. Another time I died in the back of a wagon lying on a bed of hay. When we asked specifically why I am allergic to cats, we found a lifetime a long time ago, around the first century, when I was a traveling merchant and I was jumped on and clawed by a mountain lion. The cat karma was reinforced when I found a lifetime in which I killed a cat that was my childhood pet. So it really seems that the reason I have had to be sick this lifetime has been for the purpose of learning on a conscious level that consciousness continues after the death of the physical body. It seems like dying in the past set up the traumas that have made me sensitive in this lifetime."

Case History #3

Chart pattern is a funnel with Neptune in Virgo in the third house showing extreme sensitivity and psychic disposition. Strong twelfth house shows many repressed emotions and potential health problems, as well as interest in metaphysical and spiritual work.

⊙ in ♎ in 11th house ♍ dwad	Strong emotional needs and insecurity; attention to details; concern with health
⊙ ☌ ♀	Needs to create and produce to fulfill sense of self
♀ ☌ ⚷	Fulfillment in love difficult; energy replaced through work
☽ in ♈ in 9th house	Strong personal philosophy and ideas; needs to be self-sufficient and an innovator in her work

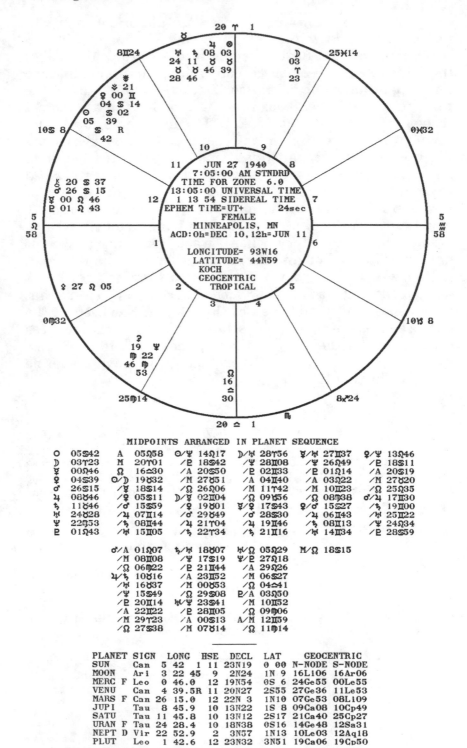

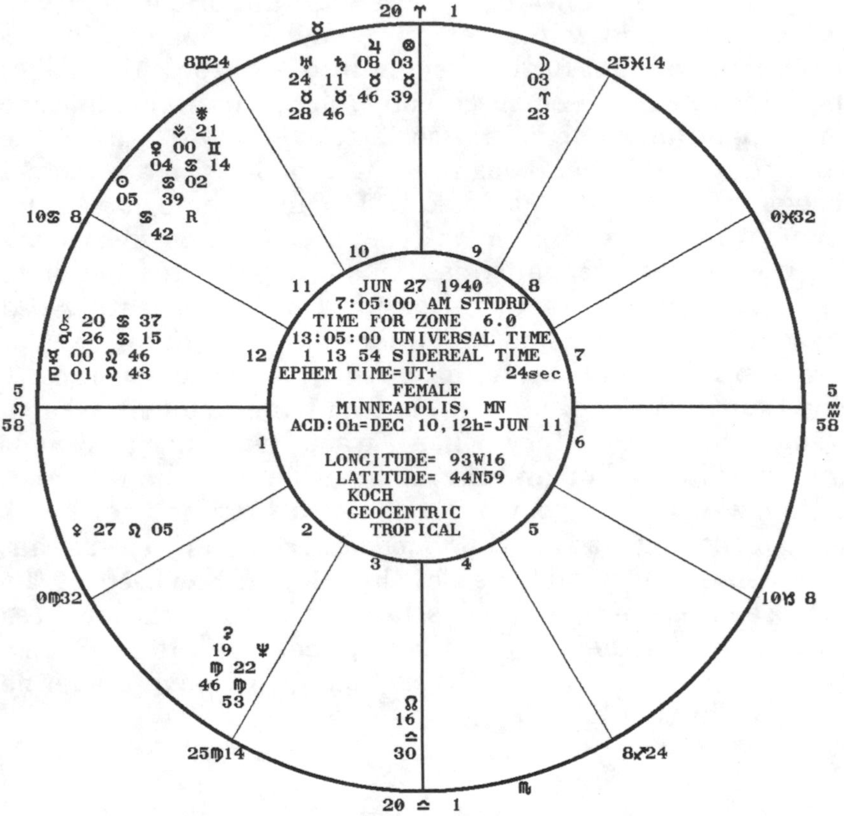
20 ♈ 1
8♊24
25♓14
10♋ 8
0♓32
5 ♌ 58
5 ♒ 58
0♍32
10♑ 8
25♍14
8♐24
20 ♎ 1
JUN 27 1940
7:05:00 AM STNDRD
TIME FOR ZONE 6.0
13:05:00 UNIVERSAL TIME
1 13 54 SIDEREAL TIME
EPHEM TIME=UT+ 24sec
FEMALE
MINNEAPOLIS, MN
ACD:0h=DEC 10,12h=JUN 11
LONGITUDE= 93W16
LATITUDE= 44N59
KOCH
GEOCENTRIC
TROPICAL
⚷ 20 ♋ 37
♂ 26 ♋ 15
☿ 00 ♌ 46
♇ 01 ♌ 43
☊ 16 ♎ 30

MIDPOINTS ARRANGED IN PLANET SEQUENCE

☉	05♋42	A	05♌58	☉/♆	14♌17	☽/♅	28♈56	☿/♅	27♊37	♀/♆	13♌46
☽	03♈23	M	20♈01	/♇	18♋42	/♆	28♊08	/♆	26♌49	/♇	18♋11
☿	00♌46	☊	16♎30	/A	20♋50	/♇	02♊33	/♇	01♌14	/A	20♋19
♀	04♋39	☉/☽	19♉32	/M	27♉51	/A	04♊40	/A	03♌22	/M	27♉20
♂	26♋15	/☿	18♋14	/☊	26♌06	/M	11♈42	/M	10♊23	/☊	25♌35
♃	08♉46	/♀	05♋11	☽/☿	02♊04	/☊	09♑56	/☊	08♍38	♂/♃	17♊30
♄	11♉46	/♂	15♋59	/♀	19♉01	☿/♀	17♋43	♀/♂	15♋27	/♄	19♊00
♅	24♉28	/♃	07♊14	/♂	29♉49	/♂	28♋30	/♃	06♊43	/♅	25♊22
♆	22♍53	/♄	08♊44	/♃	21♈04	/♃	19♊46	/♄	08♊13	/♆	24♌34
♇	01♌43	/♅	15♊05	/♄	22♈34	/♄	21♊16	/♅	14♊34	/♇	28♋59

♂/A	01♌07	♄/♅	18♉07	♅/☊	05♌29	M/☊	18♋15
/M	08♊08	/♆	17♋19	♆/♇	27♌18		
/☊	06♍22	/♇	21♊44	/A	29♌26		
♃/♄	10♉16	/A	23♊52	/M	06♋27		
/♅	16♉37	/M	00♉53	/☊	04♎41		
/♆	15♋49	/☊	29♋08	♇/A	03♌50		
/♇	20♊14	♅/♆	23♋41	/M	10♊52		
/A	22♊22	/♇	28♊05	/☊	09♍06		
/M	29♈23	/A	00♋13	A/M	12♊59		
/☊	27♋38	/M	07♉14	/☊	11♍14		

PLANET		SIGN	LONG	HSE	DECL	LAT	GEOCENTRIC N-NODE	GEOCENTRIC S-NODE
SUN		Can	5 42 1	11	23N19	0 00		
MOON		Ari	3 22 45	9	2N24	1N 9	16Li06	16Ar06
MERC	F	Leo	0 46.0	12	19N54	0S 6	24Ge55	00Le55
VENU		Can	4 39.5R	11	20N27	2S55	27Ge36	11Le53
MARS	F	Can	26 15.0	12	22N 3	1N10	07Ge53	08Li09
JUPI		Tau	8 45.9	10	13N22	1S 8	09Ca08	10Cp49
SATU		Tau	11 45.8	10	13N12	2S17	21Ca40	25Cp27
URAN	F	Tau	24 28.4	10	18N38	0S16	14Ge48	12Sa31
NEPT	D	Vir	22 52.9	2	3N57	1N13	10Le03	12Aq18
PLUT		Leo	1 42.6	12	23N32	3N51	19Ca06	19Cp50

☽ □ ☉ ♀ in ♋	Tries to fulfill her need for recognition and security by pushing her philosophical ideas; conflict between male and female aspects of her personality
♌ Asc. ♎ dwad	Needs ego gratification; needs to create a good appearance or front; relationships important
♂ in 12th house in ♋	Holds back anger and aggression
♂ ☌ ☿	Strong ability for writing, communication; nervous and respiratory systems affected
♂ * ♅	Expresses her emotions through writing and communicating
☿ ☌ ♇	Delves deeply into ideas; tendency to respiratory allergies
☿ on Asc.	Affects physical body, particularly the nervous system
♄ ♃ in 10th house	Need to be out in the world and working in practical way; need to organize projects
♄ ♃ □ Asc.	Frustration, restrictions on body; lowered vitality; socially conscious
♅ in 10th house	Unusual type of work; interest in astrology, occult disciplines; sensitive nervous system
Nodes in ♎♈ in 3rd & 9th houses	Relationships emphasized and strong communication needed to maintain the types of relationships she desires; kidneys and adrenal glands tend to be weak with ☽ in ♈
☽ 3°♈	Adrenal degree

MIDPOINTS

♂/♄ = Asc. (inverse)	Frustrations and limitations manifested through physical body; problems with spine and body structure

♄/♆ = nodes	Holding back of emotions; emotional depression
♂/♆ = ♅	Nervous diseases, respiratory allergies; metaphysical and psychic studies
♂/♅ = ♄ (inverse)	Blockage of energy in neurological system

Secondary Progressions	**Solar Arc Directions**	**Transits**	**Eclipses**
1. **1950—bad sinus infection**			
☽ ☌ Asc. Jan	♂ ☌ Asc.	♆ ☌ ☊	Sept. L. E. ☌ ☽
☽ □ ♃ March	♆ ☍ ☽	♄ ☌ ♆	
☽ □ ♄ June	MC □ ☿ ♇		
	☊ □ ♂		
2. **1963—serious problems: anti-histamines prescribed**			
MC ☌ ♄	☽ □ ♂	♄ □ ♅	July '62 S. E. ☍ Asc.
♂ □ ♄	☋ ☌ ♃		Jan. L. E. □ E. P.
	♆ ☌ ☊		
3. **1968—marriage: move to new area**			
☿ ☌ ♂	♅ □ ♆	♇ ☌ ♆	Sept. S. E. ☍ ☽
Asc. □ ♅			
♂ □ ♄			
⊙ ☌ ♇			
4. **Jan. & Feb. 1976—medical consultations & Homeopathy**			
☿ ⚺ ♅	♀ □ ♃	☊ ⚼ ⯔	S. E. ☌ ♃ April
♀ ☌ ⯔		☿ □ ♄	May L.E. ☍ ♅
♂ ⚼ ☽		♀ □ ♃ ♆	Oct. S.E. □ ☿
M. C. σ ♅		♂ ☌ ⯓	
Asc. ∠ ☊		♃ ⚺ ♅	
		♄ ∠ ♂	
		♅ □ ♃ ∠ ♆	
		♆ ⚼ ☿	
		♇ ⚼ ♅	
5. **April 1977—successful homeopathic remedy**			
☽ ☌ ASC. April	☽ ☌ ♃	☊ ⚻ ♅	April S. E. □ ♂
		☿ □ ☿	L. E. ☌ ☊
		♀ ☌ Eclipse Point	Sept. L. E. ☌ ☽
		♂ ⚼ ♂	Oct. S. E. ☌ ☊
		♃ ✱ ☿	
		♄ ♅ □ ♄	
		♄ ♅ ∠ ♆	
		♆ △ ☋ ⚼ ☿ ♇	

CHAPTER EIGHT

METABOLIC MALFUNCTIONS

Metabolic malfunctions, often called metabolic diseases, are disruptions of the body's chemistry due to malfunctioning of one or more of the glands. In the case of the disease syndromes known as diabetes and hypoglycemia there is an inability to assimilate or metabolize certain foods, notably carbohydrates and fats. This is due to a malfunctioning of the pancreas or adrenals.

Insulin is a hormone produced by the body in a set of glands located in the pancreas called the Islets of Langerhans. The Islets of Langerhans secrete insulin directly into the bloodstream. When there is not enough insulin, blood sugar rises because insulin is essential for transporting glucose (sugar) into the cells. As blood sugar levels increase, the kidneys eliminate sugar into the urine. This high level of sugar in the blood makes one particularly susceptible to infection.

Treatment for diabetics includes an alkaline diet as diabetics have a tendency to over-acidity due to increased protein and fat metabolism. Insulin injections can often be replaced through the proper combination of herbs, foods, and food supplements.

In the hypoglycemic syndrome, an excess of insulin is produced; the blood glucose level drops, and the individual feels weak and irritable. When the blood sugar gets very low, the adrenals secrete excess amounts of adrenalin and cortin. The excess amounts of these two hormones make one extremely nervous and oversensitive. Other symptoms of hypoglycemia include hunger, weakness, fatigue, anxiety, and sometimes lack of coordination and mental disturbances such as confusion. The traditional way of treating hypoglycemia was through a high protein diet. However, a new approach to diet, emphasizing vegetables, proteins and whole grains (especially buckwheat and millet which contain bioflavinoids,) has been quite successful.[1]

The hypoglycemic syndrome seems to be extremely common in the United States. Some of it comes from the typical American diet with its emphasis on sugar, carbohydrates and rich heavy foods. After doing much research with doctors and nutritionists, the following guidelines were developed for this syndrome.

1. No alcohol. A glass of white wine or sake may be taken on occasion.
2. No sugar and little honey. This includes maple syrup, rice bran syrup, molasses. Barley malt syrup and rice syrup, both of which taste like honey, may be used instead. Since they are derived from grains, they are metabolized more slowly.
3. No salt of any kind. An acid/alkaline imbalance results from the use of too much salt. Low sodium seasonings may be used instead (Veg-It or SeaSun).
4. A maximum of one portion of fruit or fruit juice daily. Fruit juices may be diluted with spring water. Certain fruits, like oranges, grapefruit and many sour apples should not be used.
5. Small amounts of red meat, as it is difficult to digest. Fish or fowl may be substituted.
6. Few heavy carbohydrates such as pasta, tortillas, etc. Whole grain cereals and breads should be used instead.
7. Dairy products should be primarily the soured milks such as yogurt, kefir, buttermilk, cottage cheese with acidopholus, or goat's milk products.

PSYCHOLOGICAL

Psychologically, the diabetic is often a very bitter person. Some circumstance in his life has made him adopt this attitude, and his body compensates accordingly by producing an increased amount of sugar. Symptoms of both

---

[1]*Hypoglycemia: A Better Approach*, Paavo Airola, N.D. Health Plus Publishers, Phoenix, AZ., 1977.

diabetes and hypoglycemia often become manifest during a period of stress in one's life. Many people have exhibited these symptoms after a traumatic shock, a death or birth in the family, an accident, or a situation where the person has been placed in a hostile environment. Under these conditions of stress there is an increased release of adrenaline and cortin. Adrenaline raises the blood sugar (an emergency mechanism) and cortin causes the liver to make more glycogen, which is converted into glucose, thereby raising the blood sugar.

ASTROLOGICAL PATTERNS

Diabetes and hypoglycemia are related to the pancreas and liver, both ruled by Jupiter. As a storage container for glycogen (the chief carbohydrate storage material) the liver is co-ruled by the Moon (Moon rules storage containers). Saturn or Neptune making hard aspects to Jupiter in the natal horoscope may indicate a propensity to these conditions. Strong Jupiterian elements in the chart, such as Sun, Moon, or Ascendant in Sagittarius, Sun conjunct Jupiter, Moon conjunct Jupiter, or Jupiter angular may point to pancreas or liver involvement with physiological symptoms. Some of the individuals who have these configurations tend to be overweight (a contributing factor to the diabetic syndrome) while others go to excess in their various habit patterns.

Mars rules the adrenal glands and thus is involved with the metabolic disease syndrome, particularly with combinations of Mars/Jupiter and Mars/Neptune (Neptune relates to toxicity and the immune system). Neptune also has rulership of the pituitary so a weak Neptune or prominent placement of Pisces might also predispose the individual to imbalances in the metabolic system. Venus rules sugar and also the kidneys which are involved in eliminating excess sugar and in helping to maintain the acid/alkaline balance.

In addition, the midpoints that are relevant in cases of metabolic diseases are:

Jupiter/Saturn - the gall bladder, pancreas, or liver involvement.

Jupiter/Neptune - an inability to deal with toxins properly.

Venus/Jupiter - assimilation of carbohydrates.

Venus/Neptune - weakened glandular functioning and enlargement of glands.

Combinations of planets that may point to a tendency toward metabolic imbalance when found in a T-square or midpoint configuration are: Saturn, Neptune, and Jupiter; Mars, Neptune, and Jupiter; Venus, Neptune, and Jupiter; Saturn, Neptune, and Venus; Mars, Neptune, and Venus; Jupiter, Saturn, and Venus; Mars, Saturn and Jupiter.

It is difficult to discern astrologically whether the manifestation will be towards hypoglycemia, which is extremely common, or diabetes. After seeing many case histories, I have found no difference in the astrological patterns; therefore some sort of testing or verification is needed.

Degree areas that are involved in these cases are 15°-19° Cancer, the pancreas; 15°-16° Virgo and 25 and 29° Virgo, the liver; and 3° Libra, adrenal malfunctions.

CASE HISTORY #1

The first horoscope reproduced here is that of a woman who was diagnosed as hypoglycemic at the age of twenty-three. She was pregnant at the time with her first child and experienced dizziness and disorientation, followed by chills and shaking. This lasted for a few hours and the next day she felt weak. Often there were feelings of fear, panic and inexplicable paranoia. She went to a clinic where she was given a glucose tolerance test, in which hypoglycemia was *not* diagnosed. Afterwards the doctor gave her a prescription for valium. Fortunately, she was aware of the nature of her condition; she read some books and put herself on a high protein diet. She also took B-vitamin supplements, iron, kelp, potassium, and protein pills. Her symptoms are completely under control now and she has just given birth to her third child. Recurrence happens only when she eats sugar or sweets.

In terms of her family history, her mother and her maternal grandfather had the same symptoms. They both experienced the most severe symptoms in their twenties. Now they keep their symptoms under control through diet and vitamin supplements.

Emotionally, there have been many changes in this woman's life. She has been married three times and the third marriage seems to be a harmonious working relationship. She is also involved in psychic and healing work which is going well. Many emotional upheavals that she experienced in her twenties have passed and she has settled into a more secure pattern with a home and family. She now has the time to take care of herself and the money to buy any foods and vitamin supplements necessary for her well-being.

Case History #1

☉ ☌ ♃ in ♏ in 12th house	Intensely passionate nature; deep need to delve into spiritual and metaphysical studies, liver and pancreas involvement
☉ ✶ dwad	Emphasis on healing and strong sensitivity
☉ ☌ ♃ □ ♄♀ in ♌ in 9th house	Determination to learn and know everything; necessity for self-transformative experiences; possibility of being didactic in her philosophy; restriction of functioning in liver and pancreas
☉♀ in mutual reception	Regeneration through spiritual and metaphysical studies
☉ △ ☽ in ✶ in 3rd house	Strong sensitivity; communicates emotions easily
☉ ⊼ ☊ in 7th house in ♊	Need to work on relationships; problems in relationships reflect on health
☽ in ✶ in 3rd house, ♎ dwad	Sensitive, imaginative, artistic; emotional relationships emphasized
☽ ☌ ⚷ in ✶	Concern for the welfare of others; sensitive to people's needs; emotional states related to health problems
☽ ⊡ ♃, ♄	Difficulty in relating to world at large

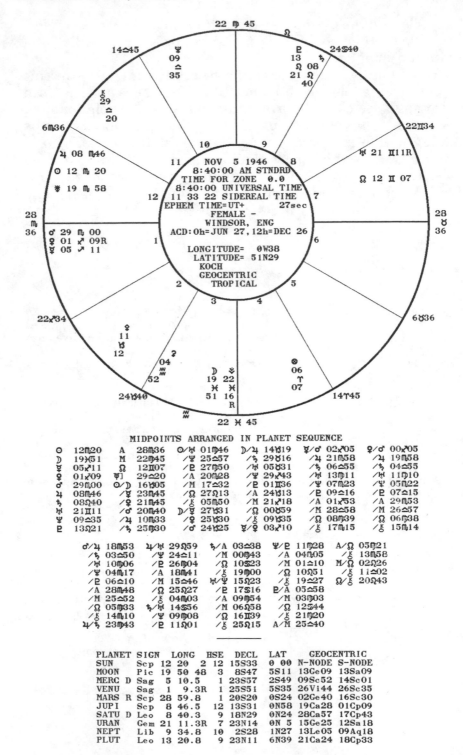

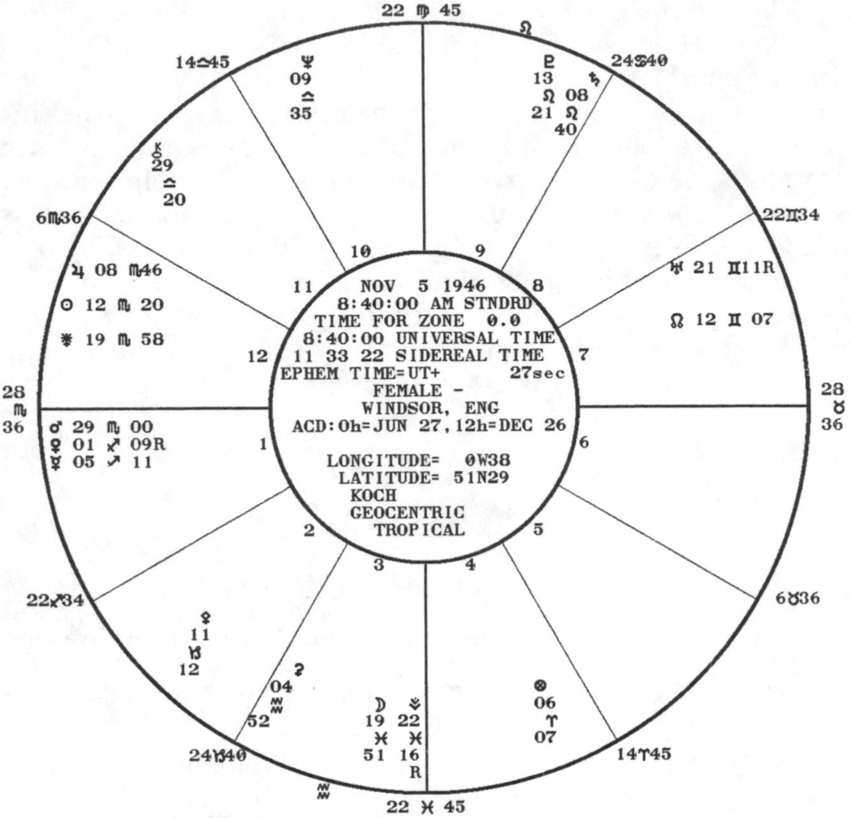
22 ♍ 45
14♎45
24♋40
22♊34
6♏36
28 ♏ 36
28 ♉ 36
22♐34
6♉36
24♑40
14♈45
22 ♓ 45
♆ 09 ♎ 35
♇ 13 ♌ 21
♄ ♌ 08 40
⚷ 29 ♎ 20
♃ 08 ♏46
☉ 12 ♏ 20
✵ 19 ♏ 58
♅ 21 ♊11R
☊ 12 ♊ 07
♂ 29 ♏ 00
♀ 01 ♐ 09R
☿ 05 ♐ 11
♀ 11 ♑ 12
04 ♒ 52
☽ 19 ♓ 51
☿ 22 ♓ 16 R
⊗ 06 ♈ 07
NOV 5 1946
8:40:00 AM STNDRD
TIME FOR ZONE 0.0
8:40:00 UNIVERSAL TIME
11 33 22 SIDEREAL TIME
EPHEM TIME=UT+ 27sec
FEMALE -
WINDSOR, ENG
ACD:0h=JUN 27,12h=DEC 26
LONGITUDE= 0W38
LATITUDE= 51N29
KOCH
GEOCENTRIC
TROPICAL

MIDPOINTS ARRANGED IN PLANET SEQUENCE

☉	12♏20	A	28♏36	☉/♅	01♍46	☽/♃	14♑19	☿/♂	02♐05	♀/♂	00♐05
☽	19♓51	M	22♍45	/♆	25♎57	/♄	29♉16	/♃	21♏58	/♃	19♏58
☿	05♐11	☊	12♊07	/♇	27♍50	/♅	05♉31	/♄	06♎55	/♄	04♎55
♀	01♐09	Ψ]	29♎20	/A	20♏28	/♆	29♐43	/♅	13♍11	/♅	11♍10
♂	29♏00	☉/☽	16♑05	/M	17♎32	/♇	01♊36	/♆	07♏23	/♆	05♏22
♃	08♏46	/☿	23♏45	/☊	27♌13	/A	24♑13	/♇	09♎16	/♇	07♎15
♄	08♌40	/♀	21♏45	/⚷	05♏50	/M	21♐18	/A	01♐53	/A	29♏53
♅	21♊11	/♂	20♏40	☽/☿	27♑31	/☊	00♉59	/M	28♎58	/M	26♎57
♆	09♎35	/♃	10♏33	/♀	25♑30	/⚷	09♑35	/☊	08♍39	/☊	06♍38
♇	13♌21	/♄	25♍30	/♂	24♑25	☿/♀	03♐10	/⚷	17♏15	/⚷	15♏14

♂/♃	18♏53	♃/♅	29♌59	♄/A	03♎38	♆/♇	11♍28	A/☊	05♍21
/♄	03♎50	/♆	24♎11	/M	00♍43	/A	04♏05	/⚷	13♏58
/♅	10♍06	/♇	26♍04	/☊	10♋23	/M	01♎10	M/☊	02♌26
/♆	04♏17	/A	18♏41	/⚷	19♍00	/☊	10♌51	/⚷	11♎02
/♇	06♎10	/M	15♎46	♅/♆	15♌23	/⚷	19♎27	☊/⚷	20♌43
/A	28♏48	/☊	25♌27	/♇	17♋16	♇/A	05♎58		
/M	25♎52	/⚷	04♏03	/A	09♍54	/M	03♍03		
/☊	05♍33	♄/♅	14♋56	/M	06♌58	/☊	12♋44		
/⚷	14♏10	/♆	09♍08	/☊	16♊39	/⚷	21♍20		
♃/♄	23♍43	/♇	11♌01	/⚷	25♌15	A/M	25♎40		

PLANET	SIGN	LONG	HSE	DECL	LAT	GEOCENTRIC	
SUN	Scp	12 20 2	12	15S33	0 00	N-NODE	S-NODE
MOON	Pic	19 50 48	3	8S47	5S11	13Ge09	13Sa09
MERC D	Sag	5 10.5	1	23S57	2S49	09Sc52	14Sc01
VENU	Sag	1 9.3R	1	25S51	5S35	26Vi44	26Sc35
MARS R	Scp	28 59.8	1	20S20	0S24	02Ge40	16Sc30
JUPI	Scp	8 46.5	12	13S31	0N58	19Ca28	01Cp09
SATU D	Leo	8 40.3	9	18N29	0N24	28Ca57	17Cp43
URAN	Gem	21 11.3R	7	23N14	0N 5	15Ge25	12Sa18
NEPT	Lib	9 34.8	10	2S28	1N27	13Le05	09Aq18
PLUT	Leo	13 20.8	9	23N11	6N39	21Ca24	18Cp33

☽ ☐ ♅ in 7th house	Many emotional changes; attracts unusual partners; hypersensitive nervous system
♂ ☌ Asc. in ♏	Good vitality and motivation; involved with growth and regeneration
Asc. ♎ dwad	Relationships and partnerships
♂ ☌ ♀ in ♐	Strong sensuality and desire nature
♂ ☌ ☿ in ♐	Need to communicate verbally
☿ ☌ ♇	Stress on nervous system; possible allergies
♀ ☌ ☿	Writing and creative work
☿ △ ♄, ♀ in ♌	Need to teach and counsel others
♆ in 10th house in ♎	Goals may be unclear; healing and psychic work; not sure of role in outside world
♆ ⁎ ☿, ♄, ♀	Opportunities for travel and spiritual growth
♆ ☐ ♆ in ♑ in 2nd house	Not clear about money she needs to bring in from her work
♅ in ♊ in 7th house	Changes in relationships; attracts unusual partners; need for independence in relationships
☿ contra ‖ ♅, ♀	Sensitive nervous system; original ideas and ways of expressing them; changes mind often

MIDPOINTS

♂ / ♄ = 3°♎	Adrenal degree
☽ / ♃ = ♂, ♀, Asc. (inverse)	Artistic and creative; possible excesses; desire for sweets and carbohydrates
♃ / ♅ = ♂, ♀, Asc.	Erratic functioning of pancreas and liver; possible problems with thyroid and hormonal balance
♃ / ♆ = ♂, ♀, Asc.	Idealistic and romantic; spiritual and artistic pursuits; hypoglycemic tendency

Secondary Progressions	Solar Arc Directions	Transits	Eclipses

1. July 1969—first symptoms when pregnant

☉ ☌ ☿	♂ □ ♅	♆ ☌ Asc.	August L. E. □ ☿
☽ ⚼ ☿ June	☉ ☌ ♀	♆ ☌ ♂	Sept. S. E. ☍ ☽
☽ ⚻ ♅ June			

CASE HISTORY #2

The second case history is that of a man in whom diabetes was discovered at the age of forty-three. As a child his life was unstable; his father was in the army in Korea; his mother drank a lot. Later they were divorced. When he was nineteen he had a bout with malaria which put him in the hospital for two months; he was severely dehydrated. At twenty he enlisted in the army and spent a good part of the time in the Orient. During this period he used many drugs inluding opium and heroin, in addition to consuming large amounts of alcohol.

After leaving the army, he went back to art school. He was using some LSD and peyote and smoking marijuana daily. He was married for three years and had a daughter.

When he finished art school, he moved around—New Mexico, Montreal, Toronto, Europe, Boston, back to New Mexico, California, and so on. He was still involved with drugs—mostly LSD, peyote and cocaine and drinking from time to time. The only period of bad health he suffered was in New Mexico in the summer of 1966. He had some kind of virus and was quite ill for a month, vomiting bile.

His daughter, who lived in New York with his ex-wife, developed multiple sclerosis and died in June 1978. This loss left him deeply depressed and he began drinking heavily. By February 1979 he had low back pains, which were related to his kidneys. In May he was diagnosed as diabetic and given insulin. Prior to this time he had noticed himself losing weight and feeling very hungry.

The following October his insulin was dropped from twenty-two units daily to four units daily. In December he had a consultation with a doctor who used natural methods of healing. He was given advice on diet, some herbs to use, vitamin and mineral supplements, and a homeopathic remedy. He tends to be fairly undisciplined in regard to diet and exercise. A sensitive artistic personality, he never completes projects and therefore never feels a sense of accomplishment or success. He also carries a great deal of bitterness beneath the surface, which is characteristic of many diabetics.

Case History #2

☉ in ♌ in 10th house	Strong vital energy; need to manifest creativity in outside world; need to be leader and in command
☉, ♑ dwad	Sense of responsibility and organization
☉ ☌ ☿	Emphasizes creative abilities
☉ □ ♅ in 7th house	Likes to be constantly stimulated; attracts unusual partners but relationships often get in the way of his artistic work; changes relationships often
☉ ∠ ☽ in ♈ in 6th house	Emotions affect his physical health; conflict between his sensitivity and concern for others and his masculine ego drive
☉ exactly △ ♃ in ♐ in 3rd house	Likes to talk about his artistic projects; easy to become involved in excesses
♈ ☽ exactly square nodes in ♑ and ♋	Working out emotional problems; problem with family and security
☽ △ ♂♀ in 10th house	Strong regenerative force; ability to carry out his projects
☽ ☊ in mutual reception	Emphasizes his strong vital force and ability to manifest his schemes in outside world
♎ Asc., ♈ dwad	Relationships important but needs to be in control and thinks of himself first
♀ ☌ ☿ in ♌ in 11th house	Creativity in speaking and writing; likes to discuss his artistic projects with friends; likes parties and social functions
☿ ∠ Asc.	Nervous system may cause health problems; health problems may arise while traveling

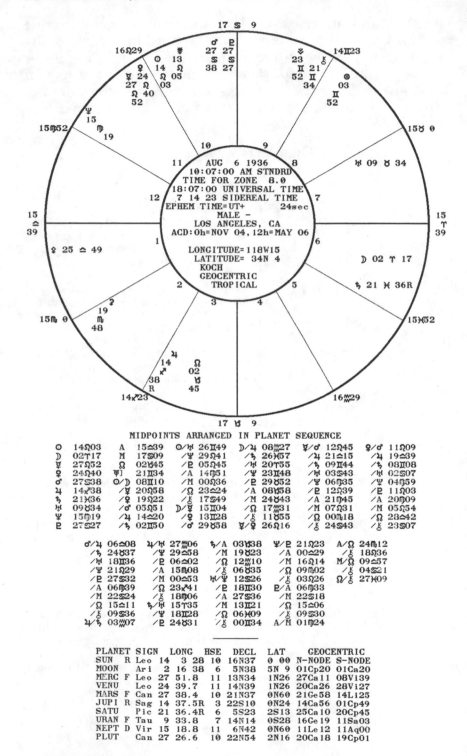

17 ♋ 9

16♌29   ♂ ♇   ⚷   14♊23
    ⚸   ☉ 13   27 27   23   ☿ 24   14 ♌   ♋ ♋   ♊ 21   27 ♌ 05   38 27   52 ♊   ⊕   ♌ 40   34   03   52   ♊ 52

♆ 15   15♍52   ♍ 19   15♉ 0

10   9

11   AUG 6 1936   8   ♅ 09 ♉ 34
       10:07:00 AM STNDRD
       TIME FOR ZONE 8.0
  12   18:07:00 UNIVERSAL TIME   7
      7 14 23 SIDEREAL TIME
    EPHEM TIME=UT+   24sec
15   MALE —   15
♎   LOS ANGELES, CA   ♈
39   ACD:0h=NOV 04,12h=MAY 06   39

    1   LONGITUDE=118W15   6   ☽ 02 ♈ 17
♀ 25 ♎ 49   LATITUDE= 34N 4
        KOCH
       GEOCENTRIC
    2   TROPICAL   5   ♄ 21 ♓ 36R
        3   4

   ♇ 19   15♓52
15♏ 0   ♏ 48

    ♃ 14   ☊ 02
     38   ♍ 45
     R
14♐23   16♒29

17 ♑ 9

MIDPOINTS ARRANGED IN PLANET SEQUENCE

☉	14♌03	A	15♎39	☉/♅	26♊49	☽/♃	08♒27	♅/♂	12♌45	♀/♂	11♌09
☽	02♈17	M	17♋09	/♆	29♋41	/♄	26♋57	/♃	21♎15	/♃	19♎39
☿	27♌52	☊	02♑45	/♇	05♋45	/♅	20♈55	/♄	09♌44	/♄	08♊08
♀	24♌40	⚷	21♊34	/A	14♍51	/♇	23♊48	/♅	03♋43	/♅	02♋07
♂	27♋38	☉/☽	08♊10	/M	00♋36	/♇	29♉52	/♆	06♍35	/♆	04♍59
♃	14♐38	/☿	20♌58	/☊	23♎24	/A	08♑58	/♇	12♋39	/♇	11♌03
♄	21♓36	/♀	19♋22	/⚷	17♋49	/M	24♉43	/A	21♍45	/A	20♍09
♅	09♉34	/♂	05♌51	☽/☿	15♋04	/☊	17♒31	/M	07♋31	/M	05♌54
♆	15♍19	/♃	14♎20	/♀	13♊28	/⚷	11♋55	/☊	00♏18	/☊	28♎42
♇	27♋27	/♄	02♏50	/♂	29♋58	☿/♀	26♋16	/⚷	24♋43	/⚷	23♋07

♂/♃	06♎08	♃/♅	27♒06	♄/A	03♑38	♆/♇	21♋23	A/☊	24♏12
/♄	24♉37	/♆	29♎58	/M	19♉23	/A	00♎29	/⚷	18♍36
/♅	18♊36	/♇	06♎02	/☊	12♒10	/M	16♋14	M/☊	09♎57
/♆	21♎29	/A	15♏08	/⚷	06♉35	/☊	09♍02	/⚷	04♋21
/♇	27♋32	/M	00♋53	♅/♆	12♋26	/⚷	03♋26	☊/⚷	27♓09
/A	06♍39	/☊	23♐41	/♇	18♊30	♇/A	06♍33		
/M	22♋24	/⚷	18♍06	/A	27♋36	/M	22♋18		
/☊	15♎11	♄/♅	15♈35	/M	13♊21	/☊	15♎06		
/⚷	09♋36	/♆	18♊28	/☊	06♓09	/⚷	09♋30		
♃/♄	03♒07	/♇	24♉31	/⚷	00♊34	A/M	01♍24		

PLANET	SIGN	LONG	HSE	DECL	LAT	GEOCENTRIC
SUN	R Leo	14 3 28	10	16N37	0 00	N-NODE S-NODE
MOON	Ari	2 16 38	6	5N38	5N 9	01Cp20 01Ca20
MERC	F Leo	27 51.8	11	13N34	1N26	27Ca11 08Vi39
VENU	Leo	24 39.7	11	14N39	1N26	20Ca26 28Vi27
MARS	F Can	27 38.4	10	21N37	0N60	21Ge58 14Li25
JUPI	R Sag	14 37.5R	3	22S10	0N24	14Ca56 01Cp49
SATU	Pic	21 36.4R	6	5S23	2S13	25Ca10 20Cp45
URAN	F Tau	9 33.8	7	14N14	0S28	16Ge19 11Sa03
NEPT	D Vir	15 18.8	11	6N42	0N60	11Le12 11Aq00
PLUT	Can	27 26.6	10	22N54	2N16	20Ca18 19Cp01

♂ ☌ ♇ on MC in ♋	Dynamic energy; possible involvement in underground plans and schemes
♂ ∠ ♆ in ♍	Toxic conditions may affect his energy
♂ ⚼ ♃ in ♐ in 3rd house	Liver and pancreas may become affected when he overdoes things
♂♇ △ ♄ in ♓ in 6th house	Good motivation and discipline in carrying out various schemes and projects
♃ in ♐ □ ♄ in ♓ in 6th house and ♆ in ♍ in 11th house	When he becomes overemotional (♆), he eats and drinks to excess (♃), and then is restricted in his health (♄)
♄ in ♓ in 6th house	Vague fears about health, digestive problems; possible allergies related to digestive system
♄ ☋ ♆	Sense of discipline and order difficult to manifest
♄ □ ⯓ in ♊ in 9th house	Health problems involve nervous and respiratory systems; feels compulsive about spreading his ideas to others
♆☽ contra ∥ ♄Asc.	Sensitive, artistic nature not able to express itself due to emotional insecurity; Difficulty with mother and women; possible craving for alcohol and drugs

MIDPOINTS

♂/♄ = ♀	Holding back of love and feelings; possible thyroid problems; problems with kidneys
♂/♇ = ♃ (inverse)	Compulsion to overdo things, go to excesses; chronic problems with liver and pancreas

Secondary Progressions	Solar Arc Directions	Transits	Eclipses
1. **July 1955—contracted malaria**			
☉ ⚻ ☽	♅ ☍ ☿	♇ ☌ ♀	June S.E. ☌ E.P.
Asc. ⚻ ☽	☿ ☌ ♆	♆ ☌ ⯰ □ ♇	Dec. S. E. □ ♄
☿ ⚹ ♂♇	♃ □ ☽	♅ ☌ ♂♇	

♂ □ ♅   ♃ ☌ ♄/♆
☽ in ♐
☽ ⊼ ♅ Sept.

2. Summer 1966—severe virus: vomited bile

☉ ∠ ♂♀	Asc. □ ☉	♅♀ ☌ ♆	May S. E. □ ☿
☿ ∠ ♀	♆ □ MC	♆ ☌ ?	
☿ ⊼ ♅	♃ ☌ Desc.	♃ ☌ MC	
♀ ☍ ☽			
♀ ⊼ ♅			
☽ ☌ ♅ June			

3. June 1978—daughter died

Asc. ☌ ?	Asc. □ ♀	♀ ☌ Asc.	March L. E. ☌ ♄
MC ☌ ☿	☽ □ ⚷	♆□ ♇	April S. E. ☍ Asc.
☉ ⊡ ♅	⚸ □ ⚵	♅ □ ☉	
☽ ☌ Asc. June	♃ □ ⚷	♄ ☌ ☿	
		♃ ☌ MC	

4. May 1979—diabetes diagnosed

♀ □ MC	♆ □ ♂♀	♅ ☌ ? ∠ ☽	Aug. L. E. ☌ ☿
♂ ☌ ♀	☽ □ ☉	♃ ☌ ♄/♆,	
		♃/♄	
☽ Q ☉ May	♅ □ ♄	♇ ☌ ♀/♃	
☽ □ ♇ June	MC □ ☿		

CHAPTER NINE

CARDIOVASCULAR DISORDERS

Cardiovascular disease is the leading cause of death in our society. In the United States alone one million people die yearly from various forms of cardiovascular disease. Some of the most common cardiovascular problems are aneurysms, atherosclerosis, hypertension, and various heart disorders.

An aneurysm is a blood-filled sac formed by an out-pouching in an arterial or venous wall. Aneurysms may occur in any major blood vessel. Atherosclerosis is a form of arteriosclerosis which includes many diseases of the arterial wall. In this disorder an artery becomes thickened with soft fatty deposits called atheromatous plaques. As atheromas grow, they may impede bloodflow in affected arteries and damage the tissues they supply. Atherosclerosis is a slow progressive disease which may start in childhood and produce no symptoms for many years. The most common disease affecting the heart and blood vessels is hypertension. Primary or essential hypertension is elevated blood pressure that cannot be attributed to any particular organic cause. Secondary hypertension is caused by disorders such as arteriosclerosis, kidney disease, and adrenal hypersecretion.[1]

The term "heart attack" includes myocardial infarctions, formation of dead cells in the heart muscle due to interruption of the blood supply to the area, and coronary occlusions, closing off of a coronary artery which may occur when the artery is suddenly plugged by a blood clot within the vessel or when fatty deposits in the wall of the vessel clog the artery.

Factors which contribute to heart attacks include high

---

[1]*Principles of Human Anatomy*, Second Edition, Gerard J. Tortora, Harper & Row, N.Y. 1980, p. 353.

blood cholesterol, high blood pressure, cigarette smoking, obesity, and lack of exercise. According to the most recent research, high blood cholesterol or serum cholesterol is not determined by the amount of cholesterol in the diet but rather by the factors which alter the synthesis or excretion of cholesterol. A reduction in cholesterol breakdown is known to result from exposure to high levels of atmospheric carbon monoxide which accounts for the importance attached to cigarette smoking and pollution.[2] High blood pressure weakens the vessel wall and encourages plaque formation. Cigarette smoking, through the effects of nicotine, stimulates the adrenal gland to oversecrete aldosterone, epinephrine and nor-epinephrine, which in turn cause constriction of blood vessels.[3] Overweight people develop extra capillaries to nourish fat tissue. The heart, therefore, has to work harder to pump the blood through more veins. Exercise strengthens the smooth muscle of blood vessels and enables them to assist general circulation. Exercise also increases cardiac efficiency and output.

The immediate physiological causes of heart disorders are inadequate coronary blood supply, anatomical diseases, and faulty electrical conduction in the heart.[4] Emotional factors include situations in which feelings have been held in restraint for many years. Sudden trauma often brings these feelings to the surface where they may exacerbate existing physiological conditions or actually lead to the development of these conditions.

Cardiovascular disorders can be alleviated and prevented in the following ways:
1. Eliminating salt and all foods containing salt in the diet as salt contributes to hypertension and high blood pressure. A low salt substitute as Veg-It or Seazun may be used instead.
2. Avoiding coffee, black tea, and other stimulants.
3. Avoiding alcohol.
4. Avoiding sugar, white flour and all refined products.

---

[2]"The lipid hypothesis: orthodoxy by default?" *Nature,* Vol. 270, Nov. 1977.
[3]*Principles of Human Anatomy*, Tortora, p. 354
[4]Ibid.

5. Avoiding the tendency to overeat.
6. Eliminating all environmental sources of metal poisoning such as aluminum and copper cooking utensils, and water to which chlorine and other chemicals have been added.

The following things should be included:

1. Plenty of exercise. Sedentary life is one of the major contributing causes of arteriosclerosis.
2. Foods and supplements rich in magnesium, which is perhaps the most important mineral for the heart. Wheat germ, almonds, cashews, soybeans, brazil nuts and peanuts are the foods highest in magnesium. Liquid chlorophyll is an excellent supplement providing magnesium. Magnesium tablets may be used.
3. Foods and supplements containing potassium. In most people with cardiovascular disorders the potassium-sodium balance is off. Potassium tablets and one of the potassium cell salts may be used. Foods highest in potassium are soybeans, lima beans, bananas, sunflower seeds, almonds, sesame seeds, and peanuts. Dulse, kelp and Irish moss are food supplements rich in potassium.
4. A liquid B-complex supplement for stress and the nervous system.
5. Vitamin E (not as an oil based capsule, but in the dry form) is often helpful.
6. Vitamin C may be needed. Vitamin C is helpful in converting cholesterol into bile acids. This has been demonstrated in animal studies.[5] It is also good for connective tissue (the heart and arteries).
7. Herbs which are beneficial to the heart—borage, red raspberry leaf (both high in magnesium), lavender, garlic, hawthorne berries and motherwort.

In addition to metabolic imbalances, the heart muscle can be affected through its neurological transmission system. The neurological transmission is primarily dependent upon the sodium-potassium balance while the muscle contraction is dependent upon the magnesium-calcium levels. These levels plus adequate blood flow (coronary circulation) insure a normal heartbeat.

---

[5]*How to Get Well,* Paavo Airola, N.D., Health Plus Publishers, Phoenix, AZ., 1974, p.42.

PSYCHOLOGICAL TRAITS

Drs. Friedman and Rosemann have catalogued the cardiovascular personality type in their book, *Type A Behaviour And Your Heart.* The type A personality strives to accomplish too much and to participate in too many events in an allotted time segment. They constantly create deadlines and are unable to relax and enjoy themselves. Because of these deadlines, they don't have time to think problems through and therefore fall into stereotyped thinking and judgments. They also tend to be extremely impatient and are strongly competitive in their work. On the surface they appear to have confidence and self-assurance but they actually experience a deep sense of insecurity. They also possess an easily-aroused hostility which is usually kept under control. As a group, they show a higher serum cholesterol, a higher serum fat, smoke more cigarettes, eat more foods high in cholesterol, and suffer more from high blood pressure. When physiological tests were administered, they indicated blood fat and hormone abnormalities.[6] Those with cardiovascular disorders tend to hold back their feelings and block the area of the heart. When they are under extreme emotional pressure and can no longer keep their feelings in check they are particularly susceptible to heart attacks.

ASTROLOGICAL INDICATIONS

Astrologically the heart is ruled by Leo and the Sun. The horoscopes of those with cardiovascular disorders exhibit a strong fixed sign emphasis. Emotionally, fixed signs tend to hold back their feelings and are often stubborn and set in their habit patterns. Physiologically the signs Taurus and Scorpio have to do with cleansing and elimination. When the body is congested, circulation becomes difficult and thus the Taurus/Scorpio axis is involved as well as the Leo/Aquarius. In a study conducted on children with congenital heart disease (see the article "Congenital Heart Problems" by Helynne Hansen, *Dell's Horoscope,* February 1977) Taurus

---

[6]*Type A Behavior And Your Heart,* Meyer Friedman, M.D. & Ray Rosenmann, M.D., Alfred A. Knopf, N.Y., 1974.

was found to be the leader among Sun signs, with Aquarius and Leo following. Likewise succedent houses were also emphasized in these horoscopes.

With a blockage of the arteries or arteriosclerosis, Jupiter is often found in Leo or Aquarius, or fifth and eleventh houses with hard aspects from Saturn. Sometimes Jupiter is found in Capricorn, Saturn's sign. In tachycardia (rapid beat) or arhythmia of the heart Uranus is often prominent, angular or conjunct the Sun or Moon. Uranus relates to the electrical system of the heart and is also the ruler of Aquarius. Many individuals with a strong Uranus in their horoscope are deficient in magnesium. Natal Uranus in the sixth house was often seen in this group with progressed fifth house cusp conjuncting natal Uranus by secondary progression at the time of the attack.

Midpoints to consider are:

Sun/Uranus - corresponds to the rhythmic function of the cells in particular and of the body in general.

Moon/Uranus - indicates emotional tension and disturbances of blood pressure.

Mars/Jupiter - rules the heart muscle.

Saturn/Uranus - heart block and disturbance of bodily rhythm.

Uranus/Neptune - heart failure and paralysis of rhythmic processes.

CASE HISTORY #1

This man held a position as executive of a chemical company in a large midwestern city. His work entailed many responsibilities; in addition to office duties he was in charge of the laboratory. He did not get much exercise, smoked a pipe and ate a typical American diet with lots of desserts. His circulation was poor and his blood pressure high. In July 1952 he went to San Francisco for a vacation with his family and became ill. In September of that year, he went to a doctor and was told he had undergone a "silent" heart attack. He was given many tests, which increased the stress he was experiencing. Various medications were prescribed and he still uses these today.

In 1959 while undergoing X-rays preparatory to the

removal of his gall bladder, it was discovered that he had an aneuryism of the descending aorta from his heart. Fortunately he did not need surgery on the gall bladder.

In 1970 cataracts began to form. The left eye was affected more than the right. He also became aware of a prostrate problem between 1968-70. During these years he went through some changes with his job because the owners were trying to sell the business. In 1971 he was transferred with the company to another state. He had refused an offer to become vice-president so his salary was reduced as a result. In September 1977 he retired and moved to California with his wife where he is now in business for himself as a consultant for people who wish to register pesticides. With his retirement some of the stress has been removed from his life. A recent physical examination indicated his circulation was poor. His diet remains the same; he does not get enough exercise; he still smokes a pipe and takes three medications daily.

Case History #1

The horoscope's emphasis is in the second and third houses, in ♒ and ♓. Both sensitivity and original inventive qualities are evident here.

☉ in ♓ ☌ ♀, ♈ dwad	Loving, sensitive nature yet has the need to be assertive with the ♈ dwad and ♂ ☌ ♀
☉ □ ♄ in ♊ 6th house	Feelings of insecurity; difficulty with his father; health problems resulting from worry, anxiety; with ♄ ruler of 2nd house, worries about finances
☉ △ ♂, ♀ in 7th house	Strengthens vital energy; importance of being involved in partnerships
☽ in ♒ ☌ ♃♅ in 2nd house	Highly sensitized nervous system; fixed sign emphasis tends to hold back emotions; tendency to high blood pressure, circulation and heart problems; innovative with tools and techniques of business
☽ in ♒, ♋ dwad	Reinforces his sensitivity, his insecurities and anxieties about finances

Grand △ ☽ △ ♄ △ MC in air	Channels his nervous sensitivity into his profession and manifests changes and innovations there; ability to communicate new ideas
♃♅ in ♒ ∠ asc.	Physical body reacts from overwork and tension
♐ asc., ♌ dwad	Expansive, philosophical nature; involvement of heart; liver and pancreas emphasized with ♐ asc. and ♃ ☌ ☽
Asc. □ nodes in ♍ - ♓	Digestive system and lymphatic system may cause problems
☿ ☌ ⚴ in ♓ in 3rd house	Need to be of service; writing and communications important
☿ ∠ asc.	Possible difficulty in expressing his ideas; nervous system interferes with physical stamina
☿ ∠ ♃♅ in ♒	Receives new original ideas but tends to overdo mental work
☿ □ ♇ in ♊ in 7th house	Need to probe deeply into his own motives; good at research
♀ in ♓ in 3rd house △ ♂♇ 7th house	Empathy in dealing with others
♀ □ ♄ in ♊ in 6th house	Holds back feelings, as ♀ rules 6th house and ♄ is in the 6th house, this undoubtedly interferes with his health
♂ ☌ ♇ in the 7th house	Deep feelings not easily expressed; explosive and volatile nature which may manifest in personal relationships
⚷ ☌ ☊ in ♓ in 3rd house	Potential for healing work; communicates ideas that are unusual

MIDPOINTS

♂/♄ = ♅ (inverse)	Difficulty expressing his individuality; possible problems with neurological system or electrical transmission system of body

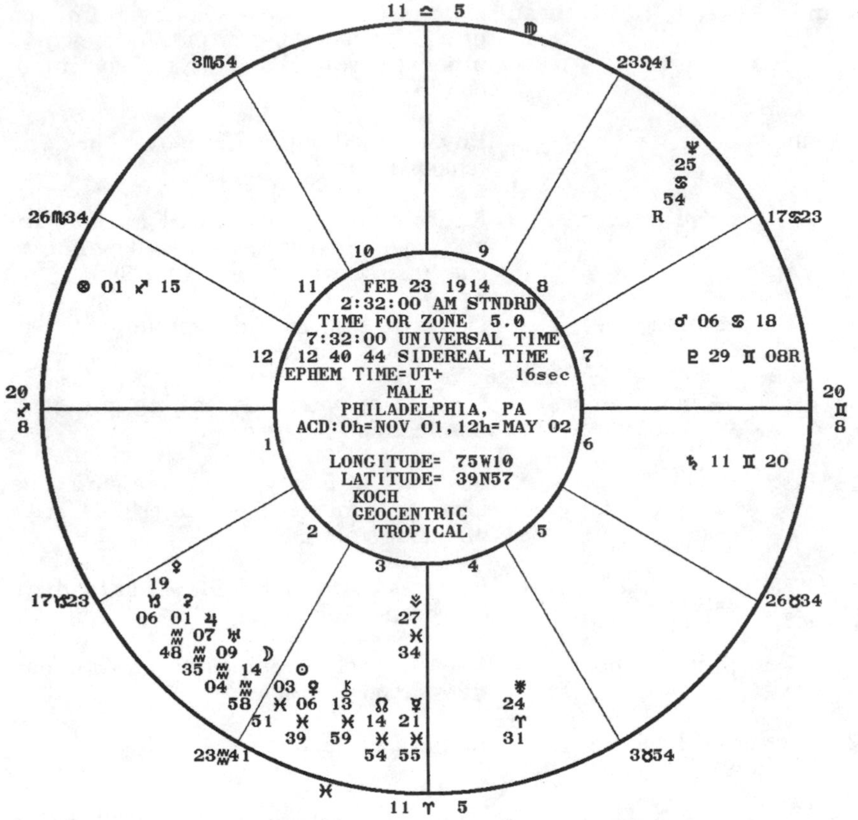
11 ♎ 5
3♏54
23♌41
26♏34
17♋23
FEB 23 1914
2:32:00 AM STNDRD
TIME FOR ZONE 5.0
7:32:00 UNIVERSAL TIME
12 40 44 SIDEREAL TIME
EPHEM TIME=UT+ 16sec
MALE
PHILADELPHIA, PA
ACD:0h=NOV 01,12h=MAY 02
LONGITUDE= 75W10
LATITUDE= 39N57
KOCH
GEOCENTRIC
TROPICAL
⊗ 01 ♐ 15
♂ 06 ♋ 18
♇ 29 ♊ 08R
♄ 11 ♊ 20
20 ♐ 8
20 ♊ 8
17♑23
26♉34
23♒41
3♉54
11 ♈ 5

MIDPOINTS ARRANGED IN PLANET SEQUENCE

☉	03♓51	A	20♐08	☉/♅	21♒28	☽/♃	11♒17	☿/♂	14♉06	♀/♂	06♉29
☽	14♒58	M	11♎05	/♆	14♉53	/♄	13♈09	/♃	29♒45	/♃	22♒07
☿	21♓55	☊	14♓54	/♇	01♉30	/♅	12♒01	/♄	01♉37	/♄	24♈00
♀	06♓39	♆]	13♓59	/A	27♑00	/♆	05♉26	/♅	00♓29	/♅	22♒52
♂	06♋18	☉/☽	24♒25	/M	22♐28	/♇	22♈03	/♆	23♉54	/♆	16♉17
♃	07♒35	/☿	12♓53	/☊	09♓23	/A	17♑33	/♇	10♉31	/♇	02♉54
♄	11♊20	/♀	05♓15	/⚷	08♓55	/M	13♐02	/A	06♒01	/A	28♑24
♅	09♒04	/♂	05♉05	☽/☿	03♓26	/☊	29♒56	/M	01♑30	/M	23♐52
♆	25♋54	/♃	20♒43	/♀	25♒49	/⚷	29♒29	/☊	18♓24	/☊	10♓47
♇	29♊08	/♄	22♈36	/♂	25♈38	☿/♀	14♓17	/⚷	17♓57	/⚷	10♓19

♂/♃	21♈57	♃/♅	08♒19	♄/A	15♓44	♆/♇	12♋31	A/☊	02♒31
/♄	23♊49	/♆	01♉45	/M	11♌12	/A	08♎01	/⚷	02♒04
/♅	22♈41	/♇	18♈22	/☊	28♈07	/M	03♍29	M/☊	27♐59
/♆	16♋06	/A	13♑52	/⚷	27♈40	/☊	20♉24	/⚷	27♐32
/♇	02♋43	/M	09♐20	♅/♆	02♉29	/⚷	19♉57	☊/⚷	14♓27
/A	28♍13	/☊	26♒15	/♇	19♈06	♇/A	24♍38		
/M	23♌41	/⚷	25♒47	/A	14♑36	/M	20♌07		
/☊	10♉36	♄/♅	10♈12	/M	10♐04	/☊	07♉01		
/⚷	10♉09	/♆	03♋37	/☊	26♒59	/⚷	06♉34		
♃/♄	09♈28	/♇	20♊14	/⚷	26♒32	A/M	15♏36		

PLANET	SIGN	LONG	HSE	DECL	LAT	GEOCENTRIC N-NODE	GEOCENTRIC S-NODE
SUN	Pic	3 51 28	3	10S 6	0 00		
MOON	Aqu	14 58 24	2	18S52	2S38	15Pi35	15Vi35
MERC D	Pic	21 54.6	3	1S51	1N29	19Pi27	07Aq08
VENU E	Pic	6 39.3	3	10S24	1S26	13Ar53	01Aq58
MARS F	Can	6 18.2	7	26N39	3N21	19Ar57	25Sa22
JUPI	Aqu	7 35.1	2	18S48	0S26	00Ca11	17Cp49
SATU	Gem	11 20.1	6	20N41	1S28	19Ca01	26Cp48
URAN R	Aqu	9 3.8	2	18S35	0S36	10Ge22	16Sa13
NEPT E	Can	25 54.1R	8	20N33	0S26	10Le07	11Aq36
PLUT	Gem	29 8.4R	7	17N42	5S45	17Ca57	20Cp07

☉/ ♅ = ♂ (inverse)   Neurological and electrical systems of body a focus area

☽ / ♆ = asc. (inverse)   Emotional sensitivity; tendency toward hypoglycemia

Secondary Progressions	Solar Arc Directions	Transits	Eclipses
1. September 1952—heart attack			
☿ ☌ ☊	♂ ☍ ☽	♂ ☌ asc.	August L.E. ☌ ☽
☉ ☌ nadir	♀ ☍ ♃	♃ ⊼ asc.	
♃ ☌ ☽		♆ □ ☉	
Asc. ☍ ♆		♀ △ asc.	
☽ ☌ ♀ August			
2. November 1959—aneruysm of descending aorta			
☉ ∠ ☉	♄ ☌ ♆	♇ ☍ ♀	March L. E. ☌ E. P.
☿ ☌ ☿	☽ □ ♇	♃ □ ♀	Sept. L. E. ☌ ☿
☽ ☌ MC Nov.		♄ ☍ ♂	
		♆ □ ♃ △ ♂	
		♅ ⊼ ☿ ⚹ ♀	
3. October-November 1970—cataracts and prostate			
☿ □ ♂	MC □ ♀	♃ □ ☽	Feb. L. E. ☍ ☉
♂ ☌ ♆	♄ ☍ ♃	♄ ⊼ asc.	
☽ ⚹ ♆ Oct.	♆ ☍ ☿	♅ ☌ MC	
☽ □ ♄ Nov.	☽ ☌ nadir	♀ □ ♇	

CASE HISTORY #2

This man has been hospitalized twelve times for cardiac dysfunction. He is a very sensitive and emotional person, as well as a gifted psychic, palmist and healer.

When he was thrity-nine his first child was born. Previously he had worked as a house painter, but at this time in 1964 he had resumed his schooling, studying dramatic art preparatory to teaching in secondary school. He was experiencing financial pressure and was also having emotional problems with his wife, who was working and supporting the family.

In December 1964 he experienced his first heart attack, which was very mild. The doctors were not sure whether or not he had had an attack. Actually he had suspected a heart problem one to two years previously but his doctor could find nothing wrong with him at that time.

From 1966-70 he taught English and Dramatic art at a high school in California. In 1968 another child was born. In 1971 he lost his job and had major problems with his car; he then went to work as a roofer. He began to experience pains in his chest from working outdoors in the cold but doctors could find nothing wrong. While he was in the hospital for observation, he walked to the next floor, disobeying regulations. When he came back to his bed, he suffered a major acute myocardial infarction. He experienced the attack in his mind's eye by seeing a rider on a black horse hit him with a lance which pierced his heart. As he left his body, he felt like he was dying. But then he saw a ray from a very bright planet. By following that ray, he came back to his body. Actually his heart had stopped beating for a minute. When he went out of his body, he knew it was not yet his time to go, that he still had more work to do here, and so he was drawn back. At the time he also developed a severe case of pneumonia with a high fever. When he finally recuperated, the doctors told him he could no longer work at a regular job, that he needed daily rest and had only another five to ten years more. Because of his strong will to live and his feelings that he had more work to accomplish in this lifetime, he refused to accept this diagnosis.

During the next several years he worked as a substitute teacher and house painter. Most of the time he was under financial pressure. He was also having problems with his marriage. From December 17-26, 1972 he was hospitalized for angina, again on January 2, 1973 for tachycardia, and on March 5, 1973 for lack of oxygen. He was not taking any medications during this period.

On April 18, 1973 he had another acute myocardial infarction and a cardiac arrest, and was given eight electric shocks with the defibrillator (an instrument that counteracts fibrillation of the heart by applying electric impulses; it is used in cardiac resuscitation). He was in the hospital twelve days and afterwards given two medications—lanoxin, similar to digitalis which is used to strengthen the heart and slow down the beat, and inderol which lowers the blood pressure and prevents abnormal beats.

This major attack, followed by two hospitalizations in 1973, was the beginning of a breakthrough for him in his work. He started to use his psychic gifts to teach palmistry and read palms. His income was earned from something he truly enjoyed doing. He has been hospitalized a few more times due to tachycardia. In 1976 he separated from his wife and embarked upon a more itinerant life style—traveling to other areas, practicing healing and reading palms. These activities provide enough income for him. He has become more aware of his diet in recent years and has added various nutritional supplements. He definitely tends to overwork and doesn't know how to slow down. He also suffers quite frequently from emotional depression.

Case History #2

Emphasis in this horoscope is in the tenth and eleventh houses in ♓ and ♈. This shows the need to identify with a group or larger social structure while dynamically pursuing his own profession.

☉ in ♈ ♂ ♀ ☿ in 10th and 11th houses, ♓ dwad	Starting new projects and communicating with others, creative and loving quality expressed in his work; ♓ dwad emphasizes his sensitivity and compassion
☉ ♂ ⚷	Tendency to be compulsive, hardworking
☉ □ ♃ in ♑ in 7th house	Needs to work out relationships with others
☉ ∠ ☽ in ♓ on MC	Emotional fantasies and daydreaming interfere with the manifestion of his ideas and his work
☉ ∠ ♂ in ♊ in 12th house	Lowered vitality; need to follow through with projects
☉ ∠ MC	Manifests his pioneering spirit in his professional life
☽ in ♓ ♂ MC	High spiritual ideals and goals; psychic

	ability, sensitivity, capacity to fantasize; can reach large numbers of people
☽ ☌ ♅	Unusual type of work; highly sensitized nervous system; sensitive to electrical vibrations
Grand water △ ☽ ♅ △ ♄ △ ♀	Ability to transform emotions; strong healing and psychic powers
☽ □ ♂ in ♊ in 12th house	Scattered energy, restlessness; need to focus his energy and follow through on projects, problems with mother
☽ ∠ ♀ ☽ contra ∥ ♀	Working out emotional problems and problems with women and his mother
♋ Asc., ♌ dwad	Emotional insecurity; ego needs to express individuality and be recognized; creativity helps to fulfill emotional needs; emphasis on heart
♀ ☌ Asc.	Probes deeply into things and works on his own transformation
Yod ☽ ♅ ⊼ ♃ ⊼ ♆	Strong psychic and healing ability; unrealistic goals; tendency toward toxic conditions of liver and pancreas
♆ ∠ Asc.	Uncertain of self image; drugs and alcohol affect physical body
♀ ☌ ☿ in ♈ in 10th house	Communication of new ideas to others
♀ □ ♃ in 7th house	Tendency to excesses; may be sugars or alcohol
Yod ♃ ⊼ ♂ ⊼ ♆	Overdoing psychic work drains his physical vitality; hypoglycemic tendency
♄ in ♏ in 5th house	Need to examine his motives deeply and transform his sexual energy in a creative manner
♄ □ ♆ in 2nd house	Confusion about handling money; vague about how his creative flow works with his responsibilities and sense of values
♄ exactly square nodes in ♌ and ♒ in 2nd and 8th house	Need to channel sexual energy; holds back emotions; blockage in circulation system

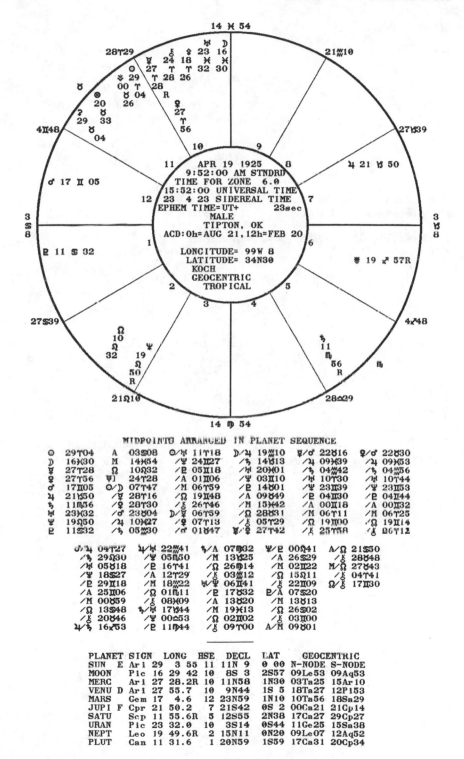

14 ♓ 54

28♈29

☊ ☿ 23 16
♄ ⚷ 24 18 ♓ ☽
☉ ♅ 27 ♈ ♈ 32 30
☄ 29 ♈ 28 26
00 ♈ 28
♂ 04 R
♀
27
♈
56

21♏10

♂ 20
? ♂
29 33 ♂
04

4♊48

27♑39

10   9

11   APR 19 1925   8
9:52:00 AM STNDRD
TIME FOR ZONE 6.0
15:52:00 UNIVERSAL TIME
12   23 4 23 SIDEREAL TIME   7
EPHEM TIME= UT+   23sec
MALE
TIPTON, OK
ACD:0h=AUG 21,12h=FEB 20

LONGITUDE= 99W 8
LATITUDE= 34N30
KOCH
GEOCENTRIC
TROPICAL

♃ 21 ♑ 50

♂ 17 ♊ 05

3
♋
8

3
♑
8

♇ 11 ♋ 32

♯ 19 ♐ 57R

27♋39

4♐48

1   2   3   4   5   6

♃ 11
♏
56
R   ♏

Ω
10
Ω
32   19
Ψ
Ω
50
R

21♌10

28♎29

14 ♍ 54

MIDPOINTS ARRANGED IN PLANET SEQUENCE

☉	29♈04	A	03♋08	☉/♅	11♈18	☽/♃	19♒10	☿/♂	22♉16	♀/♂	22♉30
☽	16♓30	M	14♓54	/Ψ	24♊27	/♄	14♑13	/♃	09♓39	/♃	09♓53
☿	27♈28	Ω	10♌32	/♇	05♊18	/♅	20♓01	/♄	04♒42	/♄	04♒56
♀	27♈56	♅]	24♈28	/A	01♍06	/Ψ	03♊10	/♅	10♈30	/♅	10♈44
♂	17♊05	☉/☽	07♈47	/M	06♈59	/♇	14♉01	/Ψ	23♊39	/Ψ	23♊53
♃	21♑50	/♅	28♈16	/Ω	19♊48	/A	09♉49	/♇	04♊30	/♇	04♊44
♄	11♏56	/♀	28♈30	/♄	26♈46	/M	15♓42	/A	00♊18	/A	00♍32
♅	23♓32	/♂	23♉04	☽/♅	06♈59	/Ω	28♉31	/M	06♈11	/M	06♈25
Ψ	19♌50	/♃	10♓27	/♀	07♈13	/♄	05♈29	/Ω	19♍00	/Ω	19♊14
♇	11♋32	/♄	05♒30	/♂	01♉47	☿/♀	27♈42	/♄	25♈58	/♄	06♈12

☉/♃	04♈27	♃/♅	22♒41	♄/A	07♍32	Ψ/♇	00♌41	A/Ω	21♋50
/♄	29♌30	/Ψ	05♍50	/M	13♓25	/A	26♋29	/♄	28♉48
/♅	05♉18	/♇	16♈41	/Ω	26♍14	/M	02♈22	M/Ω	27♉43
/Ψ	18♋27	/A	12♈29	/♄	03♒12	/Ω	15♋11	/♄	04♈41
/♇	29♊18	/M	18♒22	♅/Ψ	06♋41	/♄	22♊09	Ω/♄	17♊30
/A	25♍06	/Ω	01♍11	/♇	17♋32	♇/A	07♋20		
/M	00♍59	/♄	08♓09	/A	13♉20	/M	13♉13		
/Ω	13♋48	♄/♅	17♈44	/M	19♓13	/Ω	26♌02		
/♄	20♉46	/Ψ	00♎53	/Ω	02♍02	/♄	03♍00		
♃/♄	16♐53	/♇	11♍44	/♄	09♈00	A/M	09♉01		

PLANET	SIGN	LONG	HSE	DECL	LAT	GEOCENTRIC	
SUN	E Ari 29	3 55	11	11N 9	0 00	N-NODE	S-NODE
MOON	Pic 16	29 42	10	8S 3	2S57	09Le53	09Aq53
MERC	Ari 27	28.2R	10	11N58	1N30	03Ta25	15Ar10
VENU	D Ari 27	55.7	10	9N44	1S 5	18Ta27	12P153
MARS	Gem 17	4.6	12	23N59	1N10	10Ta56	18Sa29
JUPI	F Cpr 21	50.2	7	21S42	0S 2	00Ca21	21Cp14
SATU	Scp 11	55.6R	5	12S55	2N38	17Ca27	29Cp27
URAN	Pic 23	32.0	10	3S14	0S44	11Ge25	15Sa38
NEPT	Leo 19	49.6R	2	15N11	0N20	09Le07	12Aq52
PLUT	Can 11	31.6	1	20N59	1S59	17Ca31	20Cp34

MIDPOINTS

♅/♆ = ♃ (Inverse)

Growth through psychic and spiritual work; higher protection in cases of heart failure, (♅/♆ rules heart failure)

☿/♆ = ☽

Strong imaginative ability with tendency to fantasies

♀/♆ = ☽

Emotional and artistic sensitivity; hypoglycemic tendency

Secondary Progressions	Solar Arc Directions	Transits	Eclipses

1. December 1964—first hospitalization

♀ □ ☽	☊ ☌ ☽	♆ ☍ ☽ MC	June L. E. ☍ Asc.
♂ △ ♄	Asc. ☌ ☊	♂ ☍ ☽	
☉ ⊼ ♃	☊ ☌ ☽	♃ □ ♆ * ☽	
		♃ ∠ Asc.	
♄ □ nodes		♅ ☍ ☽	
☽ ☌ ♆ Dec.		♆ □ ♆	

2. February 1971—first major acute heart attack

MC ☌ ☉	☊ ☌ ♅	♂ ☍ ♂	Feb. L. E. ☌ ♆
☊ ☌ ♄		♃ ∠ ♃	
☉ ∠ ☉		♄ □ ♆	
☽ □ ☊ Feb.		♄ ☌ ♄/♆	
☿ ∠ ♀		♅ ⊓ ?	
♀ ∠ ☊		♆ ⊼ ☉	
♂ △ ☽			

3. 1973 Hospitalized five times: second major attack in April

♀ * ☿	Asc. ☌ ♆	♄ ☌ ♂	Jan. L. E. □ ☉
♀ ⊓ ♄		♃ ☌ ☊	June L. E. □ ☽
		♅ □ ♃	
		♀ □ Asc.	
		♆ ∠ ♃	

At the times he had most of his attacks and was hospitalized, the Moon was in Scorpio or Sagittarius, transiting his sixth house and opposite Mars.

CHAPTER TEN

EYE DISORDERS

Eye disorders, primarily cataract and glaucoma, are the leading causes of blindness today. Other visual problems as well restrict our lives making us uncomfortable and dependent on glasses or contact lenses in order to see. During periods of anxiety, stress, and emotional upset, vision may be the first part of the body to be affected. This is often because there is something we do not want to see or acknowledge about our lives. And so, symbolically, we shut off or impair our sight in some way. In the case of cataract or glaucoma, the individual may even have clairvoyant ability that he is blocking or afraid to use. Physical blindness is sometimes a necessary step in increasing one's inner vision.

When a cataract forms, the crystalline lens of the eye becomes increasingly clouded or opaque. Vision is diminished as the opacity increases. Surgical treatment, which is often performed, involves the removal of the crystalline lens.

In glaucoma there is an increase of pressure inside the eye which interferes with vision. This is due to a disturbance in the production and drainage of fluid that fills the interior of the eye in front of the lens. Too much fluid may be produced or the normal amount may not drain properly. The eyedrops that are usually prescribed constrict the pupil to allow more space for the fluid; they also help the fluid to flow through the walls of the canal. Unfortunately, these drops have many side effects. They distort the vision for the first thirty to forty minutes after they are taken, and they also make it difficult to perceive colors clearly.

Among the many causes of eye disease are poor dietary habits and the lack of certain vitamins and minerals. Vitamin B2 or riboflavin has been found to have a preventive value in treating cataracts.[1] Riboflavin is also necessary for the proper utilization of Vitamin A. Vitamin D is extremely important in the prevention of cataract. Calcium cannot be metabolized in the eye if Vitamin D is missing.[2] Vitamin D from synthetic substances may not be able to be utilized, but Vitamin D from natural sources, particularly from the sun, is very important. This is why so many researchers do not advocate wearing sunglasses.[3] Another vitamin of importance for eye disorders is Vitamin C. Studies show that vitamin C should be of organic origin for good results.[4] It can be obtained easily from vegetables, fruits and certain herbs such as hibiscus and rose hips. Vitamin C has also been used in eyedrops for glaucoma. Vitamin P or Rutin, which strengthens arterial walls, is helpful in the prevention of cataracts.[5] It is found in large amounts in buckwheat groats, a grain which can be used as a cereal.

In terms of diet, research has shown that the use of animal fats in meat, butter, cream, cheese, and eggs, which contribute to cholesterol build-up in the arteries, is an important factor in the formation of cataracts.[6] A diet low in animal products and high in grains, vegetables, fruits, nuts, seeds, and fish has usually been recommended.

Other important treatments for eye disorders include certain herbs and homeopathic remedies.[7] Stress-controlling techniques such as autogenics, biofeedback, and visualization have been very helpful, particularly in working with glaucoma. A system of eye exercises developed by Dr. William Bates has also proved invaluable in dealing with all eye problems. These exercises include palming, blinking and shifting focus.[8] Many have been able to give up their glasses or contact lenses after practicing these exercises.

---

[1] *Cataract, Glaucoma, And Other Eye Disorders*, John H. Tobe, St. Catherine's, Ontario, 1975, pp. 168–9.
[2] Ibid., pg. 175.
[3] *See Health And Light*, John Ott, Pocket Book, N.Y., 1973.
[4] Tobe, op. cit., pp. 173–4.
[5] Ibid., pg. 177.
[6] Ibid., Chapter 5.
[7] Ibid., Chapter 15.
[8] See *Better Eyesight Without Glasses*, W. H. Bates, Pyramid Books, N.Y., 1976.

ASTROLOGICAL

Astrologically, eye problems are related to the signs Aries and Libra. Aries traditionally rules the head and thus is related to the eyes. Libra is the polar opposite of Aries and is associated with the kidneys. Often there is a relationship between eye problems and malfunctioning kidneys. To quote Dr. William Davidson, "The reciprocalness between Aries and Libra and the consequent reflex influence from kidneys to eyes is well known, but not understood in medicine. But this knowledge is very helpful in refraction, the fitting of glasses. Many doctors are confounded and condemned because the glasses don't fit. It is really due to the changing condition of the kidney function".[9]

Aquarius governs the retina of the eyes and often Aquarius and Uranus are involved in problems with the retina. Since Neptune rules the pineal gland or "third eye" and so many eye problems relate to inner vision, Neptune is often found conjoined the Sun or Moon, or other planets.

Fixed Stars which affect the eyes are often found on the angles of the horoscope, or conjunct the Sun, Moon or another planet. These stars seem to influence the vibration of the planet when they are within a one degree orb—especially the conjunction, opposition and square. Examples of fixed stars relative to eye disease are in Helen Keller's horoscope, where the Pleiades conjunct Pluto and oppose her Ascendant, and the chart of John Milton, the blind poet, who had the star Antares conjunct the Ascendant and opposite Uranus, with the Pleiades conjunct the Moon in the sixth house.

Stars which affect the eyes most are the Pleiades at 29° Taurus, the Hyades at 5° Gemini, the Aselli at 6 and 7° Leo, Antares at 9° Sagittarius and Spiculum at 29° Sagittarius. Other stars are also to be considered. A complete list of stars involved in eye problems follows:

---

[9]*Lectures On Medical Astrology,* Dr. William Davidson, Astrological Bureau, Monroe, N.Y., 1973.

Star	Nature	1950 Longitude
1. Vertex	♂ ☽	27 ♈ 08
2. Capulus	♂ ☿	23 ♉ 30
3. Algol	♄ ♃	25 ♉ 28
4. Pleiades	☽ ♂	29 ♉ 06
5. Prima Hyadum (group called Hyades)	♄ ☿	5 ♊ 06
6. Bellatrix	♂ ☿	20 ♊ 16
7. Ensis	♂ ☽	22 ♊ 20
8. Castor	☿	19 ♋ 33
9. Pollux	♂	22 ♋ 35
10. Praesaepe	♂ ☽	6 ♌ 34
11. North Asellus	♂ ☉	6 ♌ 50
12. South Asellus	♂ ☉	8 ♌ 01
13. Copula	☽ ♀	24 ♍ 23
14. Foramen	♄ ♃	21 ♎ 28
15. Antares	♂ ♃	9 ♐ 03
16. Rastaban	♄ ♂	11 ♐ 15
17. Aculeus	♂ ☽	25 ♐ 04
18. Acumen	♂ ☽	28 ♐ 00
19. Spiculum	♂ ☽	29 ♐ 57
20. Facies	☉ ♂	7 ♑ 37
21. Manubrium	☉ ♂	14 ♑ 17

Midpoints to consider in diagnosing eye problems are the following:

Saturn/Neptune - health axis or cardinal point of disease
Mars/Neptune - point of toxicity, susceptibility to infection
Sun/Neptune - fluid concentration in the cells.
Moon/Neptune - over-accumulation of water in the tissues of the body.
Neptune/Pluto - disturbances of a more chronic nature in dealing with body fluids.

CASE HISTORY #1

This woman had glaucoma and was completely blind for four-and-a-half years of her life. She never expected her sight to return. During the time she was blind she learned Braille and listened to talking books on the phonograph while continuing her work. Her years of physical blindness were obviously necessary to develop her inner sight since she works as a spiritual counselor.

In 1958 cataracts which had been forming for a few years were discovered. It was at this time that she noticed what she calls "the black lace"—street lights changing their shape at night and appearing very radiant. This was a stressful period in her life. She was working weekdays in an office as a bookkeeper and receptionist and on the weekends and evenings taking dictation for a doctor and doing some counseling.

By June of 1968 she could barely see the sidewalk and had difficulty finding her way. She learned Braille and began using the talking books. In the spring of 1972 glaucoma set in. She had one operation on October 1, 1972 and a second one in November. After the second operation her left eye was restored to 20/40 vision; her right eye remained covered for a few weeks.

At present her left eye has tunnel vision (no peripheral vision), and the right eye has 20/20 vision. She has eye infections frequently when the secretions of the sebaceous gland get into her eye. In 1977 she had a cyst removed on the outer rim of her eye since the oil from the sebaceous glands hardened. There is often a lack of fluid in her eyes when she awakes in the morning; this happens especially when she is under stress.

Her general health has improved much over the years. She has published several books, continues to do spiritual counseling and teaching, and has begun to travel and lecture.

Case History #1

☉ ☌ ♀ in ♎ in 6th house	Need for ongoing relationships; helping people through counseling; being part of a healing partnership
☉ in ♎, ♉ dwad	Emphasizes the Venusian quality and the practical nature of her work

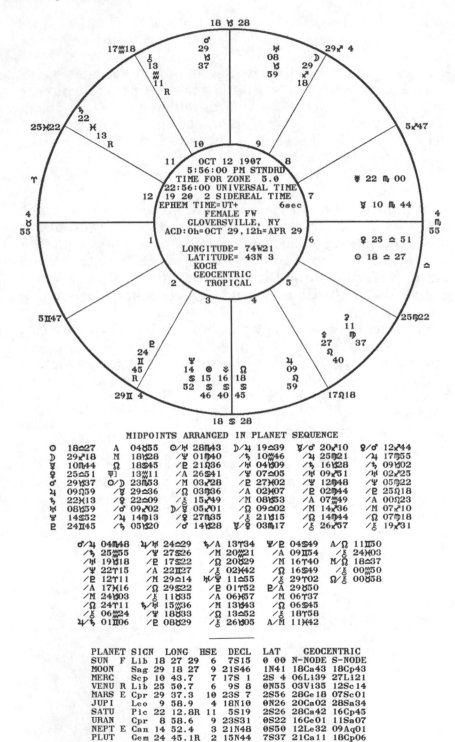

OCT 12 1907
5:56:00 PM STNDRD
TIME FOR ZONE 5.0
22:56:00 UNIVERSAL TIME
19 20 2 SIDEREAL TIME
EPHEM TIME=UT+ 6sec
FEMALE FW
GLOVERSVILLE, NY
ACD:0h=OCT 29,12h=APR 29

LONGITUDE= 74W21
LATITUDE= 43N 3
KOCH
GEOCENTRIC
TROPICAL

MIDPOINTS ARRANGED IN PLANET SEQUENCE

PLANET	SIGN		LONG	HSE	DECL	LAT	GEOCENTRIC	
							N-NODE	S-NODE
SUN	F	Lib	18 27	29 6	7S15	0 00		
MOON		Sag	29 18	27 9	21S46	1N41	18Ca43	18Cp43
MERC		Scp	10 43.7	7	17S 1	2S 4	06Li39	27Li21
VENU	R	Lib	25 50.7	6	9S 8	0N55	03Vi35	12Sc14
MARS	E	Cpr	29 37.3	10	23S 7	2S56	28Ge18	07Sc01
JUPI		Leo	9 58.9	4	18N10	0N26	20Ca02	28Sa34
SATU		Pic	22 12.8R	11	5S19	2S26	28Ca42	16Cp45
URAN		Cpr	8 58.6	9	23S31	0S22	16Ge01	11Sa07
NEPT	E	Can	14 52.4	3	21N48	0S50	12Le32	09Aq01
PLUT		Gem	24 45.1R	2	15N44	7S37	21Ca11	18Cp06

☉ □ ♅ in ♑ in 9th house	Strongly individualistic philosophy, possibly not accepted by partners; unusual relationships
☉ □ ♆ in ♋ in 3rd house	Need to incorporate a spiritual framework into counseling and service work
☽ in ♐ in 9th house	Deep interest in philosophy and metaphysics
☽ in ♐, ♏ dwad	Reiterates the ☽ ☍ ♀ theme; transforming of emotional states through metaphysical ideas
☽ ☍ ♀ in ♊ in 2nd house	Challenging groups of people through observing their motives and values
☽, ♀ T-square with ♄ in ♓ in 11th house	Health problems may stem from emotional frustrations; channelling emotions by working with groups; possible allergies and digestive problems
♉ Asc., ♊ dwad	Approaches communication and teaching in a practical business-like manner
☿ angular in ♏	Probing mind; counseling and healing others
☿ in ♏ □ ♃ in ♌	Need to communicate, to dominate conversation, tendency to overdo mental work
☿ △ ♆ in 3rd house	Increases intuitive flow and verbal ability
♀ in ♎ □ ♂ in ♑ in 10th house	Sublimation of personal emotions through professional and service work
♀ △ ♀ in ♊ in 2nd house	Ability to transform emotional and sexual energy; need to adopt a value system that fits her work
♃ in ♌ in 4th house	Buoyancy, enthusiasm; opening up home to others
♃ ⊼ ♅ in 9th house	Rebellious against traditional religious and philosophical ideas
♃, ♂, ☿ T-square	Healing and humanitarian work part of her counseling
♄ in ♓ in 11th house	Group work through teaching spiritual disciplines

☽ ☌ ♅ in 9th house	Sensitive nervous system; unusual emotional relationships; frequent changes in relationship
♆ ☌ ☊ in ♋	Communicates inner wisdom in intuitive fashion
♆ ☌ eclipse point	Inner sight and physical sight emphasized
♆ ☌ ⚵ in ♋	Works on perfecting her own inner vision and communicating it to others
☽ ∥ ♂ ∥ ♅ ∥ MC contra ∥ ♆	Highly sensitized nervous system; strong interest in occult and unusual philosophies; dynamic way of manifesting energy in her work

MIDPOINTS

☽/♆ = ♅	Strong psychic ability; unstable fluid balance especially in eyes
♂/♄ = ♅	Sudden changes in body structure; sensitive nervous system

FIXED STARS

Spiculum ☌ ☽	Has a nature of Mars and the Moon; the Moon refers to fluid imbalance in the body and has been associated with blindness
South Asellus ☌ ♃	Strong martial quality involved in her pursuit of philosophical knowledge; important star in eye problems
Facies ☌ ♅	Facies has a Sun-Mars quality; known to cause blindness and defective sight; with ♅ emphasizes second sight or strong intuition

Secondary Progressions	Solar Arc Directions	Transits	Eclipses
1. **July 1958—cataracts started**			
☉ △ ♃	♂ ☌ ♄	♇ ∠ ♆	April S. E. □ ♂
♀ ☌ ☽	‡ □ MC	♆ ☍ Asc	Oct S. E. ☌ ☉

MC ⚻ ♃
☽ ☍ Asc August

♅ □ ☿ ☌ ♃   Oct. L. E. ☌ Asc.
♄ ⧠ Asc.
♃ ☌ ☉/♀

2. June 1968—unable to see sidewalk; psychic surgery

☉ ⧠ Asc.
♂ ⚹ ♅

♄ ☍ ♀   March S. E. □ ♅
♅ □ ☿   April L. E. ☌ ♀
♃ ∠ ♆   Oct. L. E. □♆
♆ ⚻ ☿
♀ ☍ ♄ ⧠ Asc.

3. April 1972—glaucoma set in, October 1, 1972—first operation, November 1972—second operation

☉ ☍ ☿   ☊ □ ♄
Asc. ☌ ♆   ♃ □ ♆

☽ ⚹ ♄ Oct.   ☿ ☍ ♆

April
♃ ☌ ♅,
♄ ⧠ MC
♅ □ ♆,
♆ ∠ MC
October
♅ ☌ ☉
♄ ∠ Asc.
♃ ☌ ☽
♆ ∠ MC
♂ □ ☽
☉ □ ♅
☿ ☌ ☉
November
♃ ☌ ♅
♄ △ ☉
♄ ∠ Asc.
♅ □ MC
♆ ∠ MC

Jan. L. E. ☌ ♃
July S. E. ☍ MC

Dec. L. E. ⚻ ♂

4. January 1973—eye uncovered; received prescription for glasses

☉ ∠ ♃
☉ ☍ ☿
♀ □ ☉
♀ ☌ MC
MC □ ☿
☽ ⚻ ♀ Jan.

♃ ☌ MC   Jan. S. E. ☍ ♆
☊ ☌ ♇   Jan. L. E. ☍ ♂
♅ ☌ ☉/♀
♄ ⧠ ♂

CASE HISTORY #2

This case concerns a lady who has had glaucoma, and through her own experience in healing herself initiated group work in glaucoma therapy. She is presently writing a book about her work.

Her basic health and vitality level have always been good. In January 1965 she remarried and experienced stress as a result of adjusting to the relationship. Previously she had been involved with her professional life. About a year later she noticed that she had difficulty reading signs on the freeway. After an eye examination she was told she needed glasses. In 1968 she moved and her stepson came to live with them increasing the stress at home.

Glaucoma was diagnosed at the time and her quest for self-healing begun. The eye drops prescribed for glaucoma were not satisfactory to her. For the first thirty to forty-five minutes after taking them her vision was distorted. Since she was writing a book at the time and doing a lot of typing, this was inconvenient. She also found that the drops made it more difficult to see colors clearly and to drive at night. As she began to work with techniques of deep relaxation she was able to lower the dosage of the drops and eventually no longer needed them. By 1972 she found she could control the pressure in her eyes. It was at this time that she inaugurated her first workshop in self-healing techniques for glaucoma. In 1975 she started doing glaucoma therapy for others. At present, she works not only in glaucoma therapy but with healing groups for various disorders.

Case History #2

⊙ ♂ ⚥ in ♐ in 9th house	Service through travel and teaching; deep interest in philosophy
⊙ ♌ dwad	Creative and innovative in thinking and philosophy
⊙ □ ♅ in 12th house	Nervous and restless temperament; unusual and strongly individualistic philosophy; philosophical ideas of more spiritual import
Grand trine ⊙ △ ♆ △ ♂ in fire signs and houses	Strong intuitive nature and healing ability
☽ in ♒ in 11th house ♂ ♃	Working with groups in nurturing manner; uses parenting through an impersonal family
⊙ ‖ MC ‖ ♀ ‖ ☿	Need to manifest energy out in the world
☽ in ♒, ♊ dwad	Work with diverse groups; tendency to take on too many projects

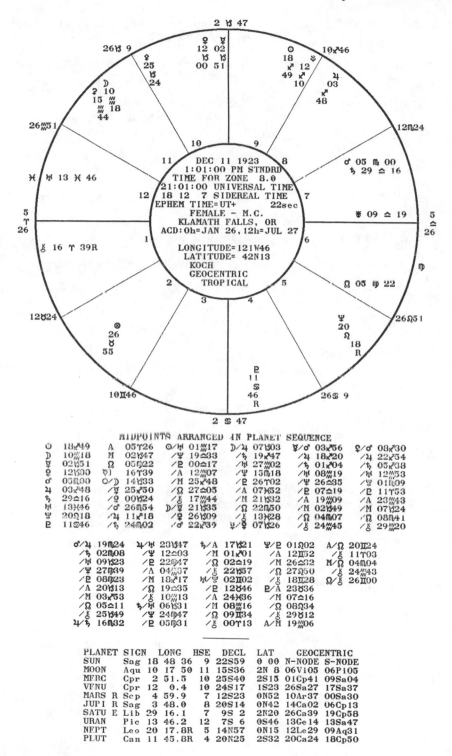

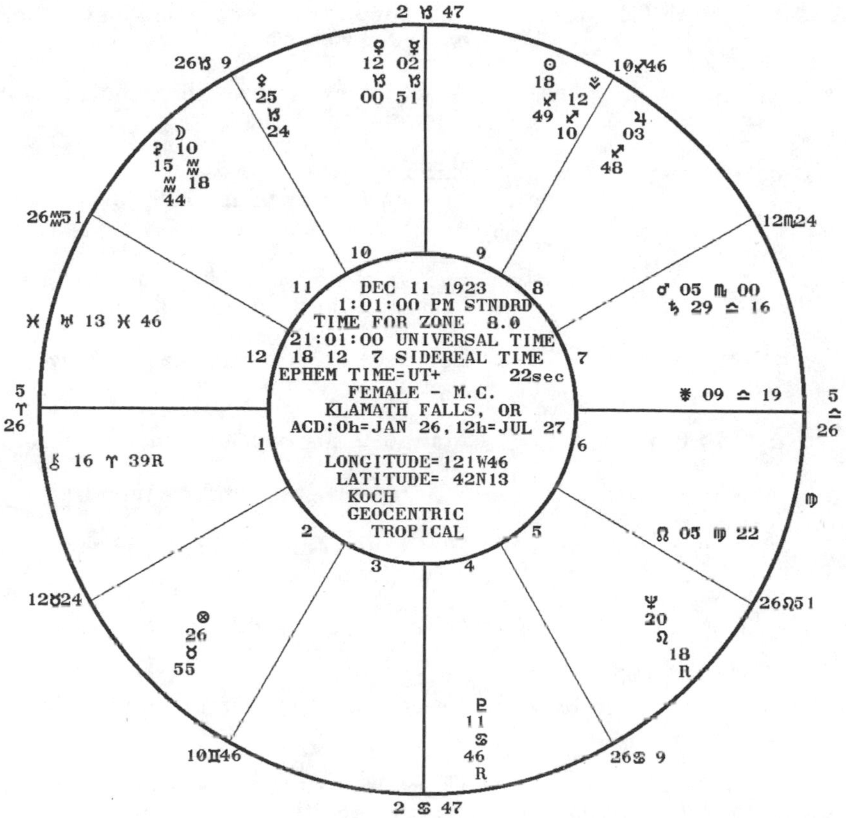
DEC 11 1923
1:01:00 PM STNDRD
TIME FOR ZONE 8.0
21:01:00 UNIVERSAL TIME
18 12 7 SIDEREAL TIME
EPHEM TIME=UT+ 22sec
FEMALE - M.C.
KLAMATH FALLS, OR
ACD:0h=JAN 26,12h=JUL 27
LONGITUDE=121W46
LATITUDE= 42N13
KOCH
GEOCENTRIC
TROPICAL

MIDPOINTS ARRANGED IN PLANET SEQUENCE

☉	18♐49	A	05♈26	☉/♅	01♒17	☽/♃	07♑03	☿/♂	03♐56	♀/♂	08♐30
☽	10♒18	M	02♑47	/♆	19♎33	/♄	19♐47	/♃	18♐20	/♃	22♐54
☿	02♑51	☊	05♍22	/♇	00♎17	/♅	27♒02	/♄	01♐04	/♄	05♐38
♀	12♑00	⚷	16♈39	/A	12♒07	/♆	15♏18	/♅	08♒19	/♅	12♒53
♂	05♏00	☉/☽	14♑33	/M	25♐48	/♇	26♈02	/♆	26♎35	/♆	01♏09
♃	03♐48	/☿	25♐50	/☊	27♎05	/A	07♓52	/♇	07♎19	/♇	11♈53
♄	29♎16	/♀	00♑24	/⚷	17♒44	/M	21♑32	/A	19♒09	/A	23♒43
♅	13♓46	/♂	26♏54	☽/☿	21♑35	/☊	22♏50	/M	02♑49	/M	07♑24
♆	20♌18	/♃	11♐18	/♀	26♑09	/⚷	13♓28	/☊	04♏07	/☊	08♏41
♇	11♋46	/♄	24♏02	/♂	22♐39	☿/♀	07♑26	/⚷	24♒45	/⚷	29♒20

♂/♃	19♏24	♃/♅	23♑47	♄/A	17♑21	♆/♇	01♌02	A/☊	20♊24
/♄	02♏08	/♆	12♎03	/M	01♐01	/A	12♊52	/⚷	11♈03
/♅	09♑23	/♇	22♍47	/☊	02♎19	/M	26♎32	M/☊	04♏04
/♆	27♍39	/A	04♒37	/⚷	22♑57	/☊	27♌50	/⚷	24♒43
/♇	08♍23	/M	18♐17	♅/♆	02♊02	/⚷	18♊28	☊/⚷	26♊00
/A	20♑13	/☊	19♎35	/♇	12♉46	♇/A	23♉36		
/M	03♐53	/⚷	10♒13	/A	24♓36	/M	07♎16		
/☊	05♎11	♄/♅	06♑31	/M	08♒16	/☊	08♌34		
/⚷	25♑49	/♆	24♍47	/☊	09♊34	/⚷	29♉12		
♃/♄	16♏32	/♇	05♍31	/⚷	00♈13	A/M	19♒06		

PLANET	SIGN	LONG	HSE	DECL	LAT	GEOCENTRIC N-NODE	GEOCENTRIC S-NODE
SUN	Sag	18 48 36	9	22S59	0 00		
MOON	Aqu	10 17 50	11	15S36	2N 8	06Vi05	06Pi05
MERC	Cpr	2 51.5	10	25S40	2S15	01Cp41	09Sa04
VENU	Cpr	12 0.4	10	24S17	1S23	26Sa27	17Sa37
MARS R	Scp	4 59.9	7	12S23	0N52	10Ar37	00Sa30
JUPI R	Sag	3 48.0	8	20S14	0N42	14Ca02	06Cp13
SATU E	Lib	29 16.1	7	9S 2	2N20	26Ca39	19Cp58
URAN	Pic	13 46.2	12	7S 6	0S46	13Ge14	13Sa47
NEPT	Leo	20 17.8R	5	14N57	0N15	12Le29	09Aq31
PLUT	Can	11 45.8R	4	20N25	2S32	20Ca24	18Cp50

☽ □ ♂ in ♏ in 7th house	Tendency to be overly emotional, to hold on to old habit patterns
☽ ⊼ ♇ in ♋ in 4th house	Need to break through and transform emotional patterns
♈ Asc., ♉ dwad	Initiating new projects and working with them in a practical manner, (eyes related to ♈)
Asc. □ ☿ in ♑	Sensitive nervous system; possible problems with hand-eye co-ordination
Asc. ⊼ ♂ in ♏	Lowered vitality; problems with eyes or tension in area of eyes
Asc. △ ♃ in 8th house	Manifests her own growth with ease
☿ ☌ MC	Writing, teaching and communicating
☿ △ ☊ in ♍ in 6th house	Ability to communicate ideas regarding health and healing
☿ ⚹ ♂ in ♏	Carries projects through to completion; acts on inspiration
☿ ☌ ♀ in ♑ in 10th house	Reaches many people through writing and teaching
♀ □ ⚷ in ♈	Crises in her life deepen compassion and healing ability
♀, ♇, ⚵ T-square	Need to transform personal emotions in order to work out relationships
♂ in ♏ in 7th house	Much energy into relationships and interaction with others; desire for power in relationships
♂ ☌ ♄ in ♎	Lessons through relationships and possible frustrations
Grand △ in water ♂ △ ♅ △ ♇	Healing and psychic ability; transforming emotional patterns through use of higher consciousness
♃ in ♐ in 8th house	Delving philosophically into occult knowledge; studying hidden motivation of others

♃ □ nodes in ♍ ♓ in 6th and 12th houses	Liver and pancreas imbalance may lead to digestive problems; need to bring philosophical ideas into practical use for healing work
♅ in ♓ in 12th house	Spurts of inspiration; necessity to commune with one's inner self
♆ in ♌ in 5th house, (part of grand fire trine)	Artistic projects take on transcendent quality; deep appreciation for spiritual qualities of art and music
♆ ☍ ☽ ? in ♒ in 11th house	Nurturing children in an unusual way; strong idealism in emotional relationships
♀ angular in ♋ in 4th house	Probing into unconscious areas; strong desire to transform emotional patterns
♀ ☍ ♀ in ♑ in 10th house	Wants to keep home fires burning and also help change the world

MIDPOINTS

♄ / ♆ = ☽ (inverse)	Emotional sensitivity and depression; possible imbalance of fluids in body
☉ / ♆ = ♃ (inverse)	Spiritual growth and expansion; liver and pancreas functioning may be irregular; with ☉ in ♐ and ♃ in ♐ this is strongly indicated

FIXED STARS

Hyades ♉ ♃	Has a Mars-Neptune influence, emphasis on spiritual growth, possibly scattered in too many directions; Hyades are important stars affecting the eyes
Bellatrix ☍ ☉	Quick mind; overdoing mental projects with the ☍ to ☉ in ♐
Aselli ☍ ☽	Eye problems and problems with fluid balance in eyes; strong emotional nature as Aselli have a Mars quality

Secondary Progressions	Solar Arc Directions	Transits	Eclipses
1. January 1965—remarried			
☉ 0♒39	Asc. □ ?	♅ ☍ ♅	Dec. '64 L. E. ☌ ⚶
♀ □♃	‡ ☌ ☋	♄ □♃	
Asc. △ ☽	♅ □ ‡	♃ □♆ ⚼ ☿	
♃ ☌ ⚶		♆ □ ♆	
☽p ☍ ☉p January		♇ ☍ ♅	
2. July 1966—difficulty with vision			
♀ □♂	♆ □ MC	♃ ☌ ♇ ☍ ♀	Oct. L. E. ☍ ♂
Asc. ⚻ ♀		♄ ⚻ ♄ ∠ ?	Nov. S. E. □ ♆
☽ ∠ ☿ June		♆ □ ♆	
☽ △ ☉ July		♅ ☌ E. P.	
☽ ☌ ♆ August			
3. October 1968—glaucoma diagnosed			
☉ □ ♂	♄ ☌ ⚶	♃ ⚼ ☽	Sept. S. E. ☌ V
♂ ☌ ♃	Asc. □ ♆	♅ ∠ ♆	Oct. L. E. □ ♀, ♇
♀ ☌ ☋	♂ ☌ ☉	♆ ☍ ⊕	
☽ ⚼♂ November	♆ □ ☿, MC		
4. August 1972—started workshops in glaucoma therapy			
♀ □ ⚶	? □ ☿	♃ * ♄ ∠ ☽	
♀ * ♀		♄ * ♆ □ E. P.	
♀ △ ♇		♆ ☌ ♃	
♂ □ ☊		♇ ∠ ♆	
♃ □ ♅			
☽ △ ♇ August			
5. September 1975—development of glaucoma therapy groups			
☉ ⚻ ♇	♀ □♃	♃ □ ‡	May S. E. □ ♆
☉ ☌ ☽	♇ □ ♃	♄ □ ♄	May L. E. ☌ ♃
	♅ ☍ ♂	♅ □ ♄	
	☽ □ MC	♆ ☌ ⚶ ∠ ‡	
		♇ ☌ ✱	

CHAPTER ELEVEN

GYNECOLOGICAL PROBLEMS

Though there are many types of gynecological problems, astrology has been most helpful in dealing with those women having difficulty conceiving and those who have had miscarriages. From a study of the natal horoscope, we can see where the imbalances are in the body, and through progressions and transits, what time periods are most beneficial for conception.

Physiologically, those who are unable to conceive or those who have had frequent miscarriages often have imbalances with the endocrine glands. The major causes of infertility stem from malfunction of the pituitary gland, of the ovaries, and obstruction of the fallopian tubes. The anterior pituitary produces FSH (follicle-stimulating hormone) and LH (Luteinizing Hormone). FSH stimulates the maturing of the Graafian Follicles leading to the production of ostrogen. LH stimulates the formation and secretion of the corpus luteum leading to the production of progesterone. Estrogen is released in the first half of the menstrual cycle and both estrogen and progesterone are released in the second half of the cycle. When the levels of estrogen and progesterone are too low, the ovulation cycle may be interrupted. Other causes of infertility include vaginal disorders, cervical abnormalities, uterine abnormalities, chronic disease states, birth control devices as the IUD, diaphragm, various jellies and sprays, and immunological reactions to sperm.[1]

---

[1]*Maternity Care—The Nurse and the Family*, Margaret Jensen et al., C. F. Mosby Co., St. Louis, 1977, Chapter 1.

PSYCHOLOGICAL

Emotional problems play an important role with women who manifest these physiological symptoms. Often the marriage or relationship is unstable and the woman fears being left alone with the child. In some cases, there has not been enough time for the relationship to become established and to work through various problem areas. The partner may not want a child at the time and the woman's subconscious mind is aware of this. In addition to difficulties within the male-female relationship, very often a woman still has problems with her mother. Until she has worked these out, she may not be ready for the responsibility of having children.

Many women also have anxieties about their age. Since they have been programmed that bearing a child after the age of thirty-five would be injurious to their health and might produce defects in the child, they are fearful to try. (In fact, many women well into their forties have had easy pregnancies and borne healthy children.) A positive outlook and maintaining good health can allay these anxieties.

Sometimes, in fact, the reasons are more subtle. It may not be a woman's role in life to have her own children. Her work may be caring for or teaching other people's children, and in some cases, adopting a child. This realization can often be a painful one and it may take many years for a woman to accept the higher plan and surrender her own will. The horoscope is helpful in indicating this and in showing where the energy can be directed so that the maternal instinct will find its outlet.

In addition to various therapies for resolving emotional problems, the following measures were found particularly helpful for these women:

1. Increased exercise, especially yoga postures which stimulate the thyroid and pituitary gland and help to balance the energy to the reproductive organs.
2. Changes in diet; inclusion of foods rich in calcium and magnesium; dulse, kelp, and other seaweeds that are rich in iodine; foods rich in B vitamins such as whole

grains; linoleic and oleic acid found in nuts, seeds, and cold-pressed oils. These are especially good for hormone production.

3. Certain herbs were found to be helpful when used daily. These include many of the herbs (raspberry leaf and blessed thistle) which tone the female reproductive system, and herbs such as sarsaparilla root that are high in plant estrogens for women who have used the birth control pill.

4. Supplementation with calcium and magnesium, (liquid chlorophyll for magnesium, carrot powder or bone meal for calcium), liquid dulse for iodine and iron, and a liquid B-complex supplement.

5. The Bach Flower Remedies and other essence remedies which deal with emotional states were found to be extremely helpful, especially in combating fears and anxieties.

6. The touching therapies such as acupressure, Jin Shinn, and polarity therapy that unblock the meridians and increase the "chi" or vital energy.

7. Visualization exercises which enabled the women to see themselves in a balanced state and carrying a healthy fetus.

ASTROLOGICAL

Women born at new and full moon tend to have more difficulty conceiving than those born at other phases, and are also more prone to problems during pregnancy. Next in line are those born during first and last quarter (Sun square Moon). It is best for women born under these phases to conceive during their ovulation time rather than during their cosmic cycle which is based on the lunar phase.

Often but by no means always the sign Aquarius is found on the cusp of the fifth house, indicating that the procreative drive manifests in a more unusual way such as adoption of children, or working with children in some other capacity. Hard aspects to the Moon from Saturn can cause delay or difficulty in conceiving; these may indicate that there are still problems to be worked out with one's own mother. Capricorn Moon sometimes falls into this category as well. Hard aspects from Mars may involve problems during pregnancy and miscarriages, or hemorrhage during delivery. Hard aspects from Uranus relate to unexpected pregnancy. In the horoscope of one of my clients, who didn't conceive until the age of thirty-seven, natal Moon is opposite Uranus. Hard aspects from Neptune often relate to the illusion of wanting to have a child where it is not practically feasible. Several women with Moon conjunct Neptune think they want a child when they are not ready to handle any more responsibilities, or want a child when their mate doesn't, or in some way are taken with the glamour of childbirth rather than the reality of it. Hard aspects from Pluto can indicate abortion, miscarriage, or stillbirth.

Several midpoint configurations show up very strongly in the horoscopes of these women.

Moon/Venus - represents the ability to conceive.

Moon/Venus = Saturn - may indicate inhibited glandular activity and is often related to a malfunctioning thyroid.

Moon/Venus = Neptune - indicates abnormal glandular activity and imbalanced hormones; found most frequently in charts of those women having difficulty conceiving.

Moon/Venus = Uranus - another common combination involving erratic activity of the endocrine glands, especially the thyroid, and in a few cases, unexpected pregnancy.

Moon/Venus = Pluto - often found in the horoscopes of those who have miscarriages or stillbirths.

Moon/Mars refers to hemorrhage, accidents, abortion, or miscarriage.

Moon/Mars = Pluto - often found in cases of miscarriage and stillbirth.

Moon/Mars = Neptune - indicates infection of female organs.

The general health midpoints, **Saturn/Neptune**, and

Mars/Saturn = Venus, indicate a holding back of love and physiologically, inhibited action of the thyroid gland.

CASE HISTORY #1

This young woman experienced two very depressing years in an attempt to conceive a child. At the time all her friends were having children and she attended many baby showers and celebrations, which made her situation even more difficult. In 1974, at the age of twenty-two, she and her husband made the decision to have a child. She started taking her temperature to determine her ovulation cycle and visited a local doctor who recommended various vitamin supplements. Her mother, who studies astrology, indicated that her horoscope showed a thyroid deficiency. This was verified by the doctor and she was given a thyroid supplement.

She had many lab tests and hormone treatments, but nothing worked. Later it was discovered that her husband had a low sperm count so he was referred to a urologist. Meanwhile she was given a fertility drug and artifically inseminated with her husband's sperm. It was about this time that she came to me for a consultation. We discussed the possibility of adoption, which her husband was against at the time, and working with children in some way. At the time she had started this, working one day a week. Mostly we focused on surrendering her will to the higher plan and flowing with what the cosmos provided. Being a Scorpio with Taurus Moon, it was not easy for her to release her fixed ideas, but she was working on it through her meditations.

She and her husband applied for adoption in 1976; there was a wait of at least a year. She also found another doctor who gave her a different fertility drug, and then tried artificial insemination again. She knew the timing to be correct now and she conceived a child through the inseminations given on September 27th and 29th, 1976. She had a healthy pregnancy and gave birth to a son on June 6, 1977. In July 1979 she conceived again through artificial insemination and gave birth to boy twins on March 21, 1980.

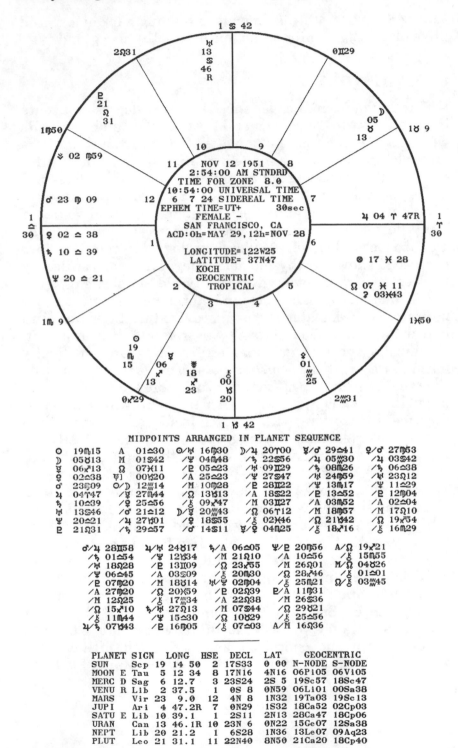

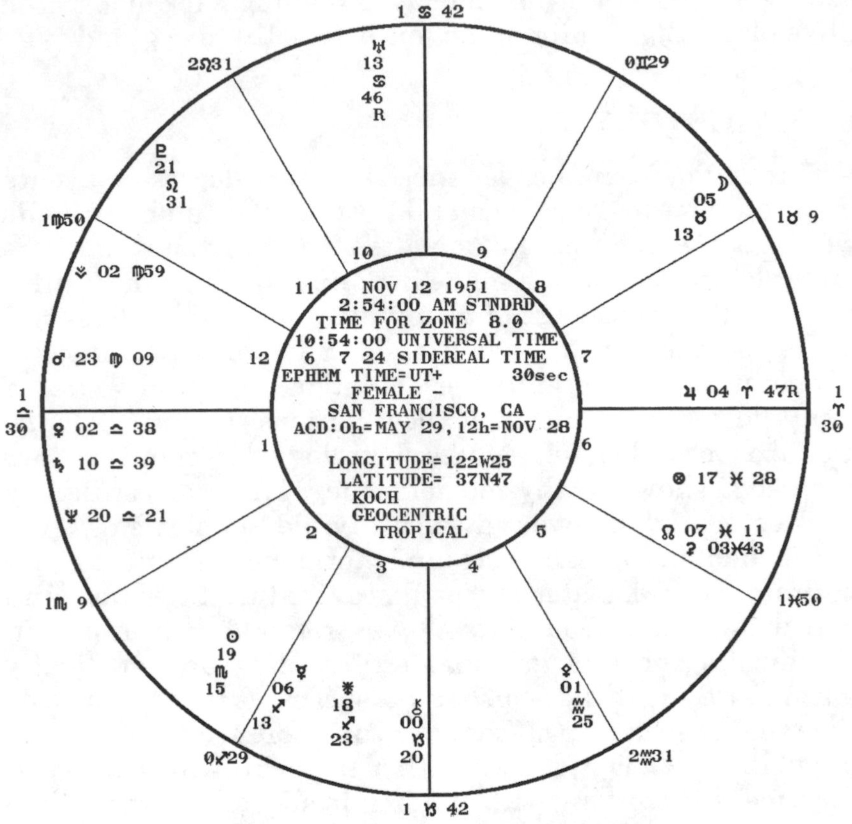
1 ♋ 42
2♌31
0♊29
♅ 13 ♋ 46 R
♇ 21 ♌ 31
☽ 05 ♉ 13
1♍50
1♉ 9
10
9
11
NOV 12 1951
8
2:54:00 AM STNDRD
TIME FOR ZONE 8.0
10:54:00 UNIVERSAL TIME
12
6 7 24 SIDEREAL TIME
7
EPHEM TIME=UT+ 30sec
FEMALE -
SAN FRANCISCO, CA
ACD:0h=MAY 29,12h=NOV 28
1
6
LONGITUDE=122W25
LATITUDE= 37N47
KOCH
GEOCENTRIC
2
TROPICAL
5
3
4
⚳ 02 ♍59
♂ 23 ♍ 09
1 ♎ 30
♀ 02 ♎ 38
♄ 10 ♎ 39
♆ 20 ♎ 21
♃ 04 ♈ 47R
1 ♈ 30
⊗ 17 ♓ 28
☊ 07 ♓ 11
⚳ 03♓43
1♏ 9
1♓50
☉ 19 ♏ 15
☿ 06 ♐ 13
⚵ 18 ♐ 23
⚷ 00 ♑ 20
⚴ 01 ♒ 25
0♐29
2♒31
1 ♑ 42

MIDPOINTS ARRANGED IN PLANET SEQUENCE

☉	19♏15	A	01♎30	☉/♅	16♍30	☽/♃	20♈00	☿/♂	29♎41	♀/♂	27♍53
☽	05♉13	M	01♋42	/♆	04♏48	/♄	22♋56	/♃	05♒30	/♃	03♋42
☿	06♐13	☊	07♓11	/♇	05♎23	/♅	09♊29	/♄	08♏26	/♄	06♎38
♀	02♎38	Ψ]	00♑20	/A	25♎23	/♆	27♋47	/♅	24♍59	/♅	23♌12
♂	23♍09	☉/☽	12♒14	/M	10♍28	/♇	28♊22	/♆	13♏17	/♆	11♎29
♃	04♈47	/☿	27♏44	/☊	13♑13	/A	18♋22	/♇	13♎52	/♇	12♍04
♄	10♎39	/♀	25♎56	/⚷	09♐47	/M	03♊27	/A	03♏52	/A	02♎04
♅	13♋46	/♂	21♎12	☽/☿	20♒43	/☊	06♈12	/M	18♍57	/M	17♌10
♆	20♎21	/♃	27♑01	/♀	18♋55	/⚷	02♓46	/☊	21♑42	/☊	19♐54
♇	21♌31	/♄	29♎57	/♂	14♋11	☿/♀	04♏25	/⚷	18♐16	/⚷	16♏29

♂/♃	28♊58	♃/♅	24♉17	♄/A	06♎05	♆/♇	20♍56	A/☊	19♐21
/♄	01♎54	/♆	12♑34	/M	21♌10	/A	10♎56	/⚷	15♏55
/♅	18♌28	/♇	13♊09	/☊	23♐55	/M	26♌01	M/☊	04♉26
/♆	06♎45	/A	03♋09	/⚷	20♏30	/☊	28♐46	/⚷	01♎01
/♇	07♍20	/M	18♉14	♅/♆	02♍04	/⚷	25♏21	☊/⚷	03♒45
/A	27♍20	/☊	20♓59	/♇	02♌39	♇/A	11♍31		
/M	12♌25	/⚷	17♒34	/A	22♌38	/M	26♋36		
/☊	15♐10	♄/♅	27♌13	/M	07♋44	/☊	29♉21		
/⚷	11♏44	/♆	15♎30	/☊	10♉29	/⚷	25♎56		
♃/♄	07♑43	/♇	16♍05	/⚷	07♎03	A/M	16♌36		

PLANET		SIGN	LONG	HSE	DECL	LAT	GEOCENTRIC	
SUN		Scp	19 14 50	2	17S33	0 00	N-NODE	S-NODE
MOON	E	Tau	5 12 34	8	17N16	4N16	06Pi05	06Vi05
MERC	D	Sag	6 12.7	3	23S24	2S 5	19Sc57	18Sc47
VENU	R	Lib	2 37.5	1	0S 8	0N59	06Li01	00Sa38
MARS		Vir	23 9.0	12	4N 8	1N32	19Ta03	19Sc13
JUPI		Ari	4 47.2R	7	0N29	1S32	18Ca52	02Cp03
SATU	E	Lib	10 39.1	1	2S11	2N13	28Ca47	18Cp06
URAN		Can	13 46.1R	10	23N 6	0N22	15Ge07	12Sa38
NEPT		Lib	20 21.2	1	6S28	1N36	13Le07	09Aq23
PLUT		Leo	21 31.1	11	22N40	8N50	21Ca20	18Cp40

Case History #1

Full Moon Type in Fixed Signs.

☉ in ♏ in 2nd house □ ♇ in ♌ in 11th house, ⊔ dwad	Transformation of values through working with groups and associations; possible difficulties with reproductive organs, poor circulation
☉ △ ♅ in ♋ in 10th house	Unusual and creative work, possibly with children, or in some aspect of nurturing or healing
☉ ∠ ♀ and Asc.	Difficulty in expressing love
☉ ⊓ ♃ in 7th house	Growth through relationships
☽ in ♉ in 8th house, ♋ dwad	Sensual, possessive tendencies; fixed habit patterns; need to nurture others in order to catalyze own transformation
☽ ⊼ ♀, Asc.	Holding back feelings; working things out with own mother and with mothering process
☽ ⊼ ☿ in 3rd house	Conflict between wanting to be at home (nurturing) and being free; tendency to nervous energy
☽ ⊓ ♂ in 12th house	Holding back of anger and aggressive tendencies; possible miscarriage or abortion; with 8th house and 12th house involvement, strong emotions
Yod with ☿ ⊼ ☽ ⊼ Asc. ♀	Inhibition in expressing love and creativity which tends to manifest through physical body
Earth grand trine ☽ △ ⚷ △ ♂	Channeling personal emotional energy into healing and service work
♎ Asc., ♎ dwad ♂ ♀	Strong need for relationships
♀ ☌ ♄	Restriction in exhibiting love and creative ability; possibly inhibited working of thyroid gland and kidney problems
♀ ☌ ♂	Passionate, strong desires but tendency to hold them back
♀ ☍ ♃ in 7th house	May invest too much energy in relationships

♀ ∠ ♇	Transforming love and sexuality; learning how to channel sexual energy
☿ in ♐ in 3rd house	Need to communicate and have intellectual freedom
☿ contra ∥ ♅, ♇	Sensitive nervous system; new and original ideas to explore
☿ □ ?, ⚷	Conflict between nurturing and taking care of others and personal freedom
☿ □ nodes in ♓, ♍ in 6th and 12th houses	Possible allergies; possible problems with digestive system
♃ in 7th house in ♈ ☍ ♄ in 1st house	Need to balance out work on relationships with personal growth
♄ □ ♅ in ♋	Difficulty in expressing personal independence and in departing from old concepts and traditions
♆ in 1st house □ ♅	Some confusion about identity and how far to express individuality
☊ in ♓ ☌ ?	Strong ability for healing, helping others

MIDPOINTS

♂/♄ = ♀, Asc.	Holding back feelings; inhibited action of thyroid
☽/♀ = ♆	Confusion about emotions; tendency to fool self at times; hormonal imbalance
☽/♂ = ♅	Sudden emotional changes; sensitive nervous system; erratic functioning of thyroid
♂/♅ =☉	Nervous and restless nature; highly intuitive; possibility of accidents; surgeries

Secondary Progressions	Solar Arc Directions	Transits	Eclipses

1. 1974—first attempts to become pregnant

Secondary Progressions	Solar Arc Directions	Transits	Eclipses
Asc. ☌ ♆	♅ □ ☽	♄ □ ♄	
Asc. ∠ ☿	⚳ □ ♄	♅ ⚻ ☊ ∠ ♘	
☿ ☍ MC		♆ ☌ ☿	

♂ ✳ ☿   ♀ ☍ ♀/♄
♂ ⊼ ☽
☽ ᵖ-6th house

2. 1976—conceived through artificial insemination—September 27th and 29th

☉ ⊼ ♅   ♄ ☍ ☽   ☉ ☍ ♄   May L.E. ☌ ☉
♆ ⊡ ☊   ☿ ☌ ♂
☽ ⊡ ☉ September   ♀ ☍ ☽
☽ ☌ ♃ September   ♂ ☌ Asc.ᵖ
                                  ♃ △ Asc., ♀
                                  ♅ ☍ ☽
                                  ♆ ✳ ♄
                                  ☽ in ♏ on 27th

3. June 6, 1977—son born

☽ ☐ ♅ June   ☿ ☌ nadir   ☿ △ ♂   April L.E. ☐ ♅
                    ⚷ ☍ ♅   ♀ ☌ △ ♂
                                       ♅ ∠ ♂
                                       ♆ ⊼ ♅
                                       ♀ ☌ ♄
                                       ☊ ☌ ♆
                                       ☽ ♒ ☍ ♀

4. July 1979—conceived twins through artificial insemination

☿ ☍ MC   ☿ ☐ ♀   ♄ ☍ ⊕   Feb. S.E. ☌ ♌
☽ ⊼ ♄ July   ♅ ☌ ♀   ♅ ☌ ☉ ☐ ♀
                    ⚷ ☍ ♅   ♆ ☌ ⚷
                    ? ☐ ♅   ♀ ☌ ♄/♆

5. March 21, 1980—twins born

☽ ☍ ☉   ♂ ☌ ♆   ☉ ☌ Desc.   Feb. S.E. ⊡ ♄
                    ♀ ☌ ⚷   ☿ ☌ ♌
                                      ♀ ☍ ☉
                                      ♃ ☍ ?
                                      ♄ ☌ ♂
                                      ♆ ☐ ♂
                                      ♀ ☌ ♆

Husband of Case #1

☉ in ♑ in 2nd house △ ♄   Strongly involved with work, holds tradi-
  on MC   tional values in terms of security and
                           material possessions

  Ⅱ dwad   Emphasis on communication
☉ contra Ⅱ ♅, ♀   Strong desire for freedom and personal
                           transformation

☉ ☐ nodes in ♈︎♎︎ in 4th   Need to balance home life and profes-
  and 10th houses   sional life; work on relationships a part
                           of this balance

☉ □ ♆ on 10th/11th house cusp	Lack of energy or etheric leak; responsibilities conflict with need to express creative energy and enjoy self with friends and associates
☽ in ♋ in 7th house, ☌ ♅, ♋ dwad	Strong empathetic nature; sensitive nervous system; love for home and family and yet need for emotional freedom and independence; women in life may be unusual
☽ □ ♂ in ♋ in 10th house	Ambitious for career opportunities; need for inner security and friendships
☽ ⊼ ☿ in ♒	Changes mind quickly; extremely sensitive nervous system affected by emotions
☽ ⊡ ♀ in ♒	Working out things with mother and with women; tendency to hold back feelings; possible problem with thyroid and circulation
☽ ∠ ♇ in ♌ in 9th house	Testing personal power; transforming personal emotions into philosophical precepts that form guidelines for work
♐ Asc., ♒ dwad	Need for freedom, ability to place ideas in a less personal and more universal framework; restates theme of ☽ ☌ ♅ and planets in ♒
☿, ♃, ⚷, ♀ in ♒ in 3rd house	Strong scientific mind capable of investigating new material and communicating ideas in a new way; sensitive nervous system; possible problems with circulation
☿ ♄ in mutual reception	Good discipline for bringing new ideas into work
☿ △ ♂ in ♎ in 10th house	Using innovative concepts in profession
♀ in ♒ ☍ ♇ in ♌	Transforming love and sexual energy; tendency to coldness in love relations; problems with circulatory system
♀ in ♒ △ ♆ in ♎	Strong creative, artistic, and spiritual energy
♀ ⊡ ♂	Difficulty expressing emotions and sexual energy

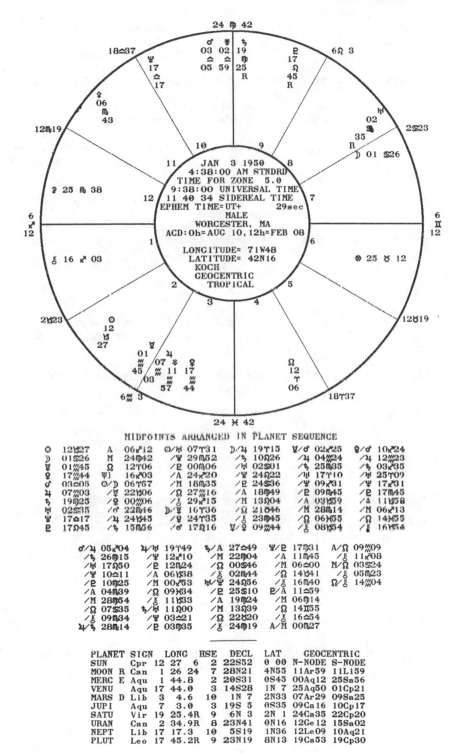

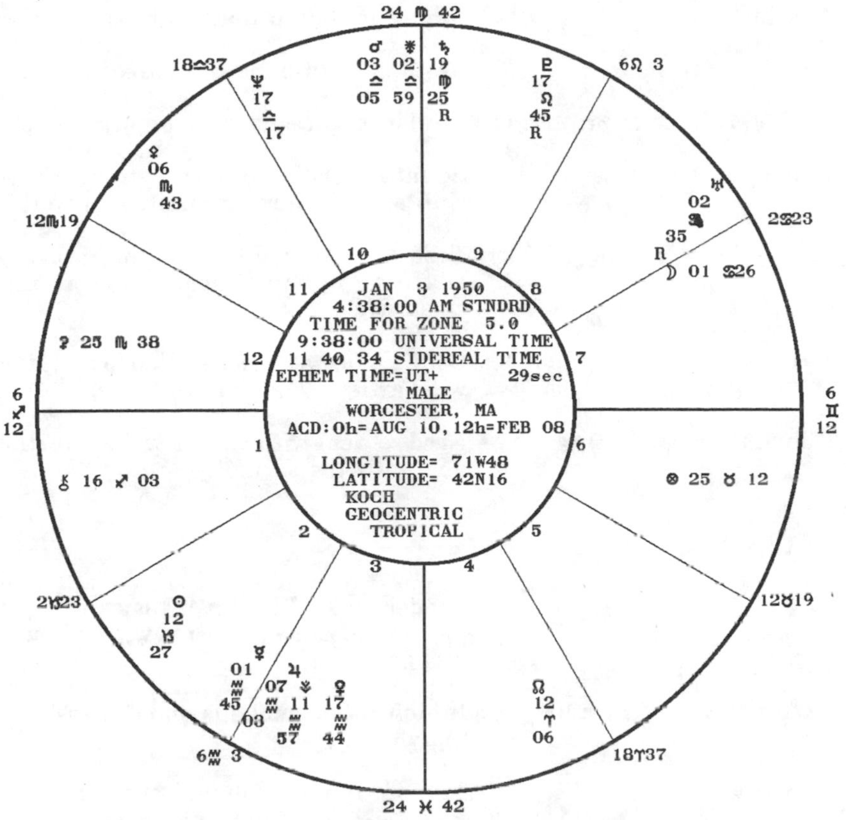
24 ♍ 42
18♎37
6♌ 3
12♏19
2♋23
6 ♐ 12
6 ♊ 12
2♑23
12♉19
6♒ 3
18♈37
24 ♓ 42
JAN 3 1950
4:38:00 AM STNDRD
TIME FOR ZONE 5.0
9:38:00 UNIVERSAL TIME
11 40 34 SIDEREAL TIME
EPHEM TIME=UT+ 29sec
MALE
WORCESTER, MA
ACD:0h=AUG 10,12h=FEB 08
LONGITUDE= 71W48
LATITUDE= 42N16
KOCH
GEOCENTRIC
TROPICAL

MIDPOINTS ARRANGED IN PLANET SEQUENCE

☉	12♑27	A	06♐12	☉/♅	07♈31	☽/♃	19♈15	☿/♂	02♐25	♀/♂	10♐24
☽	01♋26	M	24♍42	/♆	29♏52	/♄	10♌26	/♃	04♒24	/♃	12♒23
☿	01♒45	☊	12♈06	/♇	00♏06	/♅	02♋01	/♄	25♏35	/♄	03♐35
♀	17♒44	⚷	16♐03	/A	24♐20	/♆	24♌22	/♅	17♈10	/♅	25♈09
♂	03♎05	☉/☽	06♈57	/M	18♏35	/♇	24♋36	/♆	09♐31	/♆	17♐31
♃	07♒03	/☿	22♑06	/☊	27♒16	/A	18♍49	/♇	09♏45	/♇	17♏45
♄	19♍25	/♀	00♒06	/⚷	29♐15	/M	13♌04	/A	03♑59	/A	11♑58
♅	02♋35	/♂	22♏46	☽/☿	16♈36	/☊	21♉46	/M	28♏14	/M	06♐13
♆	17♎17	/♃	24♑45	/♀	24♈35	/⚷	23♍45	/☊	06♓55	/☊	14♓55
♇	17♌45	/♄	15♏56	/♂	17♌16	☿/♀	09♒44	/⚷	08♑54	/⚷	16♑54

♂/♃	05♐04	♃/♅	19♈49	♄/A	27♎49	♆/♇	17♍31	A/☊	09♒09
/♄	26♍15	/♆	12♐10	/M	22♍04	/A	11♏45	/⚷	11♐08
/♅	17♌50	/♇	12♏24	/☊	00♋46	/M	06♎00	M/☊	03♋24
/♆	10♎11	/A	06♑38	/⚷	02♏44	/☊	14♑41	/⚷	05♏23
/♇	10♍25	/M	00♐53	♅/♆	24♌56	/⚷	16♏40	☊/⚷	14♒04
/A	04♏39	/☊	09♓34	/♇	25♋10	♇/A	11♎59		
/M	28♍54	/⚷	11♑33	/A	19♍24	/M	06♍14		
/☊	07♋35	♄/♅	11♌00	/M	13♌39	/☊	14♊55		
/⚷	09♏34	/♆	03♎21	/☊	22♉20	/⚷	16♎54		
♃/♄	28♏14	/♇	03♍35	/⚷	24♍19	A/M	00♏27		

PLANET	SIGN	LONG	HSE	DECL	LAT	GEOCENTRIC	
SUN	Cpr	12 27 6	2	22S52	0 00	N-NODE	S-NODE
MOON R	Can	1 26 24	7	28N21	4N55	11Ar59	11Li59
MERC E	Aqu	1 44.8	2	20S31	0S45	00Aq12	25Sa56
VENU	Aqu	17 44.0	3	14S28	1N 7	25Aq50	01Cp21
MARS D	Lib	3 4.6	10	1N 7	2N33	07Ar29	09Sa25
JUPI	Aqu	7 3.0	3	19S 5	0S35	09Ca16	10Cp17
SATU	Vir	19 25.4R	9	6N 3	2N 1	24Ca35	22Cp20
URAN	Can	2 34.9R	8	23N41	0N16	12Ge12	15Sa02
NEPT	Lib	17 17.3	10	5S19	1N36	12Le09	10Aq21
PLUT	Leo	17 45.2R	9	23N19	8N13	19Ca53	19Cp30

♂ ☌ MC	Strong ambition and aggressiveness
♂ □ ♅ in 8th house	Restless nature; need for freedom
⚷ ☌ ♃, ♀ in ♒ in 3rd house	Inhibits expression of love and generosity
♄ in ♍ in 9th house	Scientific testing of ideas; strong leadership and organizing abilities in work
♄ ⊼ ♀ in ♒	Tendency to hold back feelings; lack of love from father; difficulty in expressing creativity
♄ contra ‖ ♆	Conflict between material side of nature with artistic and spiritual side
⚷ in 12th house □ ♀,♀	Need to deal with the nurturing function and with his sexuality

MIDPOINTS

♄ / ♆ = ♂	Tendency to hold back aggressive instincts; possible problems with adrenals and gonads
☽ / Asc. = ♄ ♅ / Asc. = ♄	Inhibition of emotions and expression of individuality
☽ / ♂ = ♀	Transforming emotional and sexual energy; possible problems with reproductive system

Secondary Progressions	Solar Arc Directions	Transits	Eclipses
1. May 1975—lab tests			
☽P ⚼ Asc. May	☉ ☌ ♃	♃ ⚼ ♄	May S.E. ⚼ ♄
	☊ □ ♃	♄ ⚼ ☉	L.E. ☌ Asc.
	Asc. ⚼ ☽	♅ △ ☽ ♅ □ ☿	
		♆ ⊼ ♇	
		♀ ☌ ☊	
2. September 27th and 29th, 1976—artificial insemination successful			
☉ ⚻ MC	Asc. ⚼ ♅	☉ ☌ ♂	May L.E. ☌ ♀
♀ ✷ ☊		☿ ☌ MC	
☽ ⚻ ♃ August		♀ □ ☿ △ ☽ ♅	
☉ △ ♂P		♂ ☌ MCP	

$$♃ \; △ \; ☿$$
$$♄ \; ⚼ \; ☉ \; ☍ \; ⚵$$
$$♀ \; ☌ \; ♇$$
$$☊ \; △ \; ♅$$

3. June 6, 1977—son born

☽ ⚼ ♀ June   V ☌ ♀   ☉ ☍ ♂   Oct. S.E. ☌ ♆
☽ ☌ ♅ June   Asc. □ ♂ ⚷   ☽ ☌ ♀
                            ♀ ⚼ □ ☿ ⚹ ☽ ♅
                            ♄ ⚼ ☉ ☍ ⚴
                            ♅ □ ♃
                            ♇ □ ☉

4. July 1979—artificial insemination successful

☉ ⚹ ☊   ♃ □ Asc.   ♀ ☌ ♆   May L.E. ☌ MC
♀ ⚼ MC   ♅ ☍ ☿   ♆ ☌ ♂
                            ♅ □ ♀
                            ♄ △ ☉
                            ♃ ☌ ♀

5. March 21, 1980—twins born

☿ △ ♄   ☽ ☍ ☿   ♃ ⚹ ♅ ☽   Feb. S.E. □ ♀
☽ ∠ MC April   ☉ ☌ ⚷   ♄ ☌ MC
                     ☊ □ ⚷   ♅ ☌ ⚷
                     ♆ □ ♀ ♇   ♆ ∠ ♃
                     ⚷ □ MC   ♇ ∠ Asc.

CASE HISTORY #2

This case history involves a woman who came to see me at the age of thirty-six. She wanted very much to have a child but had experienced difficulty conceiving due to the presence of scar tissue on her fallopian tubes. She had undergone several tests at a fertility clinic associated with a university hospital and it was determined that her right tube was closed and her left tube open with scar tissue at the end. In 1968 she had had an infection from an IUD which the doctors said may have caused the scar tissue. She also had an abortion in 1972 which possibly contributed to it as well.

The doctors told her that she ran the risk of having a mentally retarded child since she was over thirty-five but that if she really wanted to pursue it, they could perform surgery to remove the scar tissue and increase her chances of conception by thirty percent. At the time she came to see me, she was considering the possibility of surgery, but felt she should try all other methods first.

Mostly we worked with the factor of her age and getting rid of the "after thirty-five program". We also discussed alternatives such as adoption. On the physical level, her horoscope showed a thyroid deficiency. She then remembered having an underactive thyroid and being on thyroid medication from 1961-66. The thyroid deficiency was confirmed the following month by a test. She decided to balance her body and keep trying. She remembers my telling her that November of that year would be a good month in which to conceive.

In the interim she took a class in psychic healing and during the class received a strong impression that she would have a child within the next few months. The rest of her story is rather magical. She applied for adoption at the largest hospital in San Francisco, communicated with a very sympathetic social worker, and within three months of applying, obtained a baby girl one day old—in November, in fact. Several years have elapsed and she is now pregnant with her own child which is due in March 1982.

Case History #2

☉ ☌ ☿ in ♑ in 3rd house ♊ dwad	Strong emphasis on communications and writing; sense of personal responsibility
☉ ☐ ☽ in ♈ in 7th house on angle	Need to communicate emotions, work through relationships; may tend to be demanding and aggressive; emotionally sensitive
☉ ∠ ♂ in ♐	May attract men who are wanderers and without roots
☽ in ♈, ♑ dwad	Need to initiate projects yet holds back; keeps emotions bottled up
☉ ∥ ♀	Creative and loving energy
☉ contra ∥ ⚷	Constant work on self-transformation, healing herself and others
Grand trine ☽ △ ⚷ △ ♀ in fire signs in air houses	Communicates with friends and groups in loving and creative manner; capable of teaching groups or working in a counseling situation

♎ Asc., ♉ dwad	Need for relationships; may become possessive in relationships
♒ on 5th house cusp	Unusual way of having or relating to children
☿ in ♑ ∠ ♂ in ♐	May tend to overdo mental projects
☿ △ ♃♄ in ♉ in 7th house	Practical skills in communication, counseling
♀ in ♐ ⊼ ♅ in 8th house	Changes in relationships; thyroid gland may be erratic in its functioning
♀ in ♐ □ ♆ in 12th house	Tendency to be somewhat idealistic about love relationships; enjoys the adventurous quality; possible glandular imbalance
♀ in ♐ ⚼ ♃♄	Conflict between settling down in a steady relationship and needing emotional freedom
♀ in ♐ ⚼ ♇ in ♌ in 10th house	Transforming her ideals and creative visions into a healing and therapeutic manner of working with people
♂ broadly ☌ ⚷ in ♐ in 2nd house	Need to create and nurture; possible abortions and miscarriages
♂ ☍ ♅ in 2nd and 8th houses	As ♅ is ruler of 5th house, this aspect could signify abortions or miscarriages; also indicates a highly sensitized nervous system as well as breaking up energy patterns and fixed habit patterns
♂ ∠ Asc.	Diminished vital energy; more prone to accidents, inflammations, infections
♃ ☌ ♄ in 7th in ♉	Growth and expansion through personal relationships, business relationships and counseling situations
♃♄ □ ♇ in ♌ in 10th house	Need to work with people in relationship situations and learn about her own emotional patterns at the same time
♃♄ ⊼ ⚷	Work on nurturing others and healing
♃♄ grand trine with ☿ in ♑ and ⚵ in ♍, air houses	Good adjustments and creative flow with associates; able to communicate in a practical down-to-earth way

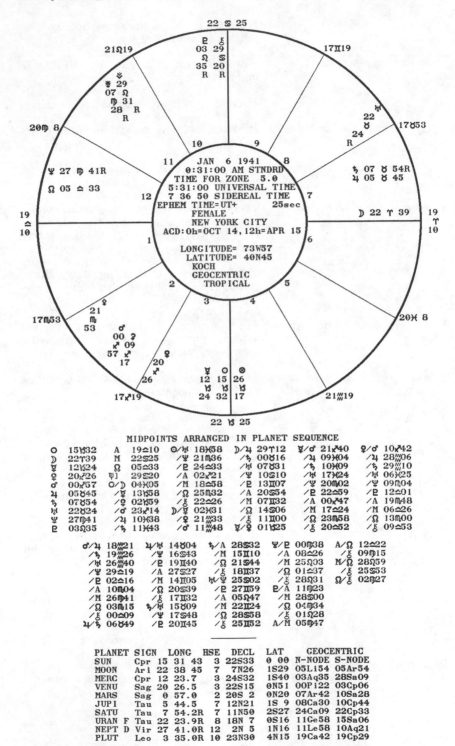

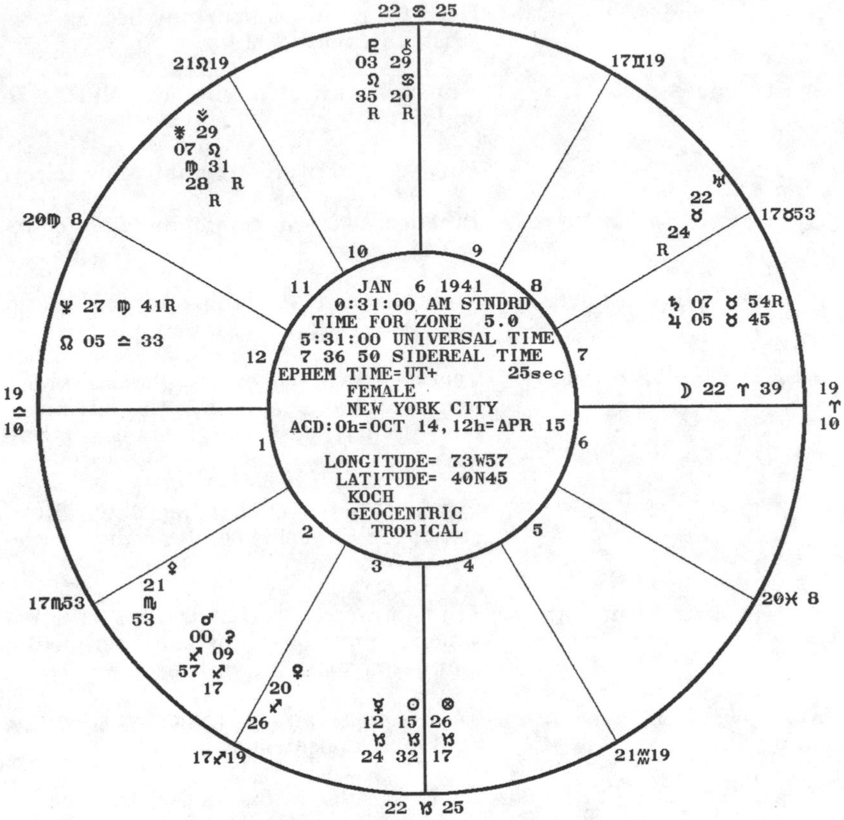
JAN 6 1941
0:31:00 AM STNDRD
TIME FOR ZONE 5.0
5:31:00 UNIVERSAL TIME
7 36 50 SIDEREAL TIME
EPHEM TIME=UT+ 25sec
FEMALE
NEW YORK CITY
ACD:0h=OCT 14,12h=APR 15
LONGITUDE= 73W57
LATITUDE= 40N45
KOCH
GEOCENTRIC
TROPICAL

MIDPOINTS ARRANGED IN PLANET SEQUENCE

☉	15♑32	A	19♎10	☉/♅	18♓58	☽/♃	29♈12	☿/♂	21♐40	♀/♂	10♐42
☽	22♈39	M	22♋25	/♆	21♏36	/♄	00♉16	/♃	09♓04	/♃	28♒06
☿	12♑24	☊	05♎33	/♇	24♎33	/♅	07♉31	/♄	10♓09	/♄	29♒10
♀	20♐26	Ψ]	29♋20	/A	02♐21	/♆	10♋10	/♅	17♓24	/♅	06♓25
♂	00♐57	☉/☽	04♓05	/M	18♎58	/♇	13♊07	/♆	20♏02	/♆	09♏04
♃	05♉45	/☿	13♑58	/☊	25♏32	/A	20♋54	/♇	22♎59	/♇	12♎01
♄	07♉54	/♀	02♑59	/⚷	22♎26	/M	07♊32	/A	00♐47	/A	19♏48
♅	22♉24	/♂	23♐14	☽/☿	02♓31	/☊	14♋06	/M	17♎24	/M	06♎26
♆	27♍41	/♃	10♓38	/♀	21♒33	/⚷	11♊00	/☊	23♏58	/☊	13♏00
♇	03♌35	/♄	11♓43	/♂	11♒48	☿/♀	01♑25	/⚷	20♎52	/⚷	09♎53

♂/♃	18♒21	♃/♅	14♉04	♄/A	28♋32	♆/♇	00♍38	A/☊	12♎22
/♄	19♒26	/♆	16♋43	/M	15♊10	/A	08♎26	/⚷	09♍15
/♅	26♒40	/♇	19♊40	/☊	21♋44	/M	25♌03	M/☊	28♌59
/♆	29♎19	/A	27♋27	/⚷	18♊37	/☊	01♎37	/⚷	25♋53
/♇	02♎16	/M	14♊05	♅/♆	25♋02	/⚷	28♌31	☊/⚷	02♍27
/A	10♏04	/☊	20♋39	/♇	27♊59	♇/A	11♍23		
/M	26♍41	/⚷	17♊32	/A	05♌47	/M	28♋00		
/☊	03♏15	♄/♅	15♉09	/M	22♊24	/☊	04♍34		
/⚷	00♎09	/♆	17♋48	/☊	28♋58	/⚷	01♌28		
♃/♄	06♉49	/♇	20♊45	/⚷	25♊52	A/M	05♍47		

PLANET	SIGN	LONG	HSE	DECL	LAT	GEOCENTRIC	
SUN	Cpr	15 31 43	3	22S33	0 00	N-NODE	S-NODE
MOON	Ari	22 38 45	7	7N26	1S29	05Li54	05Ar54
MERC	Cpr	12 23.7	3	24S32	1S40	03Aq35	28Sa09
VENU	Sag	20 26.5	3	22S15	0N51	00Pi22	03Cp06
MARS	Sag	0 57.0	2	20S 2	0N20	07Ar42	10Sa28
JUPI	Tau	5 44.5	7	12N21	1S 9	08Ca30	10Cp44
SATU	Tau	7 54.2R	7	11N50	2S27	24Ca09	22Cp33
URAN F	Tau	22 23.9R	8	18N 7	0S16	11Ge58	15Sa06
NEPT D	Vir	27 41.0R	12	2N 5	1N16	11Le58	10Aq21
PLUT	Leo	3 35.0R	10	23N30	4N15	19Ca42	19Cp29

♃ ⚻ ☊ in 12th house	Need to work in a spiritual manner to balance out relationships
☋ in 6th house in ♈	When relationships become out of balance, health problems may result
♅ in ♉ in 8th house ⚻ Asc.	Changing public image as part of her personal transformation; learning to adapt to various circumstances
♆ in ♏ ☌ ☊ in 12th house	Healing and psychic studies may play a strong part in her development
♂ in ♋ on MC	Healing others and taking care of them is important part of her work

MIDPOINTS

☽ / ♀ = ♅	Changes in relationship; erratic glandular functioning
♃ / ♆ = ☉	Growth through spiritual and psychic studies; tendency to toxic conditions, infections, hypoglycemia
♄ / ♆ = Asc.	Possible health problems throughout life; involvement in healing

Secondary Progressions	Solar Arc Directions	Transits	Eclipses
1. November 1968—IUD infection			
☿ ∠ ☉	♂ □ ♆	♃ ☌ ♆	March L.E. ☌ ☋ 6th
♂ ☌ ♀	♀ □ nodes	♄ ☌ Asc.	Oct. L.E. □ ☉, ☿
MC ⚼ ☊	♀ □ ♂	♅ □ V	
	nodes □ ♀	♆ ∠ ☿	
		♀ ⚻ ☽ ☌ ♆	
2. 1972—Conceived in March; abortion in June			
♂ ⚻ ♅ (5th ruler)	♄ 8 ?	*March*	July S.E. □ Asc., ☽
♂ ⚻ MC	☋ ☌ ♄	♃ △ ♃ ⚻ ♀	L.E. 8 ♀
♂ △ ☽	♃ □ ✳	♄ 8 ♂	
☿ ⚼ Asc.		♅ ☌ Asc.	
☽ ∠ ☽ February		♆ ⚻ ♃ ☌ ♂/?	
☽ ⚻ ☿ July		♆ ∠ Asc.	
		♀ □ V	
		June	
		♃ □ nodes	

♄ ⚹ ☉
♅ □ ☿
♆ ∠ Asc.
⚷ ☌ ♆

3. 1977—Fertility tests and on November 7th adopted child

☉ ⚹ ☽	MC ☌ ☊	♂ ☌ ⚷	Sept. L.E. □ ♀
☉ □ ♅	☽ □ ☊	♄ ☌ ☊	Oct. S.E. ☌ Asc.
☉ ⚹ MC	♂ □ nodes	♃ □ nodes	
♀ ⚼ ♀	♆ □ ⚷	☌ □ ⚷	
♀ □ ♃	? ☌ ☉	♅ ⚹ ☉ ∠ ♆	
♀ △ ☊		♆ ☌ ? / ♀	
☽ □ ♅ October		⚷ □ ☉	
☽ △ ☽ October			

CASE HISTORY #3

The next case history concerns a young woman who had one abortion, then a normal full term pregnancy and a miscarriage. At the age of seventeen she became pregnant. She had just been married and felt she wasn't yet ready for a child so a few months later she had an abortion. Three months after the abortion she conceived again and both she and her husband received the message that it was time to have a child. Exactly a year to the day after her abortion, a baby girl was born.

Three years later in August 1975 she became pregnant again. She developed a bad infection, caused by an IUD and miscarried. She came to see me a few months later because she wanted to have another child. It seemed much too early for her body to recuperate after the miscarriage and she needed to balance herself physically and emotionally. In the course of our discussion, she mentioned that her husband had not been sure about wanting the second child. Psychologically, this factor played a large part in her miscarriage. Since that time, she regained her health and moved to the East Coast where she now has another child.

Case History #3

☉ in ♐ 2nd house, ♓ dwad   Freedom-loving; tendency to spiritual and metaphysical values; expansive nature in keeping with more universal ideals and goals

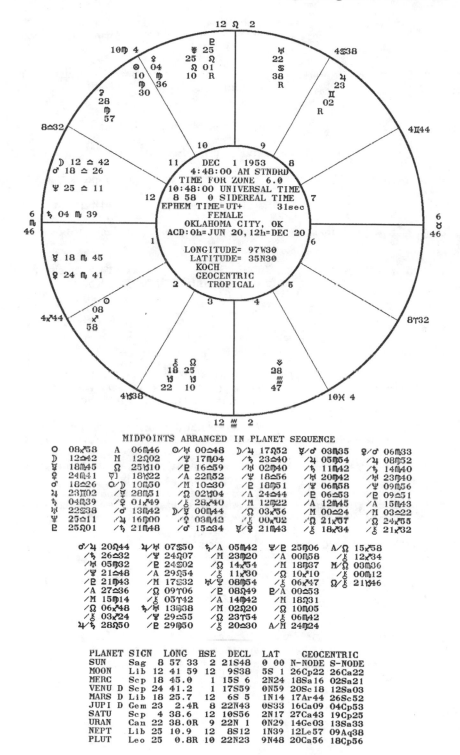

DEC 1 1953
4:48:00 AM STNDRD
TIME FOR ZONE 6.0
10:48:00 UNIVERSAL TIME
8 58 0 SIDEREAL TIME
EPHEM TIME=UT+ 31sec
FEMALE
OKLAHOMA CITY, OK
ACD: 0h=JUN 20, 12h=DEC 20

LONGITUDE= 97W30
LATITUDE= 35N30
KOCH
GEOCENTRIC
TROPICAL

MIDPOINTS ARRANGED IN PLANET SEQUENCE

PLANET	SIGN	LONG	HSE	DECL	LAT	GEOCENTRIC	
SUN	Sag	8 57 33	2	21S48	0 00	N-NODE	S-NODE
MOON	Lib	12 41 59	12	9S38	5S 1	26Cp22	26Ca22
MERC	Scp	18 45.0	1	15S 6	2N24	18Sa16	02Sa21
VENU D	Scp	24 41.2	1	17S59	0N59	20Sc18	12Sa03
MARS D	Lib	18 25.7	12	6S 5	1N14	17Ar44	26Sc52
JUPI D	Gem	23 2.4R	8	22N43	0S33	16Ca09	04Cp53
SATU	Scp	4 38.6	12	10S56	2N17	27Ca43	19Cp25
URAN	Can	22 38.0R	9	22N 1	0N29	14Ge03	13Sa33
NEPT	Lib	25 10.9	12	8S12	1N39	12Le57	09Aq38
PLUT	Leo	25 0.8R	10	22N23	9N48	20Ca56	18Cp56

☉ ✳ ☽ in ♎ in 12th house	Good vital energy; inability to deal openly with relationships may cause health problems
☉ ◻ ♅ in ♋ in 9th house	Emphasis on importance of individual freedom, independence; need to integrate new ideas into the life
☉ ∠ ♆ in 12th house	Less energy flowing through the physical body; need to integrate the intuitive and spiritual quality into life
☉ contra ‖ ♃ in ♊	Tendency to overdo, to be excessive
☽ in ♎, ♒ dwad	Independence in emotional relations
☽ ☌ ♂ in ♎ in 12th house	Strong emotional expression; possible abortion or miscarriage
♂ ☌ ♆ in 12th house	Potential for psychic and healing work; susceptibility to infections and toxic conditions; lowered immune system
☽ ◻ ♀ in ♏	Problems with mother and mothering; possible problems with reproductive system
☽ in 12th house ∠ ⚳ in ♌ in 10th house	Working with the emotions and relationships in a transpersonal way; channeling emotional energy into healing
♏ Asc., ♑ dwad	Transformations in the personal life; ♑ dwad emphasizes the ♄ on Asc., a strong sense of responsibility, shyness, secretiveness, and the tendency to block energy in the reproductive organs
☿ ☌ ♀ in ♏ in 1st house	Strong expression of energy through writing and healing
♀ in ♏ ◻ ⚳ in 10th house	Transforming emotional energy and manifesting it creatively in her work
♀ ⊼ ♃ in 8th house	Tendency to excesses resulting from strong desire nature which may lead to overindulgences that affect physical body
♂ in ♎ ◻ ♅ in ♋ in 9th house	Restless, wants to be free and unrestrained; sensitive nervous system
♅ ☌ ⚷ in ♋	Need to find a way of fulfilling nurturing instincts in a less traditional manner

♃ in ♊ in 8th house	Growth and expansion through study of metaphysics, healing
♃ △ ♆ in 12th house	Good imaginative quality; work with dreams; psychic phenomena
♃ ⚼ ♄ on Asc.	Limitations in expressing her ideas and need to be physically in control
♃ ∥ ♅ ∥ ♇	Ideas are unusual, non-traditional, relate to healing and her personal transformation
♇ in ♌ in 10th house ☍ ⚶ in ♒ in 4th house	Need to work in outside world and in humanitarian and healing professions; balance between home and profession
♆ □ nodes exactly in ♋ ♑ in 3rd and 9th houses	Communicating personal and metaphysical concepts to others; dissolving old patterns related to personal and emotional security

MIDPOINTS

☽/♀ = ♄	Holding back of emotions; possible glandular or thyroid problems
☽/♇ = ♄ (inverse)	Transforming emotions and externalizing them; possible problems with reproductive system
♀/♂ = Asc.	Need to express sexual and creative energy; sexual organs may be connected with any physical problems
♂/♆ = Asc. (inverse)	Need to manifest personal power; health problems involve the reproductive system; possible abortions, miscarriage

Secondary Progressions	Solar Arc Directions	Transits	Eclipses
1. **December 1970—conceived: March 21, 1971—abortion**			
☿ ∠ ☋	♂ ☌ Asc.	*December*	Feb. S. E. □ ☉ △ Asc.
☽ Q ☿ Dec. '70 ☽ ⚼ ♂ March '71	⚳ ☌ ♂	♂ ☌ ♄, Asc. ♃ ☌ ♀ □ ♇ ⚵ ♄ ☍ ☿ ♅ ☌ ☽	

♆ ∠ ♂, ⚷
♇ ☌ ⚳
March
☉ ☍ ⚳
♀ □ ☿
♂ ∠ ☿
♃ □ ♅
♄ ☍ ☿
♅ ☌ ☽
♆ ∠ ☽ ⚷
♇ ☌ ⚳

2. **June 1971—conceived: March 21, 1972—child born**

☿ △ MC
☉ ⚼ MC
♀ ⚹ ♂
☽ ⚻ Asc. June '71
☽ ⚻ ☿ April '72

♅ ☌ MC
⚳ ☌ ♂
Asc. ☌ ♀ □ ♇
☉ □ ⚳
♃ □ ☽

June
♃ ☌ ♇ ⚵ □ ♀ ⚶
♄ ☍ ♀ ⚼ ♇ ⚶ ⚵
♅ ∠ ♀
♆ ∠ ♂ ⚷
♇ ☌ ⚳
March
☿ ☌ ☽/♂
♀ ☍ ☿
♂ ☍ ♀ ⚼ ♇ ⚵ ⚶
♄ ⚼ ♂, ⚷
♆ ∠ ♅
♇ ⚼ ☿

Jan. '72 S. E.
☌ ☊
L. .E. ☌ MC

3. **August 10, 1975—conceived: December 13, 1975—infection and miscarriage**

☿ ⚹ ♂
♀ ⚻ ♅
♀ ∠ Asc.
☽ □ ♄ September
☽ □ Asc.
November
☽ ∠ ♃ December

☽ ☌ ♄
Asc. □ ⚶

August 10th
☿ ☌ ♇ ⚵ □ ♀ ⚶
♀ ⚼ nodes
♂ ☍ ♀ □ ♇ ⚵
♃ □ ♆

♄ □ ♆
♆ ☌ ☉
♇ ∠ ♀
☊ ☌ ♀ □ ♇ ⚵ ⚶
December
♂ ☌ ♃
♃ ☌ ☽/♂
♄ □ ♄
♅ ☌ ♄, Asc.
♆ ∠ ☊ ⚼ ☋
♇ ☌ ☽
⚷ ☍ ♆

CHAPTER TWELVE

GASTRO-INTESTINAL PROBLEMS

Most common among physical problems are those that occur within the digestive tract. Many nervous conditions and stressful situations interfere with our digestive process and thus most of us experience difficulty in this area at some point in our lives. Poor dietary habits, lack of exercise, overeating, and the ingestion of heavy starches or fats exacerbate the condition.

Problems range from dyspepsia or simple digestive upset to gastritis (inflammation of the stomach wall), colitis (inflammation of the colon or large intestine), ulcers (both duodenal and gastric) and peritonitis (inflammation of the peritoneum, the membrane lining the walls of the abdominal and pelvic cavities).

Since the digestive process starts with the teeth and the mastication of food, problems with the teeth and gums may also be involved.

In cases of severe nervousness, there can be a spasm of the muscles where the esophagus joins the diaphragm and where the diaphragm joins the stomach. The stomach is the storehouse for food and food usually remains there three or four hours before passing on. While the food is stored in the stomach, its walls undergo peristaltic contractions. This serves to mix the food with digestive juices produced there.

The inner lining of the stomach is a mucous membrane in which are tiny glands that secrete a fluid called gastric juice. This juice contains hydrochloric acid and aids in breaking down proteins into smaller substances. It also contains various enzymes.

In many cases the hyperacidity of the stomach causes gas to accumulate which often leads to a great deal of pain. When the stomach is chronically hyperacid and the individual under a great deal of tension and anxiety, a portion of the stomach wall may be irritated to form an ulcer.

The addition of the gastric juice reduces the food to a fluid called chyme which then passes into the small intestine. In the small intestine digestion proceeds to completion and in the lower portions absorption takes place. The first part of the small intestine is called the duodenum. The role of the duodenum is to neutralize the acid chyme from the stomach through antacid secretions that pour into the duodenum from the pancreas and liver. When the lining of the duodenum becomes too acid, a duodenal ulcer may result. The pancreas secretes pancreatic juice, and the liver secretes bile (stored in the gall bladder between meals) which combine with the chyme, neutralize it, and pass into the main portion of the small intestine. Here the intestinal juice possesses a number of enzymes that break down the proteins to amino acids (as well as the carbohydrates and fats.)

It takes food three hours to pass through the small intestine into the colon or large intestine. Here absorbtion takes place, especially absorption of water. As water is absorbed, the contents of the large intestine become increasingly solid. The solid contents consist of the indigestible residue of food, fragments of cellulose and similar substances, and other constituents of connective tissue. These substances make up the feces. When an individual is extremely tense, the peristaltic action of the large intestine may be slower than usual. This results in constipation. It may also happen that nervous conditions or infections cause the food to be pushed through too quickly which brings on diarrhea and a severe loss of water.

PSYCHOLOGICAL

Psychological states associated with digestive disturbances involve nervous conditions, anxieties and fears, and repressed emotions. Nervousness may lead to indigestion, constipation, or diarrhea for a short period. Deep-seated tensions and anxieties contribute to the formation of ulcers, gastritis and colitis.

Individuals who get ulcers tend to bottle up their fears in

the region of the solar plexus. As children, they may have been given little tenderness and no real nurturing. When they grow up they experience a struggle between their unsatisfied dependency needs and their more aggressive social aspirations. They therefore work very hard and assume a lot of responsibility for others. They may pride themselves on their perseverance and reliability, but when emotional conflicts and stress situations arise, the dichotomy between needing to be nurtured and nurturing comes to the fore. At these times the stomach tends to produce more acid and the condition of hyperacidity that we refer to as ulcers may develop.

Another common occurrence causing gastro-intestinal problems is the inhibition of bile production. Bile is produced by the liver and stored in the gall bladder. In cases of emotional repression, especially anger, the liver may not produce enough bile or the gall bladder may not release it which leads to constipation and other complaints.

There are many ways to avoid digestive problems. On the physical level, the most important element is diet—eating a small amount of food at a time with the following considerations:

1. Heavy proteins, like red meat, are difficult to digest. If they are eaten, on occasion, they should not be combined with carbohydrates.
2. Eggs, cheese, and milk also require a substantial amount of pancreatic enzymes for digestion and are a major cause of food allergies. Soured milk products such as yogurt or buttermilk are preferable. Products made from goat's milk rather than cow's milk are more easily handled. Dairy products should not be combined with other proteins or carbohydrates.
3. Fruit is best eaten alone and not at meals; fruit does not combine well with other foods.
4. Vegetables may be combined with other vegetables, some proteins or grains, but not with fruits.
5. Exercise before meals and at intervals during the day is important to aid digestion.
6. Meals should be eaten in a calm relaxed atmosphere without excessive radio or T.V. interference.
7. Frequent short juice fasts give the digestive tract a rest.

At these times a high enema or colonic irrigation is helpful in clearing out old fecal material from the intestines.

8. When there are digestive problems it is best to eat soups, vegetable juices and liquid foods.

9. Acidophilus (the intestinal bacteria found in yogurt and buttermilk) is helpful for digestive problems, as is liquid aloe vera (sold in bottles and made from the aloe vera plant).

ASTROLOGICAL PATTERNS

Astrologically, the entire digestive process is ruled by Virgo and, by reflex, Pisces. The stomach is governed by Cancer, the small intestines by Virgo, the duodenum (leading from the stomach to the small intestine) by Pisces, and the colon, by Scorpio.

Problems in the abdominal area may often be seen with Saturn or Mars in the sign Cancer, making hard aspects to the Sun, Moon or Ascendant. These people are often quite emotional and this may interfere with their digestion. Saturn in Cancer configurated in this way *may* indicate a lack of hydrochloric acid which is a constituent of gastric juice—often lacking in gastritis and too abundant in the case of ulcers. Mars in Cancer *may* indicate too much hydrochloric acid, and these people need to be careful with their intake of acidic foods.

Mars rules the muscles of the body, and with Mars in Virgo or Pisces, the intestinal muscles may be affected. This can lead to conditions like constipation (one of the physical causes of constipation is improper nerve-muscle co-ordination) or other abdominal conditions involving muscle spasm. Mars in Virgo or Pisces with hard aspects to Sun, Moon, Saturn, Uranus, or Neptune is often present as a signature in cases of duodenal ulcer. Saturn in Virgo or Pisces could be another indication.

Gastric ulcers are seen more with Mars or Saturn in Cancer. Gastritis (inflammation of th stomach lining caused by ulcers, digestive disorders, or other toxins) is particularly characterized by Sun conjunct Mars in Cancer or Moon conjunct Mars.

Problems in the area of the colon or large intestine may occur when there is a Scorpio or strong Plutonian emphasis in the horoscope. Sun, Moon, Ascendant, Mars, or Saturn in Scorpio with hard aspects from Mars or Pluto are often signatures for colitis or problems in the area of the bowel.

With peritonitis, the inflammation of the membrane lining the abdominal cavity, often there is Sun, Moon, or Mars in Virgo with hard aspects from Saturn, Uranus, Neptune, or Pluto.

CASE HISTORY #1

Here is a woman who has had problems both with her gastro-intestinal system and her lungs. As a young child, she had difficulty with respiratory infections and almost died of pneumonia. She began to have problems with her stomach and digestive system when she was about ten years old. Through many tests and X-rays a duodenal ulcer was discovered two years later. She was placed on a restricted diet but didn't really stick with it.

There were many emotional problems in her early years. She was deeply attached to her mother but experienced constant rejection. At thirteen her mother had a nervous breakdown and the daughter assumed responsibility for the family.

In high school she had more trouble with upper respiratory tract infections. When she was sixteen her sister died. She again had a severe case of pneumonia.

At twenty, she moved from Chicago to California to attend college. She knew no one in California and experienced a true sense of independence and being on her own. Her health was good at this time. In August 1962, she became engaged, and married that December. The following April she had a miscarriage but did have three healthy pregnancies between 1964-1967.

In 1968 she started to have problems with allergies. At this time she was having difficulty with her husband, who had finished medical school and was completing a residency in psychiatry. From 1970-1972 she underwent psychiatric treatment in which she resolved many problems with her mother, and finally dealt with her anger, which she had repressed for many years.

In 1976 gastro-intestinal problems flared up again. In February 1977 she separated from her husband and in November was divorced. From January–May 1978 she had pneumonia six times. She remarried in July 1978. In January and February 1979 she had pneumonia three times. Finally she got the message to stay home and take care of herself and gradually started to tune into her body. In the fall of 1979, she took a class in medical astrology which proved a catalyst in terms of her physical health. Presently she spends time painting and has continued her studies in astrology.

Case History #1

The chart pattern is basically above the horizon with Mars in Aries in the sixth house showing a strong motivational quality, perhaps at times driving herself too hard. Chart emphasis is on perfectionism and pushing herself towards emotional transformations.

☉ in ♍ in 10th house	Important to direct energy toward career; strong vitality; service-oriented
☉, ♎ dwad	Relationships important
☉ ☌ ☿ in ♍	Communications and writing; nervous system, respiratory allergies and digestive system indicated
☉ □ ♄ ♅ in 7th house	Working out relationships; relationships do not satisfy her need for perfection; seeks change constantly
♄ ♅ in ♉ and early ♊	Problem with throat and lungs
☽ in ♏ in 12th house, ♑ dwad	Tendency to hold back emotions, with ♏ Asc. emphasis on colon
☽ □ ♀ ♂	Strong desire to transform old emotional patterns and heal herself
☽ ∠ ♆	Tendency to be overly sensitive; susceptibility to toxins

♀ ☌ ⚶ in ♎ in 11th house	Artistic work; concern about friends and associates; attracts friends who are helpful to her
♆ ☌ ☊ in 11th house in ♍	Artistic and spritual friends; need to help friends and associates
♆ □ ♃	Variety of ideas and projects; not very practical in limiting amount of projects; plans and schemes that may not materialize; tendency towards hypoglycemia, possible difficulty in liver with detoxification.
♃ in ♊ □ nodes in ♍/♓	Emphasis on lungs and relationship to gastro-intestinal system
⚳ in 2nd house ☍ ♃	Values include caring for others; may tend to overdo this at times

MIDPOINTS

♂/♄ = Asc., ☽, ♆ (inverse)	Tendency to hold back feelings; emotionally inhibited and restricted; crystallization in body structure and possible problems with female organs
♂/♅ = Asc., ☽ , ♆ (inverse)	Emotional changes; sensitive nervous system; highly intuitive
♄/♆ = ☿ (inverse)	Problems with lungs, nervous system, respiratory allergies

Secondary Progressions	Solar Arc Directions	Transits	Eclipses
1. **August 1946—five years old, pneumonia**			
MC ∠ ♀	♇ □ Asc.	♅ ☌ ♀	June L.E. □ ☋ ☊
♂ ⚻ ☊	♃ □ ☊	♅ ☌ ♃ in ♊	
♀ ⚼ ♄		♄ ☌ ♇	
☽ ⚻ ♃ August			
☽ ⚼ ♅ August			
2. **1951—ten years old, gastro-intestinal problem and ulcer diagnosed**			
MC □ ♄	♅ □ ☿	♆ ☍ ♂ (6th, colitis)	Sept. L.E. ☌ ☋ ♓
☽ ☍ ♆ October	♂ □ ♇		
	♆ ☌ ♀	♄ □ ♇	

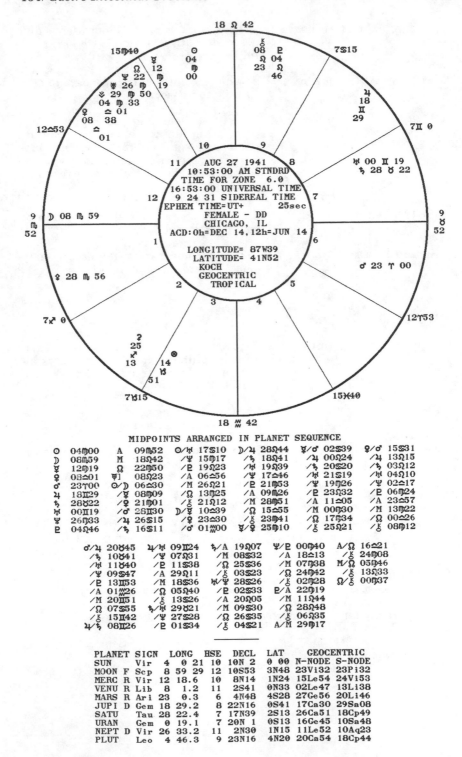

18 Ω 42

15♏40 ☉ 04 ☿ 00 ♇ 08 Ω 04 23 Ω 46 7♋15

Ω 12 ♏ 19
Ψ 22 ♏
❀ 26 ♏ 50
04 ♏ 33
☋ 08 ♎ 01
☊ 38

12♎53 ☊ 01 ♃ 18 Ⅱ 29 7Ⅱ 0

AUG 27 1941
10:53:00 AM STNDRD
TIME FOR ZONE 6.0
16:53:00 UNIVERSAL TIME
9 24 31 SIDEREAL TIME
EPHEM TIME=UT+ 25sec
FEMALE - DD
CHICAGO, IL
ACD:0h=DEC 14,12h=JUN 14

LONGITUDE= 87W39
LATITUDE= 41N52
KOCH
GEOCENTRIC
TROPICAL

☽ 08 ♏ 59
9♏52

♅ 00 Ⅱ 19
♄ 28 ♉ 22
9♍52

♀ 28 ♏ 56

♂ 23 ♈ 00

7♐ 0

☿ 25 ♐ 13

⊕ 14 ♑ 51

12♈53

7♑15

15♓40

18 ♒ 42

MIDPOINTS ARRANGED IN PLANET SEQUENCE

☉ 04♍00	A 09♏52	☉/♅ 17♌10	☽/♃ 28♋44	☿/♂ 02♌39	♀/♂ 15♌31		
☽ 08♏59	M 18♌42	/Ψ 15♏17	/♄ 18♌41	/♃ 00Ω24	/♃ 13Ω15		
☿ 12♍19	Ω 22♌50	/♇ 19♌23	/♅ 19♌39	/♄ 20♌20	/♄ 03♌12		
♀ 03♎01	♒ 08Ω23	/A 06♋56	/Ψ 17♌46	/♅ 21♌19	/♅ 04Ω10		
♂ 23♈00	☉/☽ 06♌30	/M 26♌21	/♇ 21♏53	/Ψ 19♌26	/Ψ 02♎17		
♃ 18Ⅱ29	/♅ 08♍09	/Ω 13♌25	/A 09♏26	/♇ 23♌32	/♇ 06♏24		
♄ 28♉22	/♀ 21♏01	/☌ 21♌12	/M 28♌51	/A 11♎05	/A 23♎57		
♅ 00Ⅱ19	/♂ 28♌30	☽/☿ 10♌39	/Ω 15♌55	/M 00♍30	/M 13♍22		
Ψ 26♍33	/♃ 26♌15	/♀ 23♎30	/☌ 23♍41	/Ω 17♌34	/Ω 00♎26		
♇ 04Ω46	/♄ 16♋11	/♂ 01♒00	☿/♀ 25♏10	/☌ 25♌21	/☌ 08♍12		

♂/♃ 20♉45	♃/♅ 09Ⅱ24	♄/A 19Ω07	Ψ/♇ 00♍40	A/Ω 16♎21	
/♄ 10♋41	/Ψ 07Ω31	/M 08♌32	/A 18♎13	/☌ 24♍08	
/♅ 11♉40	/♇ 11♋38	/Ω 25♌36	/M 07♌38	M/Ω 05♌46	
/Ψ 09♋47	/A 29Ω11	/☌ 03♌23	/Ω 24♍42	/☌ 13Ω33	
/♇ 13Ⅱ53	/M 18♌36	♅/Ψ 28♌26	/☌ 02♍28	Ω/☌ 00♍37	
/A 01♏26	/Ω 05Ω40	/♇ 02♌33	♇/A 22♍19		
/M 20Ⅱ51	/☌ 13♌26	/A 20Ω05	/M 11♍44		
/Ω 07♌55	♄/♅ 29♌21	/M 09♌30	/Ω 28♌48		
/☌ 15Ⅱ42	/Ψ 27♌28	/Ω 26♌35	/☌ 06Ω35		
♃/♄ 08Ⅱ26	/♇ 01♌34	/☌ 04♋21	A/M 29♍17		

PLANET	SIGN	LONG	HSE	DECL	LAT	GEOCENTRIC	
SUN	Vir	4 0 21	10	10N 2	0 00	N-NODE	S-NODE
MOON F	Scp	8 59 29	12	10S53	3N48	23Vi32	23Pi32
MERC R	Vir	12 18.6	10	8N14	1N24	15Le54	24Vi53
VENU R	Lib	8 1.2	11	2S41	0N33	02Le47	13Li38
MARS R	Ari	23 0.3	6	4N48	4S28	27Ge56	20Li46
JUPI D	Gem	18 29.2	8	22N16	0S41	17Ca30	29Sa08
SATU	Tau	28 22.4	7	17N39	2S13	26Ca51	18Cp49
URAN	Gem	0 19.1	7	20N 1	0S13	16Ge45	10Sa48
NEPT D	Vir	26 33.2	11	2N30	1N15	11Le52	10Aq23
PLUT	Leo	4 46.3	9	23N16	4N20	20Ca54	18Cp44

3. **May 1958—sixteen years old, sister died; contracted penumonia**

♀ ⚻ ♄	♂ ☍ ☽	♄ ☌ ?	May L.E. ☌ Asc.
		♅ ☌ ♂	
		Ψ □ ♇ (under-standing death and transformation)	
		♀ □ ♅	

4. **1968—allergies**

☿ ☍ ♂ (6th)	♀ □ ♇	♇♍ □ ♃□	March S.E. ☍ ♀
♀ ☌ Asc.	Ψ ☍ ♂	Ψ ☌ E.P.	☌ E.P.
		♅ ☌ Ψ	
		♄ ☌ ♂ (holding back anger)	

5. **1976—separation, divorce, gastro-intestinal problems**

☉ ☌ ♀	⚷ ☌ ☽	♇ ☌ ♀	April S.E. ☍ ☽
☿ □ ♃	♂ ☌ ♄♃ ☍ ♐	Ψ □ ☿	
♀ □ MC		♅ □ ♇	
MC ⚻ ♂	♃ □ ♂		
☽ □ ♃ November			
☽ □ ♅ December			

6. **July 1978—second marriage: pneumonia six times**

♂ □ ☉	⚷ ☌ Asc.	Ψ ☍ ♃□	March L.E. ☌ ☿
☿ □ ♇	♐ □ ⚷	♄ □ ♄☍	(health problems)
MC ∠ Asc.			Oct. S.E. ☌ ♀
☽ ∠ ♇ July			

7. **January 1979—pneumonia three times**

♀ ⚻ ♂	♂ ☌ ♅	Ψ ☍ ♃	Feb. S.E. □ ☉
♀ ∠ ♀	♇ ☌ ☿	♄ ☌ ☿♍	March L.E. □ ☊
		♇ ∠ ☉	

CASE HISTORY #2

This history concerns a woman who has suffered various digestive problems throughout her life. She also has a tendency to anemia and hypoglycemia.

When she was in grade school, she had difficulty holding down food and vomited often. If she stayed at home she felt better; she had a fear of being out in the world and realized she was extremely vulnerable. This pattern continued through high school.

At age twenty she married and moved to San Francisco.

She was dealing with many mental and emotional problems at the time and experienced symptoms of nausea, indigestion, and nervous stomach. After three years she separated from her husband.

Her path in life led her to various spiritual disciplines, through which she learned to handle her emotional problems.

In 1975 she developed intense pain in the stomach. She saw various holistic health doctors who finally diagnosed her problem as a hiatus hernia. Hiatus hernia is a protrusion of a structure through the esophageal opening of the diaphragm. She was put on a soft diet with no fruit, nuts, or raw vegetables and allowed to eat only a small amount at a time. Whenever she ate too much, or some food not on the diet, the condition would return. She experienced several nights of extreme pain. As she regulated her eating habits the symptoms subsided.

Shortly thereafter she moved again, became involved in a relationship, married for the second time and bore a child. During this period her health was good. In February 1978, her hiatus hernia flared up again. Overeating would often set it off and at this time, she was also having problems handling her daughter.

In the winter of 1979 she had a mild case of hepatitis. She was also experiencing emotional problems in her marriage.

At the present time, she has separated from her husband, works several evenings a week, and is involved in a program leading to a credential in health counseling. Her health has been good and she has not had any problems with the hiatus hernia.

Case History #2

Grand trine in earth indicates practical skills and abilities and need to be out in the world. The T-square with Moon, Mercury, Mars and Pluto points to possible overstimulation and the necessity of breaking up fixed emotional patterns.

♓ Asc.

Unable to convey exuberance of personality due to sensitivity; has difficulty in public situations; tendency to be self-sacrificing especially with ♑ dwad; healing abilities and emphasis on digestive system with ♓—♍ axis.

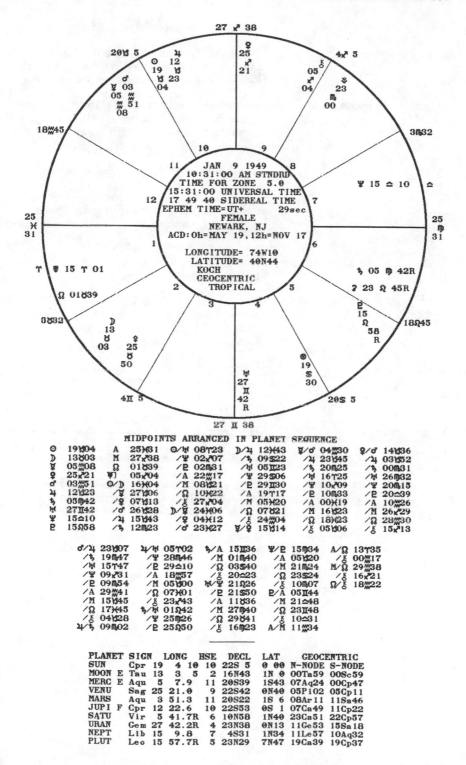

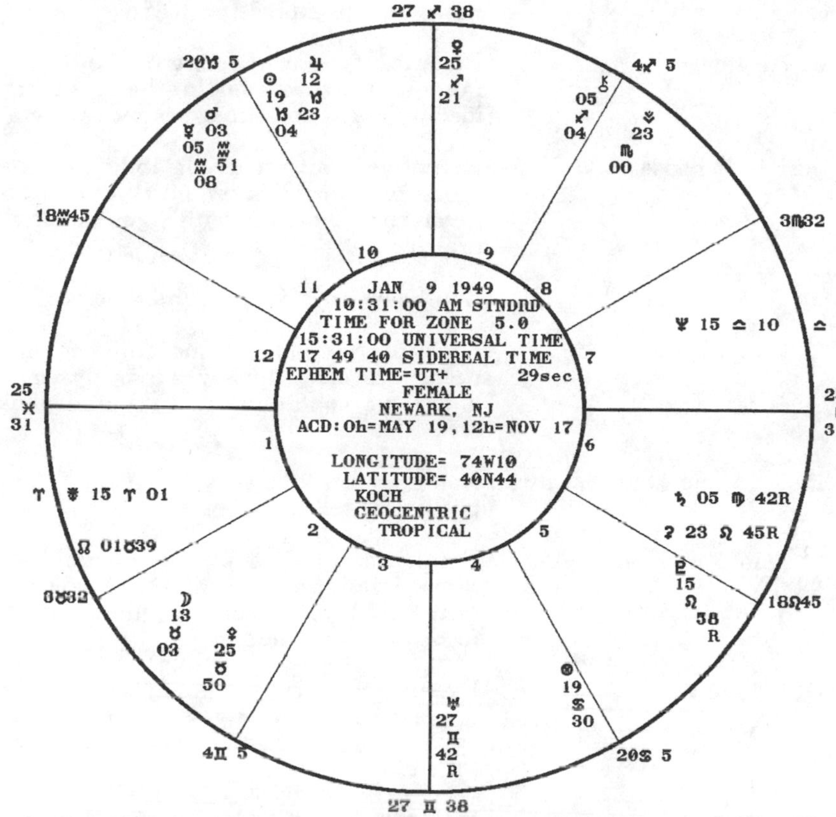
27 ♐ 38
JAN 9 1949
10:31:00 AM STNDRD
TIME FOR ZONE 5.0
15:31:00 UNIVERSAL TIME
17 49 40 SIDEREAL TIME
EPHEM TIME=UT+ 29sec
FEMALE
NEWARK, NJ
ACD:0h=MAY 19,12h=NOV 17
LONGITUDE= 74W10
LATITUDE= 40N44
KOCH
GEOCENTRIC
TROPICAL
27 ♊ 38

MIDPOINTS ARRANGED IN PLANET SEQUENCE

☉	19♑04	A	25♓31	☉/♅	08♈23	☽/♃	12♓43	☿/♂	04♒30	♀/♂	14♑36
☽	13♉03	M	27♐38	/♆	02♐07	/♄	09♋22	/♃	23♑45	/♃	03♑52
☿	05♒08	☊	01♉39	/♇	02♏31	/♅	05♊23	/♄	20♏25	/♄	00♏31
♀	25♐21	♆]	05♐04	/A	22♒17	/♆	29♋06	/♅	16♈25	/♅	26♍32
♂	03♒51	☉/☽	16♓04	/M	08♑21	/♇	29♊30	/♆	10♐09	/♆	20♏15
♃	12♑23	/☿	27♑06	/☊	10♓22	/A	19♈17	/♇	10♏33	/♇	20♎39
♄	05♍42	/♀	07♑13	/⚷	27♐04	/M	05♓20	/A	00♓19	/A	10♒26
♅	27♊42	/♂	26♑28	☽/☿	24♓06	/☊	07♉21	/M	16♑23	/M	26♐29
♆	15♎10	/♃	15♑43	/♀	04♓12	/⚷	24♒04	/☊	18♓23	/☊	28♒30
♇	15♌58	/♄	12♏23	/♂	23♓27	☿/♀	15♑14	/⚷	05♑06	/⚷	15♐13

♂/♃	23♑07	♃/♅	05♈02	♄/A	15♊36	♆/♇	15♍34	A/☊	13♈35
/♄	19♏47	/♆	28♏46	/M	01♏40	/A	05♑20	/⚷	00♒17
/♅	15♈47	/♇	29♎10	/☊	03♋40	/M	21♏24	M/☊	29♒38
/♆	09♐31	/A	18♒57	/⚷	20♎23	/☊	23♋24	/⚷	16♐21
/♇	09♏54	/M	05♑00	♅/♆	21♌26	/⚷	10♏07	☊/⚷	18♒22
/A	29♒41	/☊	07♓01	/♇	21♋50	♇/A	05♊44		
/M	15♑45	/⚷	23♐43	/A	11♉36	/M	21♎48		
/☊	17♓45	♄/♅	01♌42	/M	27♍40	/☊	23♊48		
/⚷	04♑28	/♆	25♍26	/☊	29♉41	/⚷	10♎31		
♃/♄	09♏02	/♇	25♌50	/⚷	16♍23	A/M	11♒34		

PLANET		SIGN	LONG	HSE	DECL	LAT	GEOCENTRIC	
SUN		Cpr	19 4 10	10	22S 5	0 00	N-NODE	S-NODE
MOON	E	Tau	13 3 5	2	16N43	1N 0	00Ta59	00Sc59
MERC	E	Aqu	5 7.9	11	20S39	1S43	07Aq24	00Cp47
VENU		Sag	25 21.0	9	22S42	0N40	05Pi02	05Cp11
MARS		Aqu	3 51.3	11	20S22	1S 6	08Ar11	11Sa46
JUPI	F	Cpr	12 22.6	10	22S53	0S 1	07Ca49	11Cp22
SATU		Vir	5 41.7R	6	10N58	1N40	23Ca51	22Cp57
URAN		Gem	27 42.2R	4	23N38	0N13	11Ge53	15Sa18
NEPT		Lib	15 9.8	7	4S31	1N34	11Le57	10Aq32
PLUT		Leo	15 57.7R	5	23N29	7N47	19Ca39	19Cp37

Asc., ♑ dwad	Reticence in expressing feelings
♆ in 7th house ☍ ⚷	Uncertainty in conducting relationships; inability to express self to others; attracts idealistic and artistic types as partners
♑☉ in 10th house ☌ ♃	Executive ability; teaching ability; strong sense of responsibility and need to be involved in the world with organizational projects
☉, ♋ dwad	Emphasis on emotions and stomach
♃ □ ♆ in 7th house	Looks for relationships for fulfillment but needs a career; tendency to hypoglycemia and toxic conditions in liver and pancreas
☽ in ♉ in 2nd house, ♎ dwad	Holds on to old needs and values; emphasis on relationships
☽ □ ♀ in 5th house	Transformation of old emotional patterns; children may catalyze her development; need for sensual stimulation from food and surroundings
☽ □ ♂♀ in ♒	Experiences overstimulation from friends and associates; highly sensitive nervous system; lacks magnesium; tendency to poor circulation
♅ on nadir	Inwardly knows herself to be unique but may not show it except to friends; changes residence frequently; highstrung
♅ in ♊ ☍ ♀ in ♐	Wide assortment of friends and group activities; thyroid functioning erratic and related to nervous system
♅, ♀, Asc. in T-square	Body is affected by emotional changes and activities when they become too scattered
♄ in ♍ in 6th house	Hard working; good at detail work; concerned with health and healing; possible blockage in gastro-intestinal area
♄ ⚺ ♂♀ in ♒	Nervousness related to gastro-intestinal system; friends distract her from work
♄ ⚺ ♂	Holds back anger; anemic tendencies

♄ □ ⚷ in 8th house	Need to transform old patterns and heal herself

MIDPOINTS

♄/♆ = ♀, Asc.	Vagueness in love relationships; problems with kidneys, thyroid
♂/♅ = ♆	Highly sensitive nervous system; metaphysical and psychic studies
♂/♇ = ♀ (inverse)	Problems with reproductive organs; transforming sexual energy

Secondary Progressions	Solar Arc Directions	Transits	Eclipses
1. January 1969—married, came to San Francisco, nervous stomach			
☉ ∠ ♀ ♀ ⚼ ♄ Asc. □ ♂ ☽ ☍ ♇ January	♆ □ ☿ ☿ □ ‡ ♀ □ ♆ ♄ ☍ Asc.	♇ ☌ Asc. ♄ □ ☉ (lower energy and vitality) ♆ □ ‡	March S.E. ☌ Asc.
2. 1975—26, developed hiatus hernia in summer			
☉ ☍ ♇ ☿ ∠ ♀ ☿ ∠ Asc. ♄ ⚼ ☉ Asc. ☌ ☽ Asc. ∠ ♅ ☽ □ ♂ August ☽ □ ☿ September	☉ ☍ ♇	♄ ☍ ♃ ♇ ∠ ⚶ (change in diet and health habits) ♅ ☌ ☋ ♃ ☌ Asc.	July S.E. ☍ ☉ L.E. ☌ ♂
3. March 1978—29, symptoms of hiatus hernia again			
♃ ☌ ☉ ♂ ∠ ♃ ♄ ⊼ ♂ MC ⊼ ♅ ☽ □ ♄ March	♆ ☍ ☽ ☿ □ ? (problems with children)	♆ ∠ ♂ ♃ □ Asc. ♄ □ ‡	Jan. S.E. ☍ ♆
4. November 1979—hepatitis			
♀ ☌ ♂ ☽ ∠ ☽ November ☽ ☌ ♅ November ☽ ☍ MC November	♆ □ ♇ ☿ ☍ ♄	♄ ☌ ♄ ♆ ∠ ♂ ♃ □ ☊	Feb. S.E. ☍ ♄

CHAPTER THIRTEEN

ALCOHOLISM AND DRUG ADDICTION

Both alcoholism and drug addiction are caused by a biochemical imbalance exacerbated by environmental and social conditions. The ingestion of alcohol and drugs into the body precipitates extreme changes in the body chemistry.

Most alcoholics are hypoglycemic—indicating the tendency to low blood sugar. Alcohol for them acts as a source of energy as sugar does for others. At the same time it becomes a poison filling the body with toxins and interfering with natural processes. Certain people have the type of metabolism that craves alcohol. Dr. Roger Williams, in his book, *Alcoholism And Nutrition*, explains this in his theory of *genetotrophic* problems. "A genetotrophic difficulty is one that stems from the possession of some unusually high nutritional requirement of genetic origin coupled with a failure to meet the need. The deficiency which results from using significant amounts of alcohol weakens the regulatory tissues in the hypothalamus and enhances the poisoning effect of alcohol on these tissues. This, in turn, impairs the appetite-controlling centers."

This type of person has certain genetic blocks which cause him to require a large amount of specific nutrients. If an alcoholic is supplied with the correct nutritional elements, he can produce and secrete the necessary hormones to maintain the blood sugar level. The desire for alcohol is thus decreased.

In addition to nutritional deficiencies, the liver and other body organisms can be severely damaged through the prolonged use of alcohol. As alcohol is absorbed through the stomach, it goes through the bloodstream to the liver. The liver attempts to convert the alcohol to a harmless substance and in time the liver becomes extremely toxic.

Habit-forming drugs as heroin, morphine, cocaine, nicotine, and caffeine affect the body in a similar fashion. The body craves a particular drug for its chemical reaction. It may provide the body with quick energy, it may eliminate pain; in certain ways it helps the body to feel good. Added to this, of course, are all of the psychological factors that are involved in its use. As time goes on, many of the essential vitamins, minerals, and hormones in the body are destroyed. The need for the drug becomes even greater until the correct nutritional balance can be established.

Excessive drinking often leads to deficiencies of the B vitamins, especially B-6, as well as magnesium. The following recommendations are advisable for alcoholics in order to restore a proper balance to their bodies.

1. Aloe vera juice to cleanse the liver, colon, and kidneys— ½ cup every other night for two weeks, then ¼ cup every other night for two weeks.

2. If aloe vera juice can not be obtained, dandelion root tea is good for cleansing the liver and kidneys. Boil the root for 20–25 minutes (2 tablespoons per cup of water) and drink 2 cups daily for two weeks, then 1 cup daily for 2 weeks.

3. Liquid chlorophyll (1 teaspoon in ½ glass of spring water taken 2 times daily) to supply adequate amounts of magnesium as well as vitamin A.

4. Liquid B complex supplement—2 times daily.

5. Two B-6 tablets (50 mg.) daily.

6. Vitamin C (in the form of a calcium or potassium ascorbate) about 1,000 mg. daily.

7. A liquid fast, consisting primarily of vegetable juices, vegetable broths, and herb teas is recommended for cleansing the body once the individual is able to handle it. Alcoholics tend to be malnourished; thus a long fast may not be advisable.

8. Plenty of exercise, especially outdoors, to improve circulation and build up the health.

These dietary suggestions are also appropriate:

1. Whole grains and whole grain cereals, preferably twice daily. A whole grain cereal like rice cream, buckwheat cream, millet cream, cream of barley, cream of wheat (made from wheat berries), cream of rye (made from rye berries), oatmeal,

or cornmeal should be used in the morning. (A different grain can be ground fresh each morning in a small grain and seed grinder or a coffee grinder.) In the evening, brown rice, buckwheat, millet, or another grain may be used.

2. Plenty of fresh vegetables in salads, soups, steamed, and baked.

3. Proteins are important, but nuts and seeds may be difficult to assimilate for those with liver disease. Other proteins can include bean curd (tofu), soured milks as buttermilk, yogurt, kefir and goats' milk products, fresh fish, and poultry from non-chemical sources. (Heavier meats as beef, lamb, or pork are difficult to digest as are shellfish; they also deplete the pancreatic enzymes).

4. A maximum of one portion of fruit or fruit juice every other day in order to minimize the amount of sugar.

5. A small amount of fats due to the inability of the liver to assimilate fats. Two tablespoons of cold-pressed olive oil may be used on salads every other day.

6. No sugar and little honey—barley malt syrup or rice syrup may be used instead.

7. No salt.

8. No coffee, tea, or other beverages containing caffeine such as cola drinks.

PSYCHOLOGICAL FACTORS

Alcoholics and drug addicts often come from broken families where one or more of the parents has been alcoholic. The lack of family stability and affection drives them out into the world at an early age. Finding the world a difficult place and not prepared with any vocational training, alcohol or drugs become a cushion in dealing with some of the hardcore realities. One of these realities is money, and thus many turn to dealing in drugs, which often contributes to their becoming heavy users.

Illness and depression can be another factor leading to alcoholism and drug addiction. Often, during illness, especially where there is pain involved, either alcohol or one of the pain-killing drugs such as morphine is used. The side effects are so pleasant that this then becomes a habit. In cases of severe depression, the problems seem to fade away when one is drunk or "high." Often sensitive souls turn to drugs because their sensitivity causes them to experience much emotional pain. The drugs serve to numb this sensitivity and in time, the problems no longer matter.

Many alcoholics and addicts are loners who are unable to form relationships with people and unable as well to relate to the society in which they live. A deep sense of insecurity and anxiety encompasses them. The alcohol or drug enables them to completely withdraw into their own world, where they become extremely unrealistic, dreaming of goals far beyond their capabilities.

Other traits that these personalities share are impatience and inability to endure difficult circumstances for any period of time; a lack of discipline; impulsiveness in failing to think things through before taking action; and a rebelliousness and anger directed at society. The alcoholic or drug addict often feels society or parents, or friends have "done him in", plotted against him, neglected to recognize his genius, and he thus spends much of his time in self-pity and resentment towards others.

ASTROLOGICAL THEMES

The basic theme in the horoscopes of alcoholics and drug addicts is the Neptunian one—Neptune angular, conjunct the Sun or Moon, a strong twelfth house, or several planets in Pisces. In almost all the natal charts examined, hard aspects exist between the Moon and Neptune, showing a sensitive nature and often a lack of clarity in dealing with emotional problems. Hard aspects between Saturn and Neptune are also prevalent; Saturn helps to stabilize the Neptunian energy, and without this kind of grounding Neptune can be more difficult to handle. In more than half of the cases there are hard aspects between Jupiter and Neptune; Jupiter rules the liver and pancreas and this aspect often shows problems with these organs. It is the same signature as that found in the horoscopes of those with hypoglycemia. Another common placement centers on hard aspects between Venus and Neptune; emotional confusion and the tendency to indulge oneself with rich foods, drink, or some kind of drug in order to "feel good" are indicated here.

About one third of the horoscopes studied also show hard aspects between Mars and Neptune, Mercury and Neptune, and Sun and Neptune. Mars-Neptune hard aspects are often found in the natal charts of those who misdirect their energies, feel inferior, and don't quite know how to manifest their goals. When used positively, this is a fine aspect for any kind of service work, or spiritual or psychic endeavor. With hard aspects between Mercury and Neptune thinking can be muddled and one may have certain illusions about his life; there is also a tendency to be allergic to various substances. Positively speaking, one can also have very clear insights and a strong intuitive bent.

Hard aspects between the Sun and Neptune may indicate, among other things, an alcoholic father, or alcoholic family background. An individual with this aspect works continuously to integrate the higher intuitive wisdom into his life. He can fall into the role of martyr or victim and in this case, alcohol or drugs may provide the escape-hatch.

In addition to Neptune, Pluto is often angular in these horoscopes. As Pluto rules the underworld it is often found in the charts of drug users and drug dealers. The Plutonian theme of transformation is strongly sounded by those personalities that find themselves attracted to various drugs.

Jupiter is also emphasized by being angular or conjoined Sun, Moon, or another planet in more than fifty percent of these horoscopes. Jupiter relates to excess as well as ruling the liver and pancreas.

Other characteristics these horoscopes share are a predominance of the Moon and Ascendant in fixed signs. Since the Moon has to do with habit patterns, this implies habits that are deep-rooted and difficult to break.

Degree areas given by Charles Carter for alcoholism include 9° and 25° of the fixed signs, and 11° of the cardinals. These degrees were found in about half of all the horoscopes studied with the Sun, Moon and Saturn especially in one of these degrees.

Midpoint combinations most frequently seen are:

Saturn/Neptune = Sun—indicates a weak vitality and sensitive physical vehicle.

Saturn/Neptune = Moon—emotional sensitivity and depression.

Saturn/Neptune = Jupiter—restricted functioning of the liver and pancreas.

Jupiter/Neptune = Sun, Moon, or Ascendant—this may point to a very idealistic nature, a tendency to live in a somewhat unreal world, and malfunctioning of the liver and pancreas.

Mars/Neptune = Mercury—nervous conditions resulting from drugs or alcohol

Mars/Neptune = Ascendant—difficulty in asserting one's self or making one's energy manifest.

CASE HISTORY #1

The first case history is that of a man who used many hard drugs throughout his life. As a teenager, he was very rebellious; he was expelled from several high schools and also from the military academy. He drank a lot and drove recklessly. He was well-liked by his classmates and was known to be very generous and kind-hearted; he was also very emotional.

His relationship with his mother was difficult. She was extremely domineering and tried to keep him under her wing. When he was eighteen, he met the lady whom he eventually married; at one point in their relationship, they temporarily split up, which upset him so much that he attempted suicide. As a result, he was placed in the psychiatric division of a hospital for a few weeks and then released. They married right before his nineteenth birthday. She was a responsible practical lady who understood his deep sensitivity and took care of him. At the time he was drinking quite a bit and started smoking marijuana.

Within a year and a half he had begun to use hard drugs—morphine and heroin. He was also selling LSD to make money to buy the heroin. His wife made an effort to stay with him and even tried the drugs in order to understand what he experienced. Finally, when she could handle it no longer, she moved out. However, they have always maintained a deep friendship.

Meanwhile, he had been having petit mal seizures but he didn't realize what they were. Right before a seizure he felt very high and the experience was like a daydream. The heroin and other drugs aggravated these symptoms. In addition, he never took the time to eat regularly or take care of his body.

In 1973 he got caught selling drugs and spent close to two years in a county prison. After he was released, he started drinking heavily. At this time his father was supporting him; he threatened to stop providing him with money unless he went to Synanon and started functioning as a responsible human being. The administration at Synanon immediately sent him to the hospital. He had an enlarged heart, his liver was badly damaged, his circulation was poor, and he had difficulty breathing. After his stay, he went back to Synanon and finally "got his act together". Within the structure there he was able to utilize his creative potential. He used his skill as a glass blower, made mechanical repairs and spent time counseling older people.

After one-and-a-half years at Synanon, on November 26, 1977, right before his thirty-third birthday, his body stopped functioning and he passed on to another plane.

Case History #1

☉ ☌ ♂ in ♐ in 7th house, ♒ dwad	Strong physical energy; extremely active; relationships important; needs independence and freedom within relationship
☉ ☍ ♅ in ♊ in 1st house	Restless, constantly desires changes; rebellious; sensitive nervous system; respiratory allergies
☉ △ ♀ in ♌ in 4th house	Capable of transforming old patterns; physical body has good ability to regenerate itself
☉ ⊼ ♄ in ♋	Problems with father and with own self-discipline
☽ ☌ Asc. in ♉	Extreme sensitivity; likes material comforts; fixed habit patterns; willful; sensual appetites, possible thyroid and metabolic problems

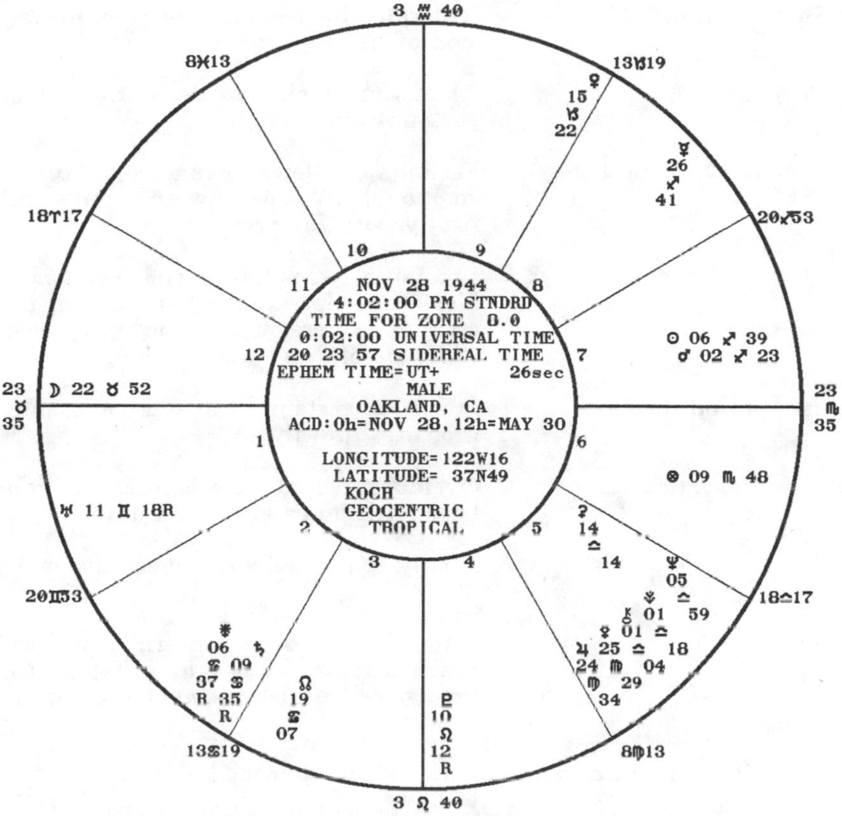

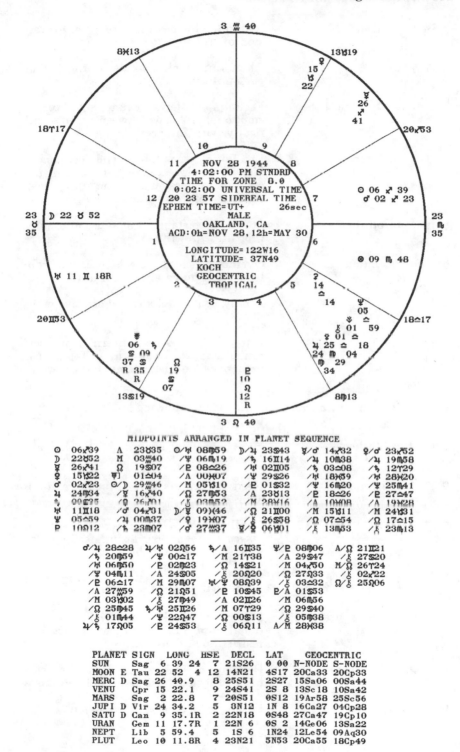

3 ♒ 40
13♑19
20♐53
23 ♏ 35
18♎17
8♍13
3 ♌ 40
13♋19
20♊53
23 ♉ 35
18♈17
8♓13
NOV 28 1944
4:02:00 PM STNDRD
TIME FOR ZONE 0.0
0:02:00 UNIVERSAL TIME
20 23 57 SIDEREAL TIME
EPHEM TIME=UT+ 26sec
MALE
OAKLAND, CA
ACD:0h=NOV 28, 12h=MAY 30
LONGITUDE=122W16
LATITUDE= 37N49
KOCH
GEOCENTRIC
TROPICAL
☽ 22 ♉ 52
♅ 11 ♊ 18R
☉ 06 ♐ 39
♂ 02 ♐ 23
⊗ 09 ♏ 48

MIDPOINTS ARRANGED IN PLANET SEQUENCE

☉ 06♐39	A 23♉35	☉/♅ 08♍59	☽/♃ 23♋43	☿/♂ 14♐32	♀/♂ 23♐52
☽ 22♉52	M 03♒40	/♆ 06♏19	/♄ 16♊14	/♃ 10♏38	/♃ 19♏58
☿ 26♐41	☊ 19♋07	/♇ 08♎26	/♅ 02♊05	/♄ 03♎08	/♄ 12♈29
♀ 15♑22	♆] 01♎04	/A 00♓07	/♆ 29♋26	/♅ 18♓59	/♅ 28♓20
♂ 02♐23	☉/☽ 29♒46	/M 05♑10	/♇ 01♋32	/♆ 16♏20	/♆ 25♏41
♃ 24♍34	/☿ 16♐40	/☊ 27♍53	/A 23♉13	/♇ 18♎26	/♇ 27♎47
♄ 09♋35	/♀ 26♐01	/⚷ 03♏52	/M 28♓16	/A 10♓08	/A 19♓28
♅ 11♊18	/♂ 04♐31	☽/☿ 09♓46	/☊ 21♊00	/M 15♑11	/M 24♑31
♆ 05♎59	/♃ 00♏37	/♀ 19♓07	/⚷ 26♋58	/☊ 07♎54	/☊ 17♎15
♇ 10♌12	/♄ 23♍07	/♂ 27♒37	☿/♀ 06♑01	/⚷ 13♏53	/⚷ 23♏13

♂/♃ 28♎28	♃/♅ 02♌56	♄/A 16♊35	♆/♇ 08♍06	A/☊ 21♊21
/♄ 20♍59	/♆ 00♎17	/M 21♈38	/A 29♋47	/⚷ 27♋20
/♅ 06♍50	/♇ 02♍23	/☊ 14♋21	/M 04♐50	M/☊ 26♈24
/♆ 04♏11	/A 24♋05	/⚷ 20♌20	/☊ 27♌33	/⚷ 02♐22
/♇ 06♎17	/M 29♏07	♅/♆ 08♌39	/⚷ 03♎32	☊/⚷ 25♌06
/A 27♒59	/☊ 21♌51	/♇ 10♋45	♇/A 01♋53	
/M 03♑02	/⚷ 27♍49	/A 02♊26	/M 06♏56	
/☊ 25♍45	♄/♅ 25♊26	/M 07♈29	/☊ 29♋40	
/⚷ 01♏44	/♆ 22♌47	/☊ 00♋13	/⚷ 05♍38	
♃/♄ 17♌05	/♇ 24♋53	/⚷ 06♌11	A/M 28♓38	

PLANET	SIGN	LONG	HSE	DECL	LAT	GEOCENTRIC N-NODE	S-NODE
SUN	Sag	6 39 24	7	21S26	0 00	N-NODE	S-NODE
MOON E	Tau	22 52 4	12	14N21	4S17	20Ca33	20Cp33
MERC D	Sag	26 40.9	8	25S51	2S27	15Sa06	00Sa44
VENU	Cpr	15 22.1	9	24S41	2S 8	13Sc18	10Sa42
MARS	Sag	2 22.8	7	20S51	0S12	19Ar58	25Sc56
JUPI D	Vir	24 34.2	5	8N12	1N 8	16Ca27	04Cp28
SATU D	Can	9 35.1R	2	22N18	0S48	27Ca47	19Cp10
URAN	Gem	11 17.7R	1	22N 6	0S 2	14Ge06	13Sa22
NEPT	Lib	5 59.4	5	1S 6	1N24	12Le54	09Aq30
PLUT	Leo	10 11.8R	4	23N21	5N53	20Ca55	18Cp49

☽ in ♉, ♒ dwad	Reiterates theme of freedom; free expression of his appetites
☽ △ ♀ △ ♃ ⚷	Abundant creative skills; warm, loving personality
☽ ∠ ♄ in ♋ in 2nd house	Feelings of inferiority; unable to express emotions; problems between parents, difficulty with finances
☽ ⚼ ♆ in 5th house	Emotional sensitivity and confusion; idealistic in love; dreamy and unrealistic; creative expression in music, poetry; possible use of drugs and alcohol
☿ in ♐ in 8th house	Study of metaphysics and philosophy promotes growth
☿ □ ♃ in ♍, (mutual reception)	Overdoes mental projects; possible problems with lungs and intestines
☿ ∥ ♀	Ability to express ideas in creative manner
☿ ⚼ ♇ in ♌	Introspection; deep concern about self could lead to studies in metaphysical area; possible allergies involving respiratory system
♀ ☌ ♇ in ♑ in 9th house	Difficulty in allowing love and creativity to flow
♀ □ ⚵ in 5th house	Has problems nurturing and helping others
♀ ∠ ♂ in 7th house	Need to express love through relationships
♀ ☍ ♄ in ♋	Holding back of love and creative energy; insecure about expressing feelings for others; tendency to be a loner
♃ in ♍ in 5th house	Growth through creative self-expression; good with detailed creative work
♄ in ♋ in 2nd house ☍ ♀	Difficulty in making money; lack of emotional and financial security, possible restrictions of thyroid
♄ □ ♆ in 5th house	Desire to escape against desire for structure; guilt about use of alcohol and drugs
♄ ∠ Asc.	Feeling of aloneness, depression

| ♆ ☌ ⚷ , ♂ in 5th house | Sensitivity to drugs; creative work involving music and film; strong healing ability |

♆ ⊡ Asc.   Confusion regarding identity

♀ at nadir   Deep probing into subconscious motives; transforming emotional heritage and family roots; possible involvement with underground and drugs; need to bring forth creative abilities

♄ in 9° cardinal   Alcohol degree

MIDPOINTS

♄ / ♆ = ☽, asc.   Emotional repression; problems with thyroid and hormonal balance

☿ / ♆ = ♂, ⚷   Sensitive nervous system, problems with lungs; respiratory allergies

Secondary Progressions	Solar Arc Directions	Transits	Eclipses

1. Feb. 1963—met wife; May 1963—suicide attempt; Oct. 1963—marriage

Secondary Progressions	Solar Arc Directions	Transits	Eclipses
☉ ⊡ ♀	♆ ☌ V	*May*	*Jan.* L.E. ☌ ☊
☿ ⊡ ☽	♀ ☌ MC	♃ ☍ ♄	July L.E. ☌ ♀
MC △ ☽	☿ ☌ ♀	♄ ⊡ ♄	S.E. ☌ E.P.
Asc. ⊼ ♀	? ⊡ MC	♅ ⊡ ♀	
☽ ☌ ♈ May	☉ ⊡ ♃	♀ ⊡ ♅	
☽ ∠ ♂ May		*Oct.*	
☽ △ Asc. Oct.		♃ ⊡ ♀ ☍ ?	
☽ △ ♃ Oct.		♄ ⊡ ♂ ⚷	
		♅ ⊡ ☉	
		♆ ∠ ♂ ⚷	
		♀ ⊡ ♅	

2. April 1973—caught stealing: sent to county jail in July

Secondary Progressions	Solar Arc Directions	Transits	Eclipses
☉ ⊡ ♆	MC ⊡ ♂	*April & July*	Jan. L. E. ☌ E.P.
☿ ⊡ ♀	♂ ⊡ ♂ , ⚷	♃ ☍ ♀	S. E. ⊡ E. P.
♂ ⊼ ☽		♅ ⊡ nodes	
Asc. ⊡ ♃		♆ ☌ ☉	
Asc. ∠ ♀		♀ ⊡ ♂ ⚷	
MC ⊡ ♂		*July*	
☽ ☍ ☉ April		♄ ☍ ☿	
☽ ☌ ♅ July			

3. January 1975—Synanon

Asc. ☍ ☿	☉ □ ♆	♃ * ♀ ⚻ ?	May S. E. ☌ ☽, Asc.
☉ ⚼ ☽	♃ ☌ V	♄ ☍ ♀	L. E. ☌ ♂
♂ □ ♃		♅ □ MC	Nov. S. E. □ ♇
		♆ △ ♇	
		♇ □ ♄	

4. November 26, 1977—died

☉ ☍ ♄	MC □ ☉	☉ ☌ ☉/♂	April S.E. □ E.P.
☉ ⚻ ♇	♆ □ ♇	☿ ⚻ ☽, Asc.	Oct. S. E. □ ☊
☿ ⚻ ☽		♀ △ ☊	
♀ ⚻ ♃		♂ ☌ ♇	
♀ ⚼ ♄		♃ ⚻ ☉, ♂	
♂ ☌ ☿		♄ ⚼ ♀	
☽ ☌ ♇ Jan.		♇ □ ♀	

CASE HISTORY #2

The next case history is that of a man who didn't use alcohol until his forty-first year. He was brought up in a family of theosophists who were vegetarian and health food faddists. His mother had given birth to him when she was forty-two; he was a blue baby (born with a bluish color due to abnormally low concentration of oxygen in the blood) and had a heart murmur. He was extremely overprotected and never moved out of his mother's home, even when he married, until after she died.

At the age of twenty-eight he was living in a Quaker camp as a conscientious objector; it was there that he met his first wife. They had a daughter the following year and a son eight years later. During this time he was doing art work, and teaching and lecturing on a variety of subjects including comparative religion and philosophy. He lived with the Hopi Indians on their reservation and also traveled to India.

When he was forty-one he left his wife and married a twenty-year-old woman. It was at this time that he started drinking. He developed a bad case of bronchitis and used the alcohol as medicine. His wife also drank heavily. The following year she gave birth to a son who was born an albino, with the muscles around the eyes quite red, and an underdeveloped ear. The doctors felt that this was due to the consumption of large amounts of alcohol during pregnancy.

During the next six years his drinking got heavier and in 1966 his mother died. This was a very low period for him; he was thrown out of his theosophy group, then lost his home, which had been his mother's house, and many possessions.

In 1974-75 he started on an upward swing and in 1976 went to a state hospital for rehabilitation. After his year at the state hospital, he went through periods of abstinence; during these times he lectured and worked with rehabilitation programs for other alcoholics. At other times, when things weren't going so well, he started drinking again.

In 1979 he hit another low and felt suicidal; nothing in his life seemed to be working. He finally went to northern California where his daughter lives. He underwent some mega-vitamin therapy, taking large quantities of B-complex vitamins, especially niacinimide and calcium. His health and energy improved greatly and he started hiking. He contacted the people he had worked with in theosophy and resumed lecturing, and also worked with rehabilitation programs. At present he spends his time lecturing and teaching but still goes on occasional binges when he feels depressed.

Case History #2

Funnel chart with ♅ in 5th house	Emphasis on strong creativity, new and unusual art forms; rebelliousness; individuality
☉ in ♌ in 10th house, ♓ dwad	Need to manifest energy in a professional way; to be out in the world, to teach, ♓ dwad brings in artistic and psychic sensitivity
☉ ☍ ♅ in 5th house	Constant changes brought into the life; strongly rebellious and individual; unusual artistic talent; possible problems with circulation and heart
☉ ∠ ♀ in 9th house	Work on transforming his life and letting go of his ego needs through study of philosophical and religious material

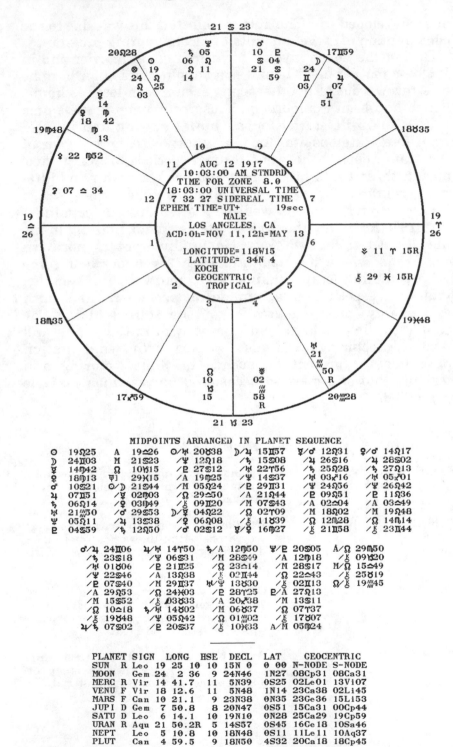

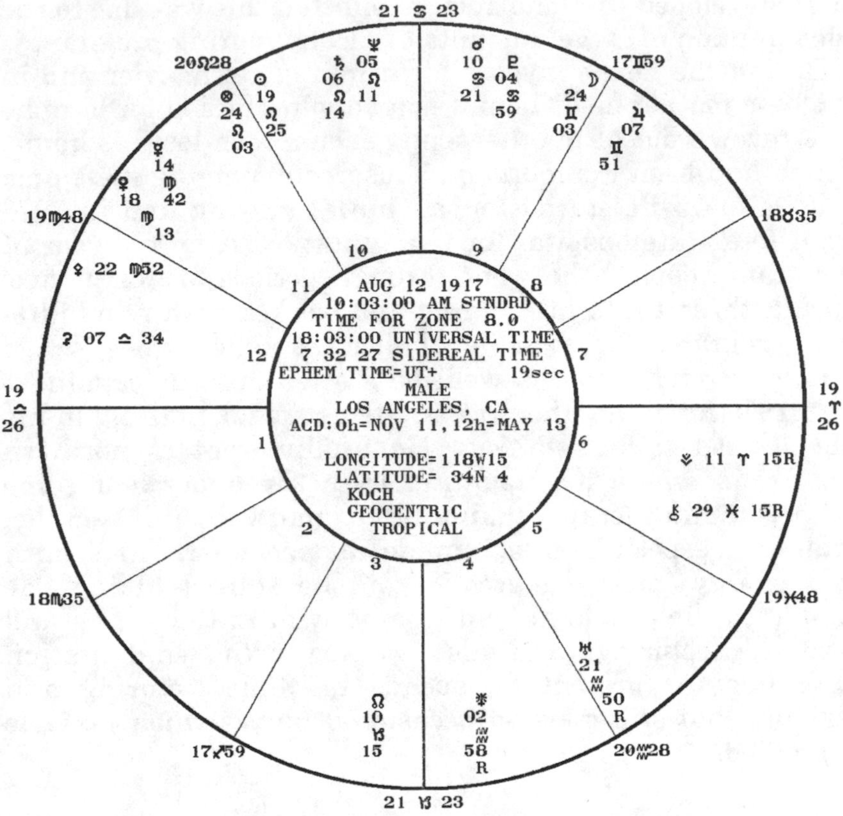
21 ♋ 23
AUG 12 1917
10:03:00 AM STNDRD
TIME FOR ZONE 8.0
18:03:00 UNIVERSAL TIME
7 32 27 SIDEREAL TIME
EPHEM TIME=UT+ 19sec
MALE
LOS ANGELES, CA
ACD:0h=NOV 11,12h=MAY 13
LONGITUDE=118W15
LATITUDE= 34N 4
KOCH
GEOCENTRIC
TROPICAL
20♌28
17♊59
19♍48
18♉35
19 ♎ 26
19 ♈ 26
18♏35
19♓48
17♐59
20♒28
21 ♑ 23
☉ 19 ♌ 25
⊗ 24 ♌ 03
♄ 06 ♌ 14
♆ 05 ♌ 11
♂ 10 ♋ 21
♇ 04 ♋ 59
☽ 24 ♊ 03
♃ 07 ♊ 51
☿ 14 ♍ 42
♀ 18 ♍ 13
⚳ 22 ♍52
⚴ 07 ♎ 34
⚵ 11 ♈ 15R
⚷ 29 ♓ 15R
♅ 21 ♒ 50 R
⚶ 02 ♒ 58 R
☊ 10 ♑ 15
1
2
3
4
5
6
7
8
9
10
11
12

MIDPOINTS ARRANGED IN PLANET SEQUENCE

☉ 19♌25	A 19♎26	☉/♅ 20♉38	☽/♃ 15♊57	☿/♂ 12♌31	♀/♂ 14♌17
☽ 24♊03	M 21♋23	/♆ 12♌18	/♄ 15♋08	/♃ 26♋16	/♃ 28♋02
☿ 14♍42	☊ 10♑15	/♇ 27♋12	/♅ 22♈56	/♄ 25♌28	/♄ 27♌13
♀ 18♍13	♆] 29♓15	/A 19♍25	/♆ 14♋37	/♅ 03♐16	/♅ 05♐01
♂ 10♋21	☉/☽ 21♋44	/M 05♌24	/♇ 29♊31	/♆ 24♌56	/♆ 26♌42
♃ 07♊51	/☿ 02♍03	/☊ 29♎50	/A 21♌44	/♇ 09♌51	/♇ 11♌36
♄ 06♌14	/♀ 03♍49	/⚷ 09♊20	/M 07♋43	/A 02♎04	/A 03♎49
♅ 21♒50	/♂ 29♋53	☽/☿ 04♌22	/☊ 02♈09	/M 18♌02	/M 19♌48
♆ 05♌11	/♃ 13♋38	/♀ 06♌08	/⚷ 11♉39	/☊ 12♏28	/☊ 14♏14
♇ 04♋59	/♄ 12♌50	/♂ 02♋12	☿/♀ 16♍27	/⚷ 21♊58	/⚷ 23♊44

♂/♃ 24♊06	♃/♅ 14♈50	♄/A 12♍50	♆/♇ 20♋05	A/☊ 29♏50
/♄ 23♋18	/♆ 06♋31	/M 28♋49	/A 12♍18	/⚷ 09♑20
/♅ 01♉06	/♇ 21♊25	/☊ 23♎14	/M 28♋17	M/☊ 15♎49
/♆ 22♋46	/A 13♌38	/⚷ 02♊44	/☊ 22♎43	/⚷ 25♉19
/♇ 07♋40	/M 29♊37	♅/♆ 13♉30	/⚷ 02♊13	☊/⚷ 19♒45
/A 29♌53	/☊ 24♓03	/♇ 28♈25	♇/A 27♌13	
/M 15♋52	/⚷ 03♉33	/A 20♐38	/M 13♋11	
/☊ 10♎18	♄/♅ 14♉02	/M 06♉37	/☊ 07♈37	
/⚷ 19♉48	/♆ 05♌42	/☊ 01♒02	/⚷ 17♉07	
♃/♄ 07♋02	/♇ 20♋37	/⚷ 10♓33	A/M 05♍24	

PLANET		SIGN	LONG	HSE	DECL	LAT	GEOCENTRIC N-NODE	S-NODE
SUN	R	Leo	19 25 10	10	15N 0	0 00		
MOON		Gem	24 2 36	9	24N46	1N27	08Cp31	08Ca31
MERC	R	Vir	14 41.7	11	5N39	0S25	02Le01	13Vi07
VENU	F	Vir	18 12.6	11	5N48	1N14	23Ca38	02Li45
MARS	F	Can	10 21.1	9	23N38	0N35	23Ge36	15Li53
JUPI	D	Gem	7 50.8	8	20N47	0S51	15Ca31	00Cp44
SATU	D	Leo	6 14.1	10	19N10	0N28	25Ca29	19Cp59
URAN	R	Aqu	21 50.2R	5	14S57	0S45	16Ge18	10Sa46
NEPT		Leo	5 10.8	10	18N48	0S11	11Le11	10Aq37
PLUT		Can	4 59.5	9	18N50	4S32	20Ca18	18Cp45

☽ in ♊ in 9th house, ♏ dwad	Many talents, versatility; work will involve traveling and possibly living in other cultures; ♏ dwad brings out a probing into metaphysical and occult philosophies
☽ □ ♀ ⚷ in ♍	Needs to work out things with his mother and other women, to allow creative energy to flow
☽ ∠ ♄ in ♌ in 10th house	Unable to express feelings; emotional inhibition; insecure about professional image
Grand △ ☽ △ ♅ △ Asc. in air,fire houses	Communication of new ideas and philosophies; artistic inventiveness
☽ ‖ ♂	Strong emotions; mother as a dominant figure in his life
♎ Asc., ♉ dwad	Emphasis on creativity and need for relationships; tendency to be fixed and stubborn
☿ ☌ ♀ in ♍ in 11th house	Writing and teaching ability; service through work with groups; particular about details in creative work
☿ □ ♃ in ♊	Takes on too many projects; friends and associates tire him; possible problems with lungs; allergies of a respiratory nature
♀ in ♍ ∠ ♄♆ in ♌ in 10th house	Idealistic about love relationships; works to integrate creativity into career
♂ ☌ ⚳ in ♎ in 9th house	Strong sense of power and vital force; potential for regenerating self and humanity through a study of ancient wisdom; with the south node involved may have misused power in previous lifetimes
♂ ⚼ ♅ in ♒	Sensitive nervous system, restlessness; energy put into creative projects; new and original ideas
♃ in ♊ in 8th house	Growth and expansion through study of metaphysical and occult sciences
♃ * ♄♆ in ♌ in 10th house	Ability to structure new ideas and focus his learning through his creative skills

♄ ∥ MC	Need to have a strong career, to be a leader and teacher, to be involved with the practical sides of life
⚷ in 6th house □ nodes in 3rd and 9th houses	In order to serve, must break through old patterns involving personal insecurities; work in communications
⚷ ☍ ⚵ in ♎ in 12th house	Needs to nurture others through relationships
♂ in ♓ in 6th house □ ☽ in ⚹	Service through healing and spiritual work; health problems from over-indulgence in alcohol and drugs

MIDPOINTS

♂ / ♆ = ♃ (inverse)	Tendency toward hypoglycemia, liver and pancreas dysfunction
☿ / ♆ = ♂, ☊ (inverse)	Creative mind, strong imagination; possible respiratory allergies; nervous condition resulting from use of alcohol or drugs
♃ / ♆ = ♀, ♅ (inverse)	Spiritual growth goes through many phases; needs to see difference between reality and imagination; chronic problems with liver and/or pancreas

Secondary Progressions	Solar Arc Directions	Transits	Eclipses

1. 1959—left his wife, developed a bad case of bronchitis in August 1959; started drinking

Secondary Progressions	Solar Arc Directions	Transits	Eclipses
Asc. □ ♅	♆ ☌ ☿	♃ ↗ ☽	April S. E. ☌ Desc.
Asc. ∠ ☊	♃ □ Asc.	♄ ☍ ♀	
☿ ∠ ♄	♂ □ ☉	♅ ☌ ☉	
☿ ⚹ MC		♆ □ ♆	
♀ ⚹ ☊		♀ ∠ Asc.	
♂ □ ♄			
☽ ☍ ☽ August			

2. September 1966—mother died

Secondary Progressions	Solar Arc Directions	Transits	Eclipses
☉ ⬓ ♅	♄ □ ☽	♃ ∠ ♃	Oct. L. E. □ ♄
☽ □ ♀ September	♀ □ ♄	♄ □ ☽	
	♅ □ nodes	♆ □ ☉	
	♀ ☍ ♅	♅♀ ☌ ♀ ⚵	
	MC □ ♃		
	⚷ ☍ V		

3. **October 1969—lost house and possessions**

☉ □ ♂ ☊	♄ □ ♄♆	Sept. L. E. □ ♇
☿ ⊼ ♅	♅ □ ♇	
♀ ⚼ ♇	♅ ☍ ⊕	
☽ □ ♅ Oct.	♇ □ ☽ ⊼ ♅ ☌ ‡	

4. **October 1976—Camarillo State Hospital for rehabilitation**

MC ☌ ♀	Asc. □ ☿	♃ □ ☉	April S. E. □ ♄
‡ ☌ Asc.	⯔ ☌ ♃	♄ ☌ ♄	
Asc. △ ♄	♅ ☌ Desc.	♅ □ ♆♄	
☉ Q ♆	⚷ ☌ V	♆ □ ☿	
☽ ☌ ☉ Oct.		♇ ☌ ? □ ♂ □ ☊☋	

☽ ∠ ♇ Oct.

5. **1979—suicidal; tried mega-vitamin therapy**

☉ ☌ Asc. ✱ ☉	Asc. □ ♀	♃ ✱ ♇ ∠ Asc
☿ ✱ ♄	♆ □ ♇	♄ ⊼ ♅ ☌ ‡
☿ ⚼ ♅		♅ □ ☉
♂ ☌ ☉		♆ □ ♀
Asc. ☍ ♃		♇ ☌ Asc.
MC ☌ ‡		
MC ⊼ ♅		
☽ □ ☽ September		

CHAPTER FOURTEEN

ARTHRITIS

Arthritis, one of the major stress-induced diseases, has become the chief cause of chronic disability in the United States and the most widespread crippling disease in the world. The term arthritis covers more than one hundred different types of joint diseases and may also arise as a side effect of a number of diseases including tuberculosis, syphillis, gonorrhea, and the viral diseases measles and influenza. Rheumatism is a general term for arthritis and is applied to almost any pain in the joints or muscles.

In arthritis, the joints become inflamed, enlarged, and swollen; the cartilage loses its elasticity, becoming dry and brittle and the ligaments and muscles which surround the joint may also become inflamed, losing tone and flexibility. Swelling and pain often increase during motion.

There are various types of arthritis with rheumatoid arthritis and osteo-arthritis the most widespread. In rheumatoid arthritis, the most painful and crippling form, one or more joints often become swollen and inflamed. If the disease progresses, there is degeneration of the joint with possible deformities and immobility. Osteoarthritis is much less crippling than severe rheumatoid arthritis because it does not cause the two bone surfaces to fuse and immobilize the joint.

Other common types of arthritis include:

Lupus (systemic lupus erysthematosus), a disease of the connective tissue producing changes in the structure and functions of the skin, joints, and internal organs; it affects seven times as many women as men.

Spondylitis (ankylosing spondylitis) is caused by an inflammation of the joints of one or more vertebrae.

Gout which results from a defect in body chemistry that

leads to high blood levels of uric acid and forms needle-like crystals in the joint.

Bursitis is the inflammation of a bursa, a sac-like structure resembling a joint located between the skin and bone in places where the skin rubs over the bone.

Among the factors leading to arthritis are prolonged periods of stress. These periods produce adrenal exhaustion as well as the malfunctioning of other glands of the endocrine system. When the glands are no longer able to produce sufficient cortisone and other hormones, a severe hormonal imbalance results. This hormonal imbalance, combined with incomplete digestion and assimilation of foods, toxins from the system (many arthritis patients suffer from constipation), and a weakened nervous system affects the structure of various tissues.

Traditional methods of dealing with arthritis, such as cortisone therapy, serve to mask the symptoms and produce so many side effects that it becomes difficult to rebalance the body. Over a long period of time cortisone can depress the functioning of the immune system and undermine the body's own healing powers.[1] The use of cortisone therapy may also lead to ulcers, gastro-intestinal disturbances, high blood pressure, insomnia and other infections.[2] Worst of all, it causes adrenal atrophy and deterioration of tissue of the joints.[3] Gold injections, another traditional form of treatment, may be highly toxic and produce damage to the liver and kidneys.[4]

Therapeutic methods of treating arthritis must include physical therapies and exercise for the joints and limbs of the body as well as cleansing regimes and nutritional programs to balance out the hormonal system and stimulate the metabolism. Natural methods of healing arthritic conditions include the following:

---

[1]Dr. Paul Dudley White, *Heart Disease* as cited in *There Is A Cure For Arthritis*, Paavo Airola, Parker Publishing Co., West Nyack, N.Y. 1968.
[2]*The Stress Of Life*, Hans Selye, McGraw Hill, N.Y. 1976, Pg. 166.
[3]*Journal of AMA*. August 27, 1960.
[4]Dr. Wm. P. Rawls, "An Evaluation Of The Present Day Therapy In Rheumatoid Arthritis". *New York Medicine*, August 5, 1947.

1. Acupuncture and other Oriental touch therapies such as acupressure and shiatsu.
2. Liquid fasts with vegetable juices, soup broths and herb teas.
3. Cleansing of the intestinal area with colonics (colon bath) and high enemas; cleansing of the skin through saunas and steam baths.
4. Various types of massage and body balancing.
5. Therapeutic exercises for strengthening joints and limbs as well as daily walking, swimming and running for mobility.
6. The herbs comfrey, alfalfa and sarsaparilla root that are high in calcium and other nutrients.
7. A balanced diet with emphasis on vegetables, whole grains, nuts and seeds, soured milk products, some fish and a small amount of fruit.
8. Supplemental vitamins, minerals, and amino acids when necessary. Niacin (vitamin B-3), pantothenic acid, biotin, and pyridoxine (B-6) are often needed in large amounts. Arthritic patients tend to be especially deficient in manganese, magnesium, iron, and calcium. (Manganese nourishes the nervous system and is found in purple, dark blue and red foods along with iron). Certain amino acids may also be required.

PSYCHOLOGICAL AND ASTROLOGICAL PATTERNS

The horoscopes of arthritic patients display a strong Saturn; often it is angular or conjoined the Sun or Moon. Most of these individuals tend to be emotionally reserved and suppress their feelings. They have particular difficulty expressing anger and turn their aggression inward. Thus their feelings of guilt may be very strong. The anger often manifests as pain, and one arthritic client mentioned that her physical therapist used to insult her while he was working on her body in order to help her release her anger.

Another shared trait is the strong sense of duty and responsibility. One of my clients is supporting both a teenage son and a ninety-year-old mother; although she has other brothers and sisters, she feels that no one else can handle that responsibility. She hates doing it, but if she didn't, she would feel guilty. There is also a tendency to exaggerate order, tidiness, punctuality, and precision. Their personal habits are extremely crystallized and it is difficult for them to adapt to other people and new circumstances.

The sense of service is strong and often the arthritic personality may go to masochistic extremes in his desire to serve as, for example, the lady supporting her mother while she suffers. Many of these individuals have Neptune angular in their horoscope and Virgo-Pisces axis on one of the angles. Another important astrological pattern is the interchange between the planets Mars, Saturn, and Neptune. All three may be involved in a T-square, or Neptune may equal the Mars/Saturn midpoint, or Saturn, the Mars/Neptune. This combination tends to emphasize the strong sense of responsibility, the self-sacrificing tendency and the quality of frustration.

Most arthritic patients have had a difficult childhood; often the father was extremely authoritarian and cold and a strong attachment to the mother ensued. Sometimes the parents were poor and the child had to work; the habit of thriftiness was inculcated at an early age. In adolescence there was much anxiety, and sexual development was often inhibited. Many female patients are frigid, and often both male and female experience sexual problems in their marriage. Their introverted tendency makes them wary of emotional entanglements and dependency.

Although these characteristics may be present for many years, it usually takes a catalyst as the death of a loved one (especially the mother), difficulty in marriage, problems with one's job, overwork and fatigue, increased responsibilities, and other stressful situations for the physical symptoms of arthritis to appear.

Once the disease begins to manifest, other psychological complications result. Expressing emotions with the physical body like pounding a fist on the table or jumping for joy becomes more difficult. Feelings of inferiority connected with the body increase as well as dependency on others due to limited mobility. This dependency on others for food, transportation and other necessities results in a loss of self esteem and increases the sense of guilt and frustration.

CASE HISTORY #1

This case history concerns a woman who had painful rheumatoid arthritis for many years and healed herself with the aid of a very unusual physical therapist. Her symptoms began about 1975, after a bout with pneumonia. Her feet hurt when she went hiking and later it became difficult to stand and walk. Her ankles especially were badly swollen. At the time she had a very demanding job; she was working six days a week and getting little sleep. Eventually it became difficult to bend her fingers and move her shoulders and arms. She went to a doctor and had a blood test which confirmed rheumatoid arthritis. The doctor recommended aspirin and told her she could get plastic joints eventually. For about six months she took twelve aspirin daily. She seriously contemplated suicide at this time but she had a young child to raise. Finally her spiritual teacher recommended a physical therapist who worked with exercises and manipulating the body as well as visualization techniques. This unusual therapist also helped her, while working on the painful areas of her body, to release her anger and frustration. After about a year, she was able to raise her arms to wash her hair and to walk stiffly. In two years time she was normal.

She also made some dietary changes, becoming a vegetarian and avoiding salt, sugar, alcohol, tomatoes, other acidic foods, and certain starches and proteins. Her desire to heal others with arthritis and related problems was strong so she started to learn these particular techniques from the physical therapist who helped her.

At the present time, in addition to working as secretary for a spiritual organization, she is also doing healing work.

Case History #1

♓/♍ axis on Asc./Desc.   Healing and spiritual work; self-sacrificing qualities

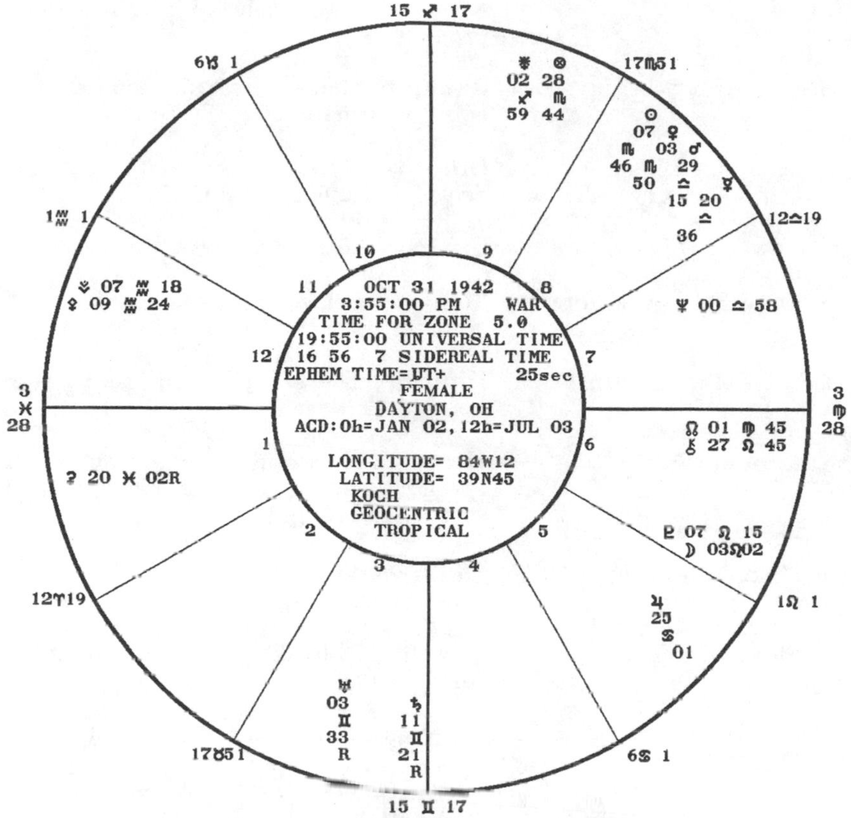

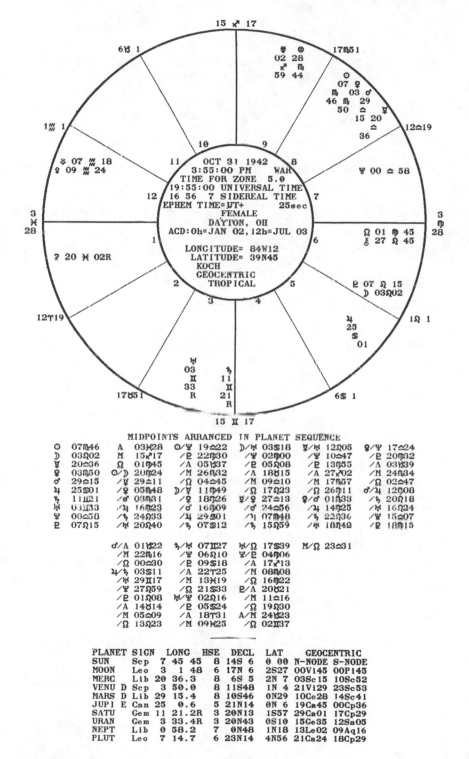

15 ♐ 17
6♑ 1
17♏51
1♒ 1
12♎19
3 ♓ 28
3 ♍ 28
12♈19
1♌ 1
17♉51
6♋ 1
15 ♊ 17
10
9
11
8
12
7
1
6
2
5
3
4
OCT 31 1942
3:55:00 PM WAR
TIME FOR ZONE 5.0
19:55:00 UNIVERSAL TIME
16 56 7 SIDEREAL TIME
EPHEM TIME=UT+ 25sec
FEMALE
DAYTON, OH
ACD:0h=JAN 02,12h=JUL 03
LONGITUDE= 84W12
LATITUDE= 39N45
KOCH
GEOCENTRIC
TROPICAL
02 ♐ 59
28 ♏ 44
☉ 07 ♏ 46
♀ 03 ♏ 50
♂ 29 ♎ 15
☿ 20 ♎ 36
♆ 00 ♎ 58
☊ 01 ♍ 45
⚷ 27 ♌ 45
♇ 07 ♌ 15
☽ 03♌02
♃ 25 ♋ 01
♅ 03 ♊ 33 R
♄ 11 ♊ 21 R
20 ♓ 02R
07 ♒ 18
09 ♒ 24

MIDPOINTS ARRANGED IN PLANET SEQUENCE

☉	07♏46	A	03♓28	☉/♆	19♎22	☽/♅	03♋18	☿/♅	12♌05	♀/♆	17♎24
☽	03♌02	M	15♐17	/♇	22♍30	/♆	02♍00	/♆	10♎47	/♇	20♍32
☿	20♎36	☊	01♍45	/A	05♑37	/♇	05♌08	/♇	13♍55	/A	03♑39
♀	03♏50	☉/☽	20♍24	/M	26♏32	/A	18♉15	/A	27♐02	/M	24♏34
♂	29♎15	/☿	29♎11	/☊	04♎45	/M	09♎10	/M	17♏57	/☊	02♎47
♃	25♋01	/♀	05♏48	☽/☿	11♍49	/☊	17♌23	/☊	26♍11	♂/♃	12♍08
♄	11♊21	/♂	03♏31	/♀	18♍26	☿/♀	27♎13	♀/♂	01♏33	/♄	20♌18
♅	03♊33	/♃	16♍23	/♂	16♍09	/♂	24♎56	/♃	14♍25	/♅	16♌24
♆	00♎58	/♄	24♌33	/♃	29♋01	/♃	07♏48	/♄	22♌36	/♆	15♎07
♇	07♌15	/♅	20♌40	/♄	07♋12	/♄	15♌59	/♅	18♌40	/♇	18♍15

♂/A	01♑22	♄/♅	07♊27	♅/☊	17♋39	M/☊	23♎31
/M	22♏16	/♆	06♌10	♆/♇	04♍06		
/☊	00♎30	/♇	09♋18	/A	17♐13		
♃/♄	03♋11	/A	22♈25	/M	08♏08		
/♅	29♊17	/M	13♓19	/☊	16♍22		
/♆	27♌59	/☊	21♋33	♇/A	20♉21		
/♇	01♌08	♅/♆	02♌16	/M	11♎16		
/A	14♉14	/♇	05♋24	/☊	19♌30		
/M	05♎09	/A	18♈31	A/M	24♑23		
/☊	13♌23	/M	09♓25	/☊	02♊37		

PLANET		SIGN	LONG	HSE	DECL	LAT	GEOCENTRIC	
SUN		Scp	7 45 45	8	14S 6	0 00	N-NODE	S-NODE
MOON		Leo	3 1 48	6	17N 6	2S27	00Vi45	00Pi45
MERC		Lib	20 36.3	8	6S 5	2N 7	03Sc15	10Sc52
VENU	D	Scp	3 50.0	8	11S48	1N 4	21Vi29	23Sc53
MARS	D	Lib	29 15.4	8	10S46	0N29	10Ce28	14Sc41
JUPI	E	Can	25 0.6	5	21N14	0N 6	19Ca45	00Cp36
SATU		Gem	11 21.2R	3	20N13	1S57	29Ca01	17Cp29
URAN		Gem	3 33.4R	3	20N43	0S10	15Ge35	12Sa05
NEPT		Lib	0 58.2	7	0N48	1N18	13Le02	09Aq16
PLUT		Leo	7 14.7	6	23N14	4N56	21Ca24	18Cp29

♈ dwad	Need to assert self and initiate new projects
Nodes on Asc./Desc. in ♓/♍	Strong emphasis on service and healing; extreme sensitivity
☉ in ♏ in 8th house	Growth and transformation dealing with death and dying; healing
♑ dwad	Tendency to rigidity, crystallization
☉ ☌ ♀ in 8th house in ♏	Manifesting love in a transpersonal way; transforming sexual energy
☉ ☐ ☽ in 6th house in ♌	Difficulty between parents; inner struggles
☉ ☐ ♀ in 6th in ♌	Heavy emphasis on transforming sexual energy; death and dying; metaphysical and spiritual studies
☉ ☐ ⚷ in 12th house in ♒	Hard working, tendency to overwork, humanitarian work
☽ in 6th house in ♌	Health and healing work; emotions related to health problems
♍ dwad	Emphasis on health concerns and service
☽ ☌ ♀	Need to transform emotions in impersonal way
☽ ☐ ♀	Problems to work out with mother
☽ ☐ ♂	Tendency to anger, emotional outbursts
☿ ☌ ♂ in ♎ in 8th house	Sensitive nervous system; energy into transpersonal psychology; study of occult and metaphysics
☿ ☐ ♃	Tendency to overdo mental work
♂ ☐ ♃	Tendency to overdo physically
♄ in ♊ in 3rd house	Communication and teaching
♄ near nadir	Strong sense of responsibility; emphasis on structure and family responsibilities
♄ △ ⚷	Sense of self-discipline and hard work

♅ in ♊ in 3rd house	New and original ideas, new ways of communicating
♅ □ ♌ ☊	Sensitive nervous system; need to ground energy through physical disciplines
♆ in 7th house	Attracting more spiritually-inclined partners
♆ grand △ with ♅ in ♊ and ⚷ ⚵ in ♒	Communications emphasized; new ideas shared with others
♂ in 6th house	Strong healing, health crises
⚴ in ♓ in 1st house	Nurturing quality, healing work

MIDPOINTS

♄ / ♆ = ♀	Chronic conditions, transforming health patterns through diet and other healing techniques
♂ / ♅ = ♆ (inverse)	Sensitive nervous system; highly intuitive and psychic
♂ / ♀ = ☽ (inverse)	Transforming emotionality and sexuality; reproductive system may need toning; hormone level may be low
♂ / ♆ = ♌ (inverse)	Emotional sensitivity; tendency to low blood sugar

Secondary Progressions	Solar Arc Directions	Transits	Eclipses

1. 1975—pneumonia and onset of symptoms

☉ ☌ ☿P □ ♄R	♃ ☌ ♂	♅ ☌ ♂	May S. E. ⚹ ☿
☿ □ ♄		♄ ⊓ ♂	Nov. S. E. ☌ ☉
			□ ♀

(Both these
aspects relate
to the lungs)

2. 1977—move to San Francisco in January; running and standing painful, ankles swollen

☿ ☌ MC	MC □ ☿	♆ ☌ MC	April S. E. ☍ ♂
			(Swelling)

Asc. □ ♀   ♄ ∠ ☊   ♇ ∠ ♂   Oct. S. E. ☌ ☿
MC □ ☿
♄ ⚼ ☉
☽ ♍ January

3. 1978—rheumatoid arthritis confirmed by blood tests; in July started physical therapy

☉ ∠ ♂   ♂ ⚼ Asc.   ♄ ☌ ♂ July   April S. E. ⚼
                                                         E. P.

♂ △ ♃ₚ   ♆ □ ⚸   ♆ ☌ MC
Asc. 8 ☉   ♂ ∠ ☿
☿ □ ☽
☽ ☌ MCₚ July
☽ ☌ ♂ₚ August

4. 1979—some movement and walking

☉ ∠ ♂   ♇ ☌ ☿   Feb. S. E. ☌ Asc.
                                          ⚼ ♀
♃ ☌ ☊   Aug. S. E. ☌ ♂
♆ ☌ ☉
☽ ∠ ♃
♀ ∠ ♂
♄ □ Asc.
♄ ∠ ♅
☿ □ ♂

5. 1980—normal movement of limbs; started healing others

☉ ☌ MC   ♀ 8 ♄   ♆ ⚹ ☿   Feb. S. E. 8 ♂
☽ ☌ MC January   ⚸ □ MC   ♀ ☌ ☿   (Healing
                                                  others)
(Strong emphasis   ♀ □ MC (profes-
 on work)   sional work)
                    ☽ □ ♄
                    ♃ 8 Asc.

CASE HISTORY #2

The second case history is that of a young man whose arthritic symptoms began at the age of twenty-three. At that time, 1970, he experienced much pain around the area of the sciatic nerve. He saw an orthopedic surgeon who put him in a corset and gave him exercises to do. The pain continued and his back began to stiffen. His symptoms were diagnosed as osteoarthritis and in November 1973 he was placed in traction for a week.

In August 1976 he moved to the east coast where he worked and lived for two years. He found a chiropractor there who was able to give him weekly adjustments which alleviated his condition. He was also very much aware of his diet during that time going on frequent vegetable juice fasts, eliminating sugars and most other carbohydrates and proteins, maintaining himself on vegetables, fruits and some grains. He was fired from his job in May 1978 and moved back to the San Francisco area. He feels that everything went downhill from that time on.

His spine has continued to stiffen and he has pain in his hips, knees, back and shoulders. He walks with his body slightly bent over. He vacillates between being overly disciplined—doing his exercises, maintaining his diet, undergoing a two-week juice fast, to sitting back and smoking marijuana, eating "junk food" and ignoring his condition.

There is a very strong destructive urge within him and part of him would rather die. He is very intelligent, has read many books on arthritis, knows all the right things to do, but prefers to suffer. He also has a great deal of hostility toward society, feels frustrated in his work (electrical repairs), and wants to be involved in a more creative and professional occupation. As of this writing, his spine was diagnosed by both an M.D. and chiropractor as being that of an eighty-year-old man. He still seeks help but manages to negate any positive achievements.

Case History #2

♎ Asc., ♑ dwad	Need to relate to others; possible indecisiveness and extremism; tendency to be crystallized in habit patterns; emphasis on back and spine
♆ ☌ Asc.	Uncertainty regarding identity; highly intuitive and sensitive, tendency for escapism through alcohol and drugs; hypoglycemic tendency; prone to allergies
☉ in ♋, ♍ dwad	Receptivity; need for financial and emotional security; concern with health; need to be of service to others
☉ ☌ MC	Wants to be strongly involved in career or profession; with Sun on MC need for recognition in outside world

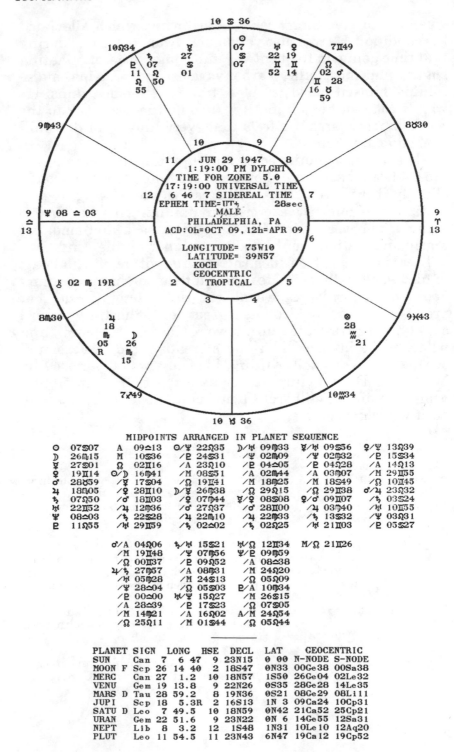

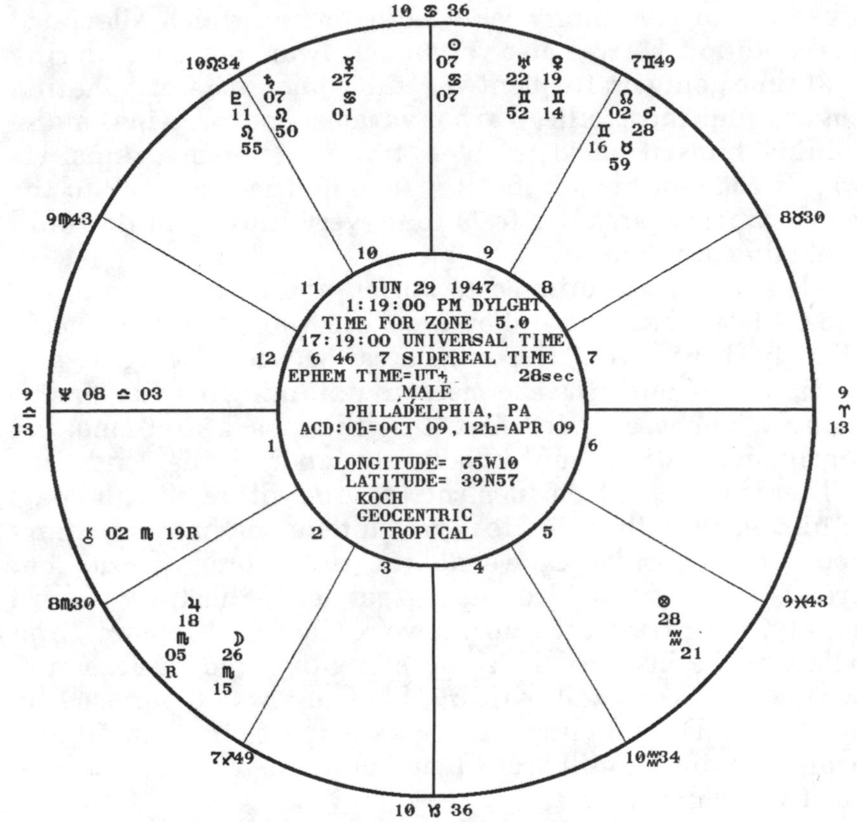
10 ♋ 36
10♌34
7♊49
9♍43
8♉30
9 ♎ 13
Ψ 08 ♎ 03
9 ♈ 13
⚷ 02 ♏ 19R
8♏30
9♓43
7♐49
10♒34
10 ♑ 36
JUN 29 1947
1:19:00 PM DYLGHT
TIME FOR ZONE 5.0
17:19:00 UNIVERSAL TIME
6 46 7 SIDEREAL TIME
EPHEM TIME=UT+ 28sec
MALE
PHILADELPHIA, PA
ACD:0h=OCT 09,12h=APR 09
LONGITUDE= 75W10
LATITUDE= 39N57
KOCH
GEOCENTRIC
TROPICAL

MIDPOINTS ARRANGED IN PLANET SEQUENCE

☉	07♋07	A	09♎13	☉/♆	22♌35	☽/♅	09♍33	☿/♅	09♋56	♀/♆	13♌39
☽	26♏15	M	10♋36	/♇	24♋31	/♆	02♏09	/♆	02♍32	/♇	15♋34
☿	27♋01	☊	02♊16	/A	23♌10	/♇	04♎05	/♇	04♌28	/A	14♌13
♀	19♊14	☉/☽	16♍41	/M	08♋51	/A	02♏44	/A	03♍07	/M	29♊55
♂	28♉59	/☿	17♋04	/☊	19♊41	/M	18♍25	/M	18♋49	/☊	10♊45
♃	18♏05	/♀	28♊10	☽/☿	26♍38	/☊	29♌15	/☊	29♊38	♂/♃	23♌32
♄	07♌50	/♂	18♊03	/♀	07♍44	☿/♀	08♋08	♀/♂	09♊07	/♄	03♋24
♅	22♊52	/♃	12♍36	/♂	27♌37	/♂	28♊00	/♃	03♍40	/♅	10♊55
♆	08♎03	/♄	22♋28	/♃	22♏10	/♃	22♍33	/♄	13♋32	/♆	03♌31
♇	11♌55	/♅	29♊59	/♄	02♎02	/♄	02♌25	/♅	21♊03	/♇	05♋27

♂/A	04♌06	♄/♅	15♋21	♅/☊	12♊34	M/☊	21♊26
/M	19♊48	/♆	07♍56	♆/♇	09♍59		
/☊	00♊37	/♇	09♌52	/A	08♎38		
♃/♄	27♍57	/A	08♍31	/M	24♌20		
/♅	05♍28	/M	24♋13	/☊	05♌09		
/♆	28♎04	/☊	05♋03	♇/A	10♍34		
/♇	00♎00	♅/♆	15♌27	/M	26♋15		
/A	28♎39	/♇	17♋23	/☊	07♋05		
/M	14♍21	/A	16♌02	A/M	24♌54		
/☊	25♌11	/M	01♋44	/☊	05♌44		

PLANET		SIGN	LONG	HSE	DECL	LAT	GEOCENTRIC N-NODE	S-NODE
SUN		Can	7 6 47	9	23N15	0 00		
MOON	F	Scp	26 14 40	2	18S47	0N33	00Ge38	00Sa38
MERC		Can	27 1.2	10	18N57	1S50	26Ge04	02Le32
VENU		Gem	19 13.8	9	22N26	0S35	28Ge28	14Le35
MARS	D	Tau	28 59.2	8	19N36	0S21	08Ge29	08Li11
JUPI		Scp	18 5.3R	2	16S13	1N 3	09Ca24	10Cp31
SATU	D	Leo	7 49.5	10	18N59	0N42	21Ca52	25Cp21
URAN		Gem	22 51.6	9	23N22	0N 6	14Ge55	12Sa31
NEPT		Lib	8 3.2	12	1S48	1N31	10Le10	12Aq20
PLUT		Leo	11 54.5	11	23N43	6N47	19Ca12	19Cp52

☉ □ ♆, Asc.	Lack of energy and etheric leak
☽ in ♏, ♍ dwad	Healing ability; tendency to have fixed habit patterns; need to transform emotional reactions in more objective manner; emphasis on health; desire for perfection
☽ ☌ ♃	Growth through healing, metaphysical studies
☽ ☍ ♂	Tendency to be overly emotional; outbursts of anger
♀ in ♊	May express creativity in mental way; multi-talented; difficulty in staying with one relationship
♀ ☌ ⚷	Tendency to celibacy; need to work in creative way
♀ ☌ ♅	Unusual creative talent; talent for writing and communication; erratic functioning of thyroid gland related to neurological system
♄ in ♌ in 10th house	Strong sense of responsibility; need to assume leadership and authority in profession
♄ ☌ ♀	Healing work; focus on personal transformation
☿ △ ☽	Ability to express ideas fluently
☊ in 8th house in ♊	Study of healing arts, metaphysics; using new ideas as a catalyst to growth
☽ contra ∥ ☿	Changes mind easily, indecisive
☿ in 10th house in ♋	Strong sense of responsibility; need to assume leadership and authority in profession

MIDPOINTS

☉/☽ = ♂ (inverse)	Importance of healing work; personal health crises
♂/♅ = ☿ (inverse)	Sensitive nervous system; respiratory allergies;

♂/♆ = ⚷, ♀ (inverse)	Possible difficulty in perceiving emotional situations clearly; tendency to low blood sugar and difficulty metabolizing carbohydrates
♂/♄ = ♃ (inverse)	Restriction in functioning of liver and pancreas

Secondary Progressions	Solar Arc Directions	Transits	Eclipses

1. **August-September 1970—sciatic problem; consulted orthopedic surgeon**

☿ ☌ ♀	MC □ ⚷	♆ ☌ ☽	Feb. L.E. □ ☊
♀ ∠ ☊	⚷ ∠ Asc.	♅ ☌ Asc.	Aug. L.E. □ ☽
MC □ ⚷	♀ ⚼ ☽	♄ ∠ ☉	
☽ ∥ ♆	☿ ☌ ♂/♆	♇ ∠ ♇	
☽ ∠ ♃ Sept.		♃ ☌ ⚷	
(Jupiter rules the sciatic nerve)			

2. **November 1973—in the hospital in traction**

MC ∥ ♄	♅ ∠ ☊	♃ □ ♄	June S.E. ☌ ☉
MC ∠ ♀	♄ □ ☊	♄ ⚼ ♃	Dec. L.E. ☌ ♀
MC ∥ ☿	☊ ∠ ♇	♅ □ ☿	Aug. L.E. □ ♄/♆
♂ ⚻ ♃	♀ ∠ ♂	♆ ⚻ ☉	
♂ ☌ ☉/☽	Asc. ⚼ ♀	♇ ☌ ♆ □ ☉	
♂ ⚼ ⚷	☿ ∠ ☉		
	☉ □ ⚷		
	♆ ☌ ☉/☽		

3. **August 1976—moved to New Jersey for two years and had chiropratic adjustments**

MC ☌ ♄	MC ☌ ♄	♃ ☍ ☽	May L.E. ☌ ☽
☿ ∥ ☿	MC ∠♅	♄ ☌ ♄	Oct. S.E. ☌ ⚷
MC ∠ ♅	♂ ∠ ♇	♅ ☌ ⚷	
Asc. ⚻ ☊	♀ ∠ ☊	♆ △ ♇	
♂ ∥ MC		♇ ☌ ♆, Asc.	
♂ ☌ ♀			
Asc. ☌ ⚷			
☽ ☍ ♀ August			

4. **May 1978—fired from job and moved back to San Francisco area**

♀ ☌ ☿	☿ □ ☽	♂ ☌ ♄♇	March L.E. □ ☉
☽ □ Asc.	♆ □ ♄	♃ ☌ ☉	Sept. L.E. □ ♅
☉ ☌ ♄	♆ ⚼ ♅	♄ □ ☽	Oct. S.E. ☌ ♆ Asc.
Asc. ⚼ ♀	⚷ ☍ ☊	♆ ☍ ♀ ∠ ⚷	
		♇ △ ⩡ ⚻ ♂	

CHAPTER FIFTEEN

CANCER

The rapid increase of the dis-ease known as cancer reflects the conditions of the times in which we live. Increased societal stresses, the proliferation of pollutants in the air we breath and the water we drink, the depletion of our soil and subsequent effect on the nutritional value of the foods grown in it, place our bodies in a lowered state of resistance. Added to this, the tensions of our daily life and emotional traumas cause us to turn inward and our individual power becomes thwarted.

The combination of these factors can affect the metabolic structure of our bodies in a variety of ways. The weakened action of the pancreas and the liver often manifests as hypoglycemia and diabetes. In more extreme states it can contribute to the metabolic diseases known collectively as cancer.

There are many explanations for the change in the physiology of the cell which are referred to as malignant cells or cancer cells. Stephanie and Carl Simonton in their book *Getting Well Again* have explored the thesis that our emotional states have the power to change the physiology of the cells. To this end, the Simontons have worked with various types of therapy and with the technique of visualization where the mind can visualize the body in a totally healthy state, and thereby change the malignant cells to normal ones. Others have proposed that a virus or invading bacteria is responsible for cellular change and depletes the individual immune system as well. Still others have emphasized the environmental causes of cancer—pollution in the air and water and increased amounts of radiation to which we are all subject.

Detoxifying the body through juice fasting, enemas and colonic irrigations has proved helpful in many cases as it helps to cleanse the liver and pancreas and allows the metabolic system to regain its balance. Certain homeopathic remedies have been beneficial depending on the individual and his particular constitution. Body therapies are also important in helping the individual to relax and stimulate the vital energy.

None of these treatments, however, is effective without handling the emotional and psychological roots of the condition.

It is significant that many children are being born with various types of cancer or being diagnosed as having cancer in their early years. If we accept the belief in re-embodiment or reincarnation, then we accept the fact that each of us has chosen to come into this lifetime with certain karmic patterns—physical, emotional, and spiritual—with which we have been working over a span of several lifetimes for our own evolution.

The genetic blueprint that predisposes to cancer runs in certain families and is, therefore, part of the karmic pattern of that family.

Some children come in for a brief time to teach their parents various lessons of compassion and non-attachment; others need to develop these qualities themselves for some future work they will be doing. Therefore their early years may often involve a certain amount of suffering and dealing with the death of their peers through working in children's healing groups. Often they are being trained as doctors, healers and therapists at an early age.

In some cases hormonal preparations were given to the mothers of these children. One of these, DES, or Diethyl-stilbestrol, was a preparation prescribed as a contraceptive. The daughters of some of these women developed vaginal cancer as a result.[1]

PSYCHOLOGICAL

Now let us consider some of the psychological causes and stress situations that are involved in the cancer personality.

---

[1] *Women And The Crisis In Sex Hormones*, Barbara Seaman and Gideon Seaman, M.D. p. 11

Many of these people are strong individuals who present a weak facade due to various emotional insecurities. Some of them have been rejected by their families; others have had difficulties with one or both parents. Angular Moons are prevalent in these horoscopes, implicating emotional factors; the Moon also has several hard aspects, indicating problems to be worked out with the mother as well. A therapist in Michigan told me that when he regressed his cancer patients back to the fetal state, they all felt unwanted.

In some cases, there is a great deal of anger and resentment which has been held in check. Since the emotion anger corresponds to the liver in the Oriental system of healing, we can understand why the liver and pancreas play such an important role in the physiology of cancer. The planet Jupiter, which rules the liver and the pancreas as well as tumors and unrestrained growth, figures prominently in these horoscopes—being angular or conjoined the Sun or Moon.

The predominance of fixed signs astrologically points to yet another trait shared by many of these individuals—that of rigid habit patterns which are difficult to break. This dominance in the fixed signs also indicates a very strong will. In addition to the Sun, Moon, and Ascendant being in fixed signs, the nodes of the Moon were also found to have a fixed sign emphasis. The nodes of the Moon, like the Moon itself, relate to the emotional make-up and patterning of the soul through various incarnations.

Another shared trait is extreme sensitivity and vulnerability to outside forces. Many of the cancer patients I have worked with feel victimized by society, and it is difficult for them to build up confidence in themselves. Astrologically, this extreme sensitivity and tendency to become victims is shown by the strong placement of the planet Neptune. Neptune is often angular, conjunct the Sun or Moon, or there may be several planets in Pisces. Neptune can be the mystic or seer when properly channelled; he can also be the martyr or victim when the energies are turned inward. Neptune also governs the lymphatic system and the lymphocytes which are responsible for immunity.

Cancer has often been termed an underground disease and

the secretive guarded nature of those who develop it has been observed. Astrologically, the planet Pluto and the sign Scorpio are very prominent in these horoscopes. A strong Plutonian personality can keep things well hidden— problems may begin to fester before they are forced to the surface and show themselves. The Plutonian personality also must face the issue of death and dying and the continuous process of transformation. Healing qualities are strong in these individuals, and it is not coincidental that so many of them have to go through their own self-healing process before they can manifest this energy in their work with others.

A picture then emerges of a sensitive being who often holds his feelings in check or allows himself to be victimized by others. When the disease syndrome known as cancer is discovered, it is time to examine all of these old patterns and to transform the energy. With all of the water planets (Moon, Neptune and Pluto) prominent the emotional side of the nature is emphasized as well as the potential for expansion and rebirth.

ASTROLOGICAL PATTERNS

General astrological configurations, therfore, include the predominance of fixed signs, a prominent Moon with several hard aspects to it, and often angular Jupiter, Neptune and Pluto.

There are also several midpoints that are important in working with cancer in addition to the midpoints for general health diagnosis. They are:

Moon/Neptune - overaccumulation of water in the tissues of the body.

Mars/Jupiter - relationship between the liver and adrenals, increased metabolic changes.

Jupiter/Saturn - restrictive action of the liver and pancreas.

Jupiter/Uranus - unexpected cellular growth and change.

Jupiter/Neptune - toxic conditions of the liver and pancreas, increase of water in the blood.

Jupiter/Pluto - expansion of cellular growth, regeneration of the organs.

Midpoint patterns commonly found in the horoscopes of cancer patients are:

Saturn/Neptune = Pluto - this combination indicates a chronic condition or one where the body undergoes a strong regenerative process.

Moon/Neptune = Pluto - emotional upheaval and catharsis, transforming the balance of liquids in the body.

Jupiter/Neptune = Moon - another very emotional combination indicating faulty metabolism, often found in the charts of those with hypoglycemia and allergies.

Jupiter/Pluto = Ascendant - with the Ascendant representing the physical body this grouping emphasizes the regenerative quality of the body organs, especially liver and pancreas.

Jupiter/Pluto = Venus - Venus represents the blood sugar and with Jupiter and Pluto relates to improper carbohydrate metabolism.

Jupiter/Neptune = Venus - also refers to faulty carbohydrate metabolism, and abnormal sugar level in the blood.

CASE HISTORY #1

The first case pertains to a lady whose bout with cancer was a true catalyst to her spiritual growth. As a child and adolescent she was physically very healthy with strong recuperative powers. At age sixteen she was involved in an automobile accident and suffered a severe concussion and multiple fractures of the ribs.

Having been brought up in a strict Catholic background, she had a strong belief in the Immaculate Conception, and never wanted to have sex. This pattern was broken after her marriage, but her sex urge diminished when she became pregnant. As she was growing up, she had no belief in God or a spiritual framework of existence. She had two strong fears—one was of cancer and the other of death. Her father died when she was sixteen and she became extremely angry. Later she underwent therapy and got in touch with the causes of her anger.

In May 1978, her twenty-ninth year, when she was about eight months pregnant, a small nodule was discovered on her breast. The mammogram first reported it negative, but later it was found to be positive. She had a mastectomy on May 10, used little medication, and four weeks later, had a baby boy by caesarean section. She recovered quickly from both operations and was in good spirits.

In September 1978 she developed a pain in her hip. She was told by the oncologist that it was probably a disc affecting the sciatic nerve. A few months later, X-rays revealed a large tumor on the femur. The doctors decided that her ovaries should be removed, because estrogen often feeds malignant growths. Even though the estrogen receptor analysis was negative they went ahead and removed her ovaries on January 23, 1979. At this time, she became discouraged.

Soon after the operation she was introduced to the Simonton technique of meditation and visualization. She says she was "awakened to the universal life force" at that time, and since then her life has been very joyful with many wonderful teachers coming to her.

Malignancy also was discovered in areas of her spine and ribs. She has been treated with both radiotherapy and chemotherapy. In October 1979, when she was carrying her child upstairs, she leaned on her weak side, her legs gave way, and the sciatic nerve was damaged.

In a channelling with a reputable spiritual channel she was told that the six years of birth control pills had contributed much to her disease. Her Catholic upbringing had been a strong factor in causing her to reject and negate feelings concerning her body. She was advised to get in touch with her subconscious to reprogram her attitudes about her body.

She started working with an herbalist and a psychic healer and began to feel more comfortable. The cancer, however, spread and in August 1980 she left her body and passed on to another plane of consciousness.

Case History #1

The general pattern is a funnel chart with the Moon in Aquarius on the MC. This points to an extremely emotional nature, and a highly individualistic personality. It also shows one who is deeply concerned with humanity and may be involved with humanitarian projects and endeavors.

☉ in ♏ in 5th house, ♉ dwad	Strong involvement in healing, particularly with children; transforming of sexual energy through creativity and healing
☉ □ ♀ in 3rd house	Tendency to poor circulation
T-square with ♀ ☊ □ ☉ □ ☽ in fixed signs	Deep-rooted habit patterns hard to break; transforming of emotional and sexual energy; feeling of a personal mission involving the nurturing of others
☉ ∠ ♃ in ♐ in 7th house	Tendency to overdo in extending energy to people and various projects; liver and pancreas affected
☉ ⚼ ♅ in 1st house in ♋	Rebellious against traditional modes; tries to integrate new ideas and change into her life and healing work
☉ ⚻ Asc.	Lowered energy and vitality
☽ in ♒, ♏ dwad	Emphasizes interest in service and humanitarian work, health and healing
☽ in ♒, ♅ in ♋ in mutual reception	Nurturing and caring for others a strong part of her work
Grand trine in air signs Asc. △ ☽ △ ♆	Strongly inspired; good creative flow; work involves a deep spiritual commitment and communication
☽ ☍ ♀	Needs to work with old emotional patterns and change them; needs to channel sexual energy and use it in a more detached and less emotional manner; possible problems involving reproductive system
♊ Asc., ♑ dwad	Diversified interests; need to communicate but tendency to hold back
Asc. ⚹ ♀ ☊	Working with others in a caring, nurturing manner
☿ in ♎ in 5th house ☌ ⚷	Sensitive nervous system; writing, communicating with others through some creative mode; working with children
☿ △ ♅ in 1st house	Good intuitive flow; utilization of new ideas

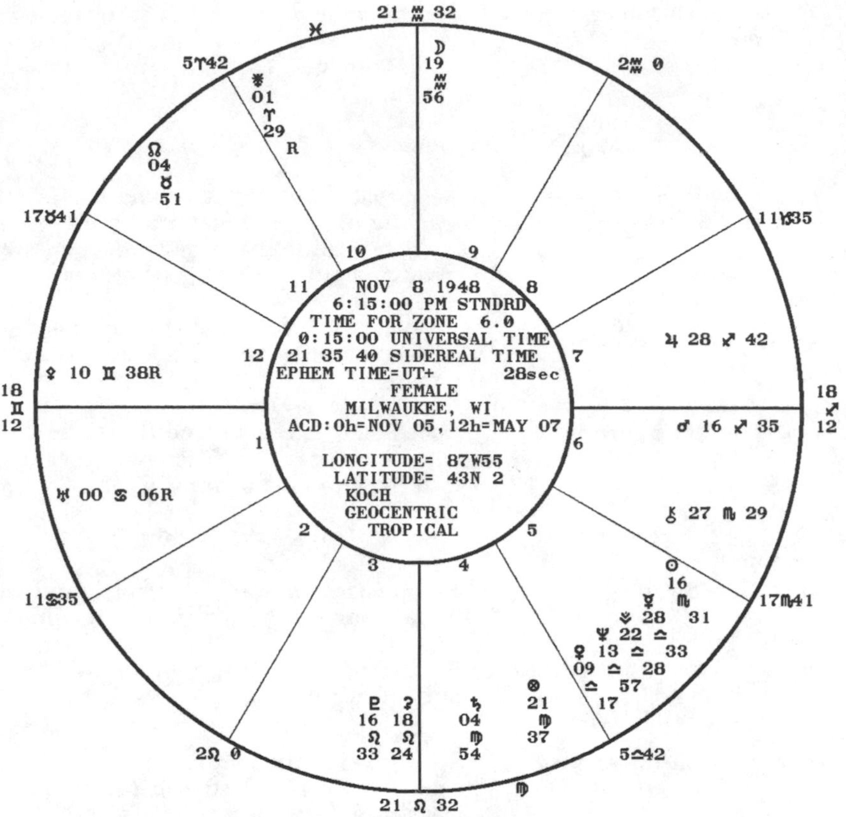

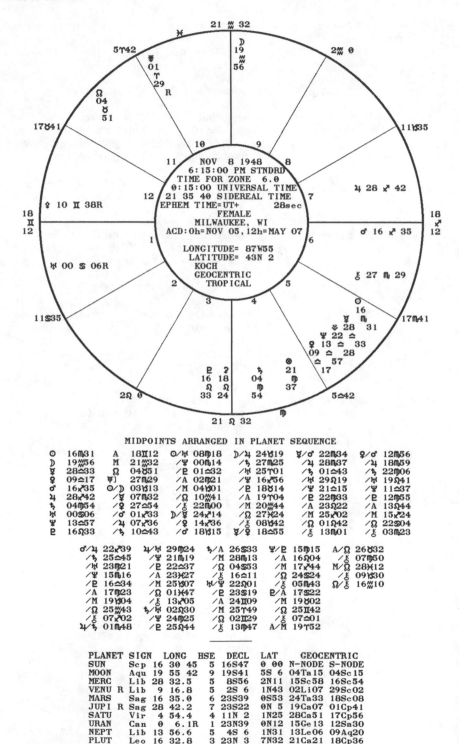

MIDPOINTS ARRANGED IN PLANET SEQUENCE

☉	16♏31	A	18♊12	☉/♅	08♍18	☽/♃	24♑19	☿/♂	22♏34	♀/♂	12♏56
☽	19♒56	M	21♒32	/♆	00♏14	/♄	27♏25	/♃	28♏37	/♃	18♏59
☿	28♎33	☊	04♉51	/♇	01♎32	/♅	25♈01	/♄	01♎43	/♄	22♍06
♀	09♎17	Ψ]	27♏29	/A	02♍21	/♆	16♐56	/♅	29♌19	/♅	19♌41
♂	16♐35	☉/☽	03♑13	/M	04♑01	/♇	18♉14	/♆	21♎15	/♆	11♎37
♃	28♐42	/☿	07♏32	/☊	10♒41	/A	19♈04	/♇	22♍33	/♇	12♍55
♄	04♍54	/♀	27♎54	/⚷	22♏00	/M	20♒44	/A	23♌22	/A	13♌44
♅	00♋06	/♂	01♐33	☽/☿	24♐14	/☊	27♓24	/M	25♐02	/M	15♐24
♆	13♎57	/♃	07♐36	/♀	14♐36	/⚷	08♑42	/☊	01♌42	/☊	22♋04
♇	16♌33	/♄	10♎43	/♂	18♑15	☿/♀	18♎55	/⚷	13♏01	/⚷	03♏23

♂/♃	22♐39	♃/♅	29♍24	♄/A	26♋33	♆/♇	15♍15	A/☊	26♉32
/♄	25♎45	/♆	21♏19	/M	28♏13	/A	16♌04	/⚷	07♍50
/♅	23♍21	/♇	22♎37	/☊	04♋53	/M	17♐44	M/☊	28♓12
/♆	15♏16	/A	23♓27	/⚷	16♎11	/☊	24♋24	/⚷	09♑30
/♇	16♎34	/M	25♑07	♅/♆	22♌01	/⚷	05♏43	☊/⚷	16♒10
/A	17♍23	/☊	01♓47	/♇	23♋19	♇/A	17♋22		
/M	19♑04	/⚷	13♐05	/A	24♊09	/M	19♉02		
/☊	25♒43	♄/♅	02♌30	/M	25♈49	/☊	25♊42		
/⚷	07♐02	/♆	24♍25	/☊	02♊29	/⚷	07♎01		
♃/♄	01♏48	/♇	25♌44	/⚷	13♍47	A/M	19♈52		

PLANET		SIGN	LONG	HSE	DECL	LAT	GEOCENTRIC	
SUN		Scp	16 30 45	5	16S47	0 00	N-NODE	S-NODE
MOON		Aqu	19 55 42	9	19S41	5S 6	04Ta15	04Sc15
MERC		Lib	28 32.5	5	8S56	2N11	15Sc58	16Sc54
VENU	R	Lib	9 16.8	5	2S 6	1N43	02Li07	29Sc02
MARS		Sag	16 35.0	6	23S39	0S53	24Ta33	18Sc08
JUPI	R	Sag	28 42.2	7	23S22	0N 5	19Ca07	01Cp41
SATU		Vir	4 54.4	4	11N 2	1N25	28Ca51	17Cp56
URAN		Can	0 6.1R	1	23N39	0N12	15Ge13	12Sa30
NEPT		Lib	13 56.6	5	4S 6	1N31	13Le06	09Aq20
PLUT		Leo	16 32.8	3	23N 3	7N32	21Ca21	18Cp36

☿ ✳ ♃ in 7th house	Counseling, working to improve relationships with others
♀ ☌ ♆ in 5th house in ♎	Idealistic and compassionate nature; tendency to express self through music and poetry
♀ ♆ △ ⚷ in 12th house	Spiritual philosophy a part of her creative work
♂ in ♐ in 6th house ☍ Asc.	Energy channelled toward work and service; possible problems with liver, pancreas, sciatic nerve; possible accidents, surgeries
♂ ∠ ♇ in ♏ in 5th house	Reproductive system and problems in childbirth; health concerns a result of old emotional patterns
♃ in 7th house in ♐ ☍ ♅	Unusual partners who stimulate thinking and philosophical ideas; eclectic in her attitudes, tendency to be involved with too many causes; erratic functioning of pancreas and liver
♃ ⊡ ♀	Philosophical awareness helps to catalyze her growth and communication with others
♄ in ♍ in 4th house	Problems in childhood; strong authoritarian influence; need to perform service in work; concerned with own health
♄ △ ♃ in 7th house	Personal relationships help her to fulfill herself through service
♄ ⚻ ☉	Lessons learned through transformation of energy
♄ △ ☊ in 11th house grand △ with ♃ in 7th house	Working with groups and partnerships in a practical way through service-oriented disciplines
♂ in ♏ in 6th house ☐ ☽	Health problems involve reproductive organs and relate to emotions
Asc. ‖ ♅ and ♀ contra ‖ ♂ ♃	Rebellious, independent, highly sensitive nervous system; working on own growth

MIDPOINTS

♂ / ♆ = ☉	Sensitivity to toxins, lowered immune system, hypoglycemic tendency

☽ / ♆ = ♂, Asc.	Strong emotionality, hypersensitivity; susceptibility to infections, overaccumulation of water in cells
♃ / ♄ = Asc., ♂ (inverse)	Insecurity, lack of endurance; restrictions in functioning of gall bladder, liver and pancreas

Secondary Progressions	Solar Arc Directions	Transits	Eclipses

1. May 10, 1978—mastectomy; June 9, 1978—caesarean birth

Secondary Progressions	Solar Arc Directions	Transits	Eclipses
⊙ ☌ ♂ △ ♀	? □ ♂	*May 10*	March L. E. □ ♅
Asc. □ ♆	☿ ☌ ♂	⊙ ☍ ⊙ □ ☽	April S. E. ☍ ⚷
☿ ∠ ♀		☿ ☍ ⚷	
☿ ⚹ ♆		♀ ☌ Asc.	
♀ ⊓ ♅		♂ ⊓ ♃	
♂ □ ♀		♃ ⊓ ☽	
♃ △ ♄, ☊		♄ ☌ nadir	
☽ □ ♂ ⊼ ♀ June		♅ ☌ ⊙	
⊙ = ♆ / ♀		♆ ☌ ♂, Desc.	
		♇ ☌ ♆	
		June 9	
		⊙ ☌ Asc.	
		☿ ☌ ‡	
		♀ □ ⚷	
		♂ □ ♂	
		♃ ⊓ ♂	
		♄ □ ♂	
		♅ ∠ ♃ ☌ ⊙	
		♆ ☌ ♂	
		♇ ☌ ♆	

2. September 1978—pain in hip: January 23, 1979—ovaries removed

Secondary Progressions	Solar Arc Directions	Transits
☿ ☌ ♂ in ♐ (hip, sciatic nerve)	⊙ ☌ ♂	*Sept. 1978*
♀ ☌ ⊙	♀ ☌ V	♂ ☌ ☿, ☋
♀ □ ♇	♃ □ ☿	♃ △ nodes
♂ □ ♀	♇ □ ♂	♅ ∠ ♃ ☌ ⊙
	? □ Asc.	♆ ☌ ♂
		♇ ☌ ♆
		Jan. 23, 1979
		⊙♂ □ nodes
		☿ □ ⚷
		♀ ☌ ♂
		♃ □ nodes
		♄ ∠ ☿
		♅ □ ☽, MC
		♆ ☌ Desc.
		♇ △ ☽ ∠ ♄

3. October 1979—damage to hip while carrying child upstairs

☉ ☍ Asc. ☊ □ ♄	♅ □ ☽	Aug. S. E. □ ♂
☿ ☌ ♂	♃ ☌ ♄	Sept. L. E. □ ♂
Asc. ⊼ ♂	♄ ∠ ♅	
☽ ⊡ ♀ September	♆ ☌ Desc.	
☽ ⚹ ☉ September	♀ ∠ ♄	

4. August 1980—passed over

♀ ⊼ Asc. August ♆ ☌ ☉	♃ □ ♂	Aug. S. E. ☌ ♀ ?
	♄ □ ♃	
	♅ □ MC	
	♆ ☌ Desc.	
	♀ ∠ ♄	

CASE HISTORY #2

This history concerns a woman who has healed herself successfully of cancer. She has been an artist all her life, started a school for people who professed no creative talent, worked with handicapped children and was the director of a child development center. Later she opened her own art school and worked with a doctor in a stress-reduction program at a local hospital.

In 1974 she underwent a mastectomy to remove a lump on her breast. At this time she was ending a thirteen-year relationship with a man who had been the most important person in her life. After the mastectomy she had no problems but in 1978, another lump grew back on the chest wall at the same site. The oncologists insisted on chemotherapy and radiation, but she felt strongly that this was not the type of treatment to pursue. She speaks of this time period as the darkest in her whole life because she had to make a major decision and at the same time continuously "buck the authorities" who were pushing the chemotherapy.

She finally enrolled in a Laetrile program in which she was given Laetrile shots daily and drank lots of vegetable juices. She feels this program created more stress for her and she is not sure how much it helped. Then she heard about a new program at UCLA which used tomoxofin, a drug that suppresses hormone production. She went to UCLA and found, for the first time, some onocologists who did not believe she needed chemotherapy. She started taking two tablets of tomoxofin daily and has continued this for two years now. In addition, she improved her diet. She had been a vegetarian before the mastectomy. In 1978 she saw a chiropractic doctor who felt that her low vitality resulted from having always been hypoglycemic. He put her on a diet of root vegetables, which are cleansing for the system, and she continued this for two years. In 1980, she added some protein and grains to her diet. She also started meditation in 1978 and says she read the I-Ching which continuously supplied her with a message of encouragement and hope.

Out of her meditations and other studies evolved her Institute. She has fifty private clients a month in addition to teaching, and works with creative processes at several universities. She takes good care of herself and feels her physical vitality to be very high.

Case History #2

This horoscope shows a strong mutable influence with the majority of planets above the horizon, indicating an outgoing expansive personality.

☉ in ♊ in 11th house, ♑ dwad	Communication work with groups; structure and teaching a part of her work
☉ ☌ ☽ in ♊	Balsamic Moon type indicates one who is oriented to the future, a planter of seeds
☉ ☌ ☿	Intellectually curious; good writing ability
☉ □ ♂ in 9th house in ♓	Lack of physical energy; tendency to overdo things of a mental nature
☉ ⟑ ♄ in 4th house in ♏	Problems with father and with men; possible restrictions in home life; potential health problems involving the reproductive system
☽ in ♊, ♌ dwad	Creative application of her energy in communications and group work
☽ Q ♂	This aspect suggests some involvement with health through the Moon or organs ruled by the Moon, and with Mars, surgeries, accidents

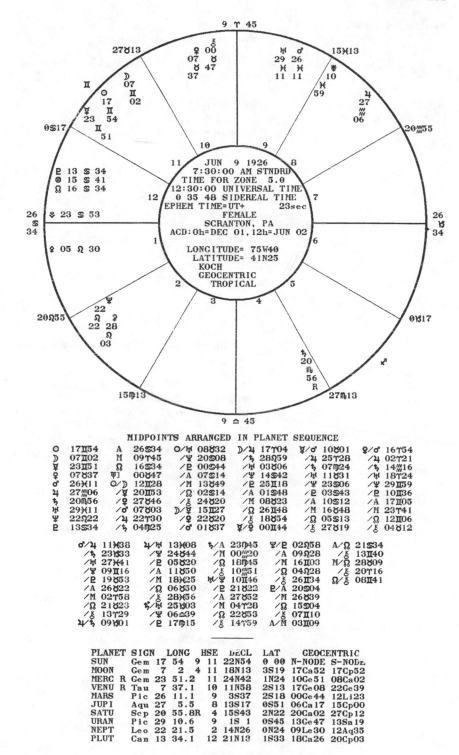

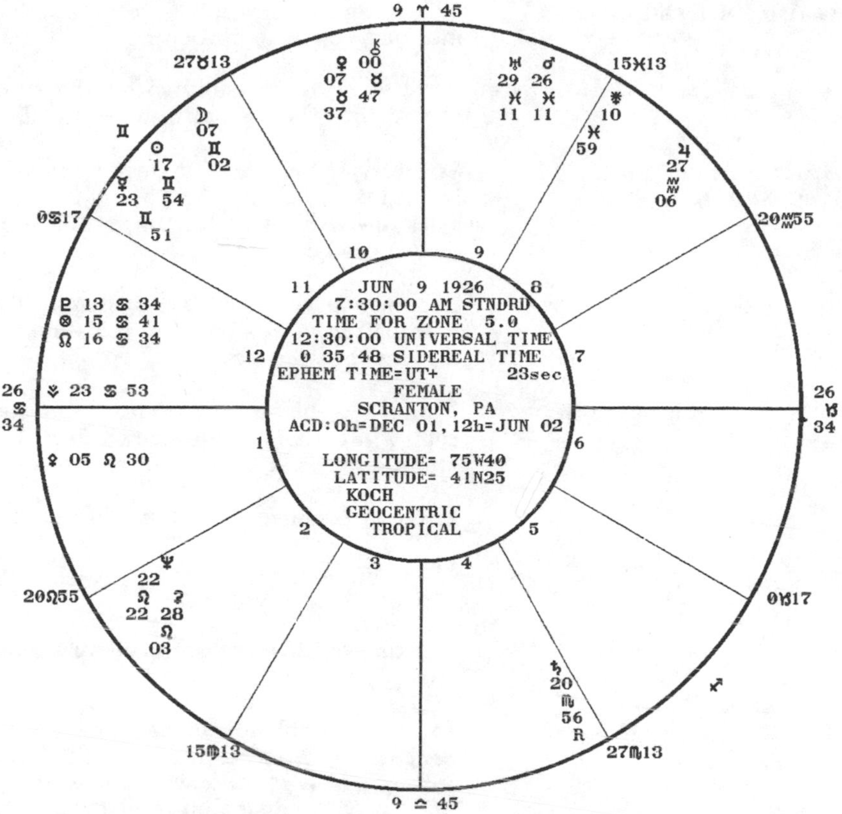
9 ♈ 45
27♉13
15♓13
0♋17
20♒55
26 ♋ 34
26 ♑ 34
20♌55
0♑17
15♍13
27♏13
9 ♎ 45
JUN 9 1926
7:30:00 AM STNDRD
TIME FOR ZONE 5.0
12:30:00 UNIVERSAL TIME
0 35 48 SIDEREAL TIME
EPHEM TIME=UT+ 23sec
FEMALE
SCRANTON, PA
ACD:0h=DEC 01,12h=JUN 02
LONGITUDE= 75W40
LATITUDE= 41N25
KOCH
GEOCENTRIC
TROPICAL

MIDPOINTS ARRANGED IN PLANET SEQUENCE

☉	17♊54	A	26♋34	☉/♅	08♉32	☽/♃	17♈04	☿/♂	10♉01	♀/♂	16♈54
☽	07♊02	M	09♈45	/♆	20♋08	/♄	28♌59	/♃	25♈28	/♃	02♈21
☿	23♊51	☊	16♋34	/♇	00♋44	/♅	03♉06	/♄	07♍24	/♄	14♒16
♀	07♉37	♆]	00♉47	/A	07♋14	/♆	14♋42	/♅	11♉31	/♅	18♈24
♂	26♓11	☉/☽	12♊28	/M	13♉49	/♇	25♊18	/♆	23♋06	/♆	29♊59
♃	27♒06	/☿	20♊53	/☊	02♋14	/A	01♋48	/♇	03♋43	/♇	10♊36
♄	20♏56	/♀	27♉46	/⚷	24♉20	/M	08♉23	/A	10♋12	/A	17♊05
♅	29♓11	/♂	07♉03	☽/☿	15♊27	/☊	26♊48	/M	16♉48	/M	23♈41
♆	22♌22	/♃	22♈30	/♀	22♉20	/⚷	18♉54	/☊	05♋13	/☊	12♊06
♇	13♋34	/♄	04♍25	/♂	01♉37	☿/♀	00♊44	/⚷	27♉19	/⚷	04♉12

♂/♃	11♓38	♃/♅	13♓08	♄/A	23♍45	♆/♇	02♌58	A/☊	21♋34
/♄	23♑33	/♆	24♉44	/M	00♒20	/A	09♌28	/⚷	13♊40
/♅	27♓41	/♇	05♉20	/☊	18♍45	/M	16♊03	M/☊	28♉09
/♆	09♊16	/A	11♉50	/⚷	10♒51	/☊	04♌28	/⚷	20♈16
/♇	19♉53	/M	18♓25	♅/♆	10♊46	/⚷	26♊34	☊/⚷	08♊41
/A	26♉22	/☊	06♉50	/♇	21♉22	♇/A	20♋04		
/M	02♈58	/⚷	28♓56	/A	27♉52	/M	26♉39		
/☊	21♉23	♄/♅	25♑03	/M	04♈28	/☊	15♋04		
/⚷	13♈29	/♆	06♎39	/☊	22♉53	/⚷	07♊10		
♃/♄	09♑01	/♇	17♍15	/⚷	14♈59	A/M	03♊09		

PLANET	SIGN	LONG	HSE	DECL	LAT	GEOCENTRIC N-NODE	S-NODE
SUN	Gem	17 54 9	11	22N54	0 00		
MOON	Gem	7 2 4	11	18N13	3S19	17Ca52	17Cp52
MERC R	Gem	23 51.2	11	24N42	1N24	10Ge51	08Ca02
VENU R	Tau	7 37.1	10	11N58	2S13	17Ge08	22Ge39
MARS	Pic	26 11.1	9	3S37	2S18	00Ge44	12Li23
JUPI	Aqu	27 5.5	8	13S17	0S51	06Ca17	15Cp00
SATU	Scp	20 55.8R	4	15S43	2N22	20Ca02	27Cp12
URAN	Pic	29 10.6	9	1S 1	0S45	13Ge47	13Sa19
NEPT	Leo	22 21.5	2	14N26	0N24	09Le30	12Aq35
PLUT	Can	13 34.1	12	21N13	1S33	18Ca26	20Cp03

♋ Asc., ♉ dwad	Nurturing and healing in a practical manner; cooking, gardening
⚷ ☌ Asc.	Hard working; possibly with children or caring for others; careful with details
Grand trine in water— Asc. ⚷ △ ♄ △ ♂ ♅	Strong spiritual quality, deeply involved in philosophical teachings and spiritual work, sense of discipline in putting forth new ideas
☿ □ ♂ ♅	Supersensitive nervous system; communication of new ideas of a metaphysical and healing nature
☿ △ ♃ in 8th house in ♒	Ability to bring forth ideas that are somewhat unusual and innovative; this stimulates her growth and expansion
☿ ⊼ ♄	Possible problems with nervous system
♀ ☌ ♂ in ♉ in 10th house	Professional healer; use of artistic capabilities in healing work
♀ ∠ ♂	Working to integrate spiritual and sexual energy
T-square ♃, ♄, ♆	Idealistic, tendency to be unrealistic in concepts for projects and failure to follow through; in a positive way, the energy of ♄ is used to discipline and ground the projects; this T-square points to possible problems with the liver and pancreas, and a tendency to hypoglycemia
♃ □ ♇ in 12th house	Working in a more spiritual and inner way on her own growth
♆ in 2nd house in ♌	Could tend to be overly generous with money, allowing money to slip through her fingers easily
♆ ☌ ?	Nurturing in a more spiritual way, through the use of the arts and music
♇ ☌ ☊ in 12th house	Healing and nurturing others; learning through her own growth and transformation
♇ ‖ Asc.	Strong Plutonian emphasis; needing to continuously work on own evolution

MIDPOINTS

♂/♆ = ☽	Possible feelings of insecurity, over-sensitivity; susceptibility to infection, particularly in female organs; hypoglycemic tendency
♂/♄ = ☽ (inverse)	Tendency to hold back feelings; problems with bones or structure of body
♂/♀ = ♄	Hard-working, overcomes obstacles; possible problems with reproductive system
♃/♄ = ♆ (inverse)	Toxic conditions involving pancreas, liver and gall-bladder

Secondary Progressions	Solar Arc Directions	Transits	Eclipses

1. September 1973—mastectomy

Secondary Progressions	Solar Arc Directions	Transits	Eclipses
☿ ☌ ♆	♀ ☌ ⚷	♃ ⚼ ☉	June L. E. □ ♂
♂ □ Asc.	♆ ⚻ ♀	♄ ⚼ ♄	June S. E. ∠ ♆
☉ ∠ ☉	Asc. ⚹ ♃	♅ □ ⚷ E. P.	July L.E. ☌ E.P.
♃ ∠ MC		♅ ⚹ ♆ △ ♀	Dec. L. E. ☌ ☉
MC ⚼ MC		♆ ☍ ☽	
☽ □ MC_P ⚻ ⚷ =		♀ ∠ ♄	
♃/♆ September			
☉ = ♆/♀			

2. January 1979—lump returned: removal by surgery

Secondary Progressions	Solar Arc Directions	Transits	Eclipses
☉ □ ♀	☿ ⚼ ♅	♃ ☌ ⚷ ♀	Sept. L. E. ☌ ♂♂
♀ □ MC	☊ □ ☽	♃ ☌ ♃/♀	Oct. S. E. ☌ Nadir
♂ ☌ ♂	⚷ ☍ ♂	♄ ⚹ ♀	Feb. S. E. □ ☽
☽ ∠ ♂ January	♆ ∠ ⚷	♅ ☌ ♄	
	☉ ∠ ☿	♆ ☍ ☉	
		♀ △ ☉	

Appendix A

CALCULATION OF MIDPOINTS

Midpoints should always be calculated by the planets' order in the zodiac. There are several ways of calculating midpoints. Two of the simplest will be illustrated here.

Method I

1. Subtract the difference between the two planets. If ♀ is 4♊ and ♂ 16♏, ♊ to ♏ would be five signs or 150°, 16 – 4 = 12, that gives 150° + 12° = 162°.
2. Divide 162° by 2 giving 81°.
3. Add 81° to 4°♊ – 60° would be two signs. Adding this, plus 21° more, to 4°♊, gives 25° ♌ (i.e. 2 signs, plus 21°).

Method II

The following table can be used:

0	♈ –	0°
0	♉ –	30°
0	♊ –	60°
0	♋ –	90°
0	♌ –	120°
0	♍ –	150°
0	♎ –	180°
0	♏ –	210°
0	♐ –	240°
0	♑ –	270°
0	♒ –	300°
0	♓ –	330°

1. ♀ in 4♊ is 60° (for 0° ♊) + 4 = 64°.
   ♂ in 16♏ is 210° (for 0° ♏) + 16 = 226° (64° + 226° = 290°).

2. Divide by 2 (290° ÷ 2 = 145°).
3. 145° = 120° (0° ♌) + 25 = 25° ♌

CALCULATION OF VERTEX

Subtract the latitude of the birth from 90 ; this is the co-latitude. The I.C. of the horoscope (4th house cusp) is then used as the M.C. and for that M.C., the ascendant at the co-latitude becomes the vertex. The anti-vertex is always exactly opposite the vertex.

ASTROLOGICAL BIRTH CONTROL

The concept of Astrological Birth Control has been a very murky issue since the work of Dr. Eugen Jonas was first introduced into this country by Sheila Ostrander and Lynn Schroeder in their book, *Psychic Discoveries Behind the Iron Curtain*. Dr. Jonas, a gynecologist and psychiatrist who was head of the Psychiatric Department of the State clinic in Nagysurany, Czechoslovakia, had been experimenting with a cosmic fertility cycle based on the angle between the Sun and Moon in a woman's birth chart. Since many good results were achieved through his work, the Czech government allowed him to set up the Astro Research Center for Planned Parenthood in Nitra, Czechoslovakia. More recently, an organization was started in Vienna, known as Astra International, in order to make Jonas' work available to people all over the world.

However, it is of prime importance to understand that we do not have Dr. Jonas' completed work available in this country. The information that has been popularized is based only on a partial knowledge of his discoveries. I quote from a letter written by Dr. Jonas himself to Jim Shere, an Astrologer and former president of the ICHA (International Committee for a Humanistic Astrology) presently residing in Occidental, Ca. The letter is dated Jan. 23, 1971.

"Nobody from the USA has so far been to see me in Czechoslavakia and nobody has asked for any work or publications of mine. Nevertheless I have learned from some extracts of papers that were published in your country that some people had come to see me from the USA and they write such things about my work that I was greatly surprised with what ideas people can have. All the information about myself and

my work that I had read and understood is not based
on truth"

Using Jonas' theories, Robert Kimball, an astrologer from
Santa Rosa, Ca. and Bill Kautz from Palo Alto, California
did statistical research utilizing 800 cases (see Dean's *Recent
Advances in Natal Astrology*). They found that for most
American women, conception seems to occur at the normal
ovulation time and not during the lunar phase. They also
found the astrological predetermination of sex to be less than
seventy percent effective in this country. However, it is
important to note that the cases they used were women who
already had children, and worked backwards to determine
their dates of conception, rather than using recent cases of
women as they conceived. Another astrologer, Judi Zeisler of
San Francisco, California, is currently doing research on
this. To date, she has only 133 cases, but has found the
cosmic cycle to be extremely relevant in these cases.

The most practical solution to the birth control problem
seems to be to incorporate both cycles and to determine
carefully the ovulation time through the basal temperature
and vaginal mucous method. Both of these methods, along
with much fine information on mental birth control and
tables for the Sun-Moon angle are given in the *Natural Birth
Control Book* by Art Rosenblum. (Aquarian Research
Foundation, Philadelphia, Pennsylvania). This book has
been carefully revised every two years to report new de-
velopments on the fertility cycles and feedback from women
who are using various forms of this method. Included in the
book are instructions for calculating the lunar angle for those
who do not have an astrological chart.

Two other books are worth mentioning here—*Lunaception*
by Louise Lacey and *Mental Birth Control* by Mildred
Jackson, N.D. and Terri Teague, N.D. Louise reports on the
twenty-nine women who worked with regulating their ovulation cycle by leaving a light on in the bedroom on the
fourteenth, fifteenth and sixteenth nights of their menstrual
cycle. In this way ovulation became more regular and only
five days of abstention from sexual intercourse was required.
The women also charted their basal temperature and vaginal
mucous changes to confirm when ovulation was taking

place. Among those who followed these instructions, there were no unwanted pregnancies. Louise did not know about the cosmic cycle when she did this study, so consequently it was not observed by these women. Again, only twenty-nine women participated.

The second book, *Mental Birth Control*, deals with some important concepts in working with the mind and subconscious. It is helpful to anyone using any type of birth control, and should certainly be included by those observing their two fertility cycles.

I
BIBLIOGRAPHY—GENERAL ASTROLOGY

1. Arroyo, Stephen, *Astrology, Psychology, and the Four Elements*, CRCS Publications, Davis, Calif., 1975.
2. Bach, Eleanor and Climas, George, *Ephemerides of the Asteroids*, Ceres, Pallas, Juno, Vesta, 1900–2000, Celestial Communications, N.Y., 1973.
3. Carter, Charles, *Encyclopedia of Psychological Astrology*, Theosophical Publishing House, London, England 1924.
4. Dean, Geoffrey, *Recent Advances in Natal Astrology*, The Astrological Association, Kent, England, 1977.
5. Dobyns, Zipporah, *Finding the Person in the Horoscope*, TIA Publications, Los Angeles, 1973.
6. Dobyns, Zipporah P. (Introduction by) *The Asteroid Ephemeris*, TIA Publications, Los Angeles, 1977.
7. Donath, Emma Belle, *Asteroids in the Birth Chart*, Gemini World, Dayton, Ohio, 1976.
8. Ebertin, Reinhold, *Combination of Stellar Influences*, Ebertin-Verlag, Aalen, Germany, 1960.
9. Ebertin, Reinhold and Hoffman, Enid, *Fixed Stars and Their Interpretation*, Ebertin-Verlag, Aalen, Germany, 1971.
10. Hand, Robert, *Horoscope Symbols*, Para-Research, Rockport, Mass., 1981.
11. Jansky, Robert, *Interpreting the Eclipses*, Astro-Computing Services, San Diego, Calif. 1979.
12. Moore, Marcia and Douglas, Mark, *Astrology, the Divine Science*, Arcane Publications, York Harbor, Maine, 1971.
13. Neely, James and Tarkington, Eric, *Ephemeris of Chiron* 1890–2000, with an Introduction by Tony Joseph, ed. by Malcolm Dean, Phenomena Publications, Toronto, Canada, 1978.
14. Oken, Alan, *A Modern Guide to Astrological Awareness*,

Alan Oken's Complete Astrology, Bantam, Toronto, N.Y. and London, 1980.

15. Robson, Vivian E., *The Fixed Stars and Constellations in Astrology*, Samuel Weiser, N.Y., 1969.

16. Rudhyar, Dane, *The Astrology of Personality*, Servire/ Wassenaar, the Netherlands, 1963.

II

BIBLIOGRAPHY—MEDICAL ASTROLOGY

1. Baker, Douglas Dr., *Esoteric Healing*, Part III, *Flower Remedies and Medical Astrology*, Samuel Weiser, N.Y., 1978.

2. Cornell, H. L., *Encyclopedia of Medical Astrology*, Llewellyn Publications, St. Paul, Minn., 1972.

3. Davidson, Wm., M.D., *Lectures on Medical Astrology*, Astrological Bureau, Monroe, N.Y., 1973.

4. Ebertin, Elsbeth and Reinhold, *Anatomiche Entsprechen Die Tierkreis Grad*, (Anatomical Correspondences to Zodiacal Degrees), Ebertin-Verlag, Aalen, Germany, 1971. translated and adapted by Mary L. Vohryzek, Aquarian Agent, March-April 1976, Vol. 4, #11, pp. 29–41.

5. Garrison, Omar V., *Medical Astrology*, University Books, N.Y., 1971.

6. Jansky, Robert, *Modern Medical Astrology*, Astro-Analytics, Venice, Calif., 1974.

7. Jansky, Robert, *Astrology, Nutrition and Health*, Para-Research, Rockport, Mass., 1977.

8. Lane, Alice, *Guide to Cell Salts and Astro-Biochemistry*, Zebra Books, N.Y., 1975.

9. Millard, Margaret, M.D., *Casenotes of a Medical Astrologer*, Samuel Weiser, N.Y., 1980.

10. Perry, Inez and Carey, George, *The Zodiac and the Salts of Salvation*, Samuel Weiser, N.Y.

11. Roberts, Ursula, *Hints For Harmony of Body and Soul*, Hendon, London.

12. Sawtell, Vanda, *Astrology and Biochemistry*, Health Science Press, Devon, England, 1975.

III

BIBLIOGRAPHY—GENERAL HEALTH

1. Asimov, Isaac, *The Human Body: Its Structure and Operation*, Signet, New American Library, N.Y., 1963.
2. Graedon, Joe, *The People's Pharmacy,* St. Martin's Press, N.Y., 1976.
3. Miller, Benjamin and Keane, Claire, *Encyclopedia and Dictionary of Medicine and Nursing*, W. B. Saunders Co., Philadelphia, Penn., 1972.
4. Williams, Roger, *Biochemical Individuality,* University of Texas Press, Austin, Texas, 1956
5. McNaught, Ann and Callander, Robin, *Illustrated Physiology,* Churchill Livingstone, N.Y., 1979
6. Tortora, Gerald J., *Principles of Human Anatomy*, Harper & Row, N.Y., 1980.

IV

BIBLIOGRAPHY—PSYCHOLOGICAL ASPECTS OF DISEASE

1. Luce, Gay Gaer, *Body Time*, Pantheon Books, Random House, N.Y., 1971.
2. Pelletier, Kenneth, *Mind as Healer, Mind as Slayer,* Delta, N.Y., 1977.
3. Selye, Hans, *The Stress of Life,* McGraw Hill, N.Y., 1976.
4. Sheehy, Gail, *Passages: Predictable Crises of Adult Life*, E. P. Dutton and Co., N.Y., 1974.

V

BIBLIOGRAPHY—HOLISTIC HEALTH

1. Airola, Paavo, *How to Get Well,* Health Plus Publishers, Phoenix, Ariz., 1974.
2. Ballentine, Rudolph, M.D., *Diet and Nutrition: A Holistic Approach,* Himalayan International Institute, Honesdale, Pa. 1978.
3. Bricklin, Mark, *The Practical Encyclopedia of Natural Healing,* Rodale Press, 1977.

4. Clark, Linda, *Get Well Naturally*, Ace Books, N.Y., 1965.
5. Heritage, Ford, *Composition and Facts About Foods and Their Relationship to the Human Body*, Health Research, Mokelumne Hill, Calif., 1971.
6. Hill, Ann (ed. by), *A Visual Encyclopedia of Unconventional Medicine*, Crown Publishers, N.Y., 1979.
7. Jackson, Mildred, N. D. & Teague, Terri, *The Handbook of Alternatives to Chemical Medicine*, Terri Teague and Mildred Jackson, Oakland, Calif., 1975.
8. Jackson, Mildred, N. D. and Teague, Terri, *Mental Birth Control,* Lawton-Teague Publications, Oakland, Calif., 1978.
9. Lacey, Louise, *Lunaception,* Warner Books, N.Y., 1976.
10. Parvati, Jeannine, *Hygieia; A Woman's Herbal*, Freestone Collective, 1978.
11. Rosenblum, Art, *The Natural Birth Control Book,* Aquarian Research Foundation, Philadelphia, Penn., 1976.
12. *A Barefoot Doctor's Manual,* Running Press, Philadelphia, Penn., 1977.
13. *Well-Being Magazine,* articles on various aspects of Holistic Health, published monthly by Well-Being Productions, Suite 921, 41 E. 42nd St., N.Y. 10017.

VI

BIBLIOGRAPHY—ALLERGIES AND ASTHMA

1. Coca, Arthur F., M.D., *The Pulse Test,* Arco Publishing Co., New York, 1956.
2. Mandell, Dr. Marshall and Scanlon, L. W., *Dr. Mandell's 5-Day Allergy Relief System*, Simon & Schuster, New York, 1979.
3. Prick, Dr. J. J. G. and Van De Loo, Dr. K. J. M., *The Psychosomatic Approach to Primary Chronic Rheumatoid Arthritis*, Chapter X "The Psychosomatic Approach to Bronchial Asthma", pp. 137-155, F. A. Davis Co., Philadelphia, Penn., 1964.
4. Worden, Bhavani, "How Not to Get Hay Fever This Year", *Well-Being Magazine,* Issue #45, April 1981 Published in the *Vegetarian Times,* New York.

VII

BIBLIOGRAPHY—
METABOLIC MALFUNCTIONS

1. Airola, Paavo, N. D., *Hypoglycemia: A Better Approach,* Health Plus Publishers, Phoenix, Ariz., 1977.

VIII

BIBLIOGRAPHY—CARDIOVASCULAR DISORDERS

1. DeBakey, Michael M.D. and Gotto, Antonio M.D. *The Living Heart,* David McKay Co., N.Y., 1977.
2. Friedman, Meyer M.D. and Rosenman, Ray M.D., *Type A Behavior and Your Heart,* Alfred A. Knopf, N.Y., 1974.

IX

BIBLIOGRAPHY—EYE PROBLEMS

1. Bates, W. H., *Better Eyesight Without Glasses,* Pyramid Books, N.Y., 1976.
2. Eden, John, *The Eye Book,* Penguin Books, N.Y., 1978.
3. Huxley, Aldous, *The Art of Seeing,* Harper Bros., London, England, 1942.
4. Ott, John, *Health and Light,* Pocket Books, N.Y., 1973.
5. Rodale, J. I., *The Natural Way to Better Eyesight,* Pyramid Books, N.Y., 1971.
6. Tobe, John H., *Cataract, Glaucoma, and Other Eye Disorders,* St. Catherine's, Ontario, Canada, 1975.

X

BIBLIOGRAPHY—FEMALE PROBLEMS

1. Jensen, Margaret et al., *Maternity Care—the Nurse and the Family,* D. F. Mosby Co., St. Louis, Mo., 1977.
2. Odsess, Carol and Murwitz, Deena (compiled and edited by), *Taking Control:* A Guide to Self Healing for Women, P.O. Box 2324, Santa Cruz, Calif., 1978.
3. Seaman, Barbara and Seaman, Gideon, M.D., *Women*

and the Crisis in Sex Hormones, Rawson Associates Publishing Inc. N.Y., 1977.

XI

BIBLIOGRAPHY— GASTROINTESTINAL PROBLEMS

1. Prick, Dr. J. J. G. and Van De Loo, Dr. K. J. M., "Peptic Ulcer From the Psychosomatic Point of View" pp 161-174 in *The Psychosomatic Approach to Primary Chronic Rheumatoid Arthritis,* F. A. Davis Co., Philadelphia, Penn., 1964.

XII

BIBLIOGRAPHY—ALCOHOLISM

1. Williams, Roger, *Alcoholism: The Nutritional Approach,* Univ. of Texas Press, Austin, Texas, 1978.

XIII

BIBLIOGRAPHY—ARTHRITIS

1. Adams, Ruth and Murray, Frank, *All You Should Know About Arthritis,* Larchmont Books, N.Y., 1979.
2. Airola, Paavo O., *There is A Cure For Arthritis,* Parker Publishing Co., West Nyack, N.Y., 1968.
3. Prick, J. J. G., M.D. and Van De Loo, K. J. M., M.D., *The Psychosomatic Approach to Primary Chronic Rheumatoid Arthritis,* F. A. Davis Co., Philadelphia, Penn., 1964.

XIV

BIBLIOGRAPHY—CANCER

1. Fredricks, Carlton, *Breast Cancer: A Nutritional Approach,* Grosset & Dunlap, N.Y., 1977.
2. Gerson, Max, M.D., *A Cancer Therapy:* Results of 50 Cases, Totality Books, Del Mar, Calif., 1958.
3. Griffin, G. Edward, *World Without Cancer,* The Story of

Vitamin B-17, American Media, Westlake Village, Calif., 1974.
4. Hutschnecker, Arnold A. M.D., *The Will to Live*, Simon & Schuster, N.Y., 1969.
5. Kelley, Dr. Wm. Donald, *One Answer to Cancer*, The Kelley Foundation, 1969.
6. Le Shan, Lawrence, *You Can Fight For Your Life,* M. Evans & Co., N.Y., 1976.
7. Manner, Dr. Harold W., *The Death of Cancer,* Advanced Century Publishing Co., Chicago, Ill., 1978.
8. Simonton, O. Carl M.D., Simonton, Stephanie M. and Creighton, James, *Getting Well Again*, J. P. Torcher Inc., Los Angeles, Calif., 1978.

INDEX